S0-AET-623

Apple Training Series
iLife '04

Michael Rubin

Apple
Certified

Apple Training Series: iLife '04
Michael Rubin
Copyright © 2004 by Michael Rubin

Published by Peachpit Press. For information on Peachpit Press books, contact:

Peachpit Press
1249 Eighth Street
Berkeley, CA 94710
(510) 524-2178
Fax: (510) 524-2221
http://www.peachpit.com
To report errors, please send a note to errata@peachpit.com
Peachpit Press is a division of Pearson Education

Editor: Serena Herr
Production Coordinator: Lisa Brazieal
Project Editor: Nancy Peterson
Technical Editors: Steve Guttman, Fred Johnson, and Jay Payne
Copy Editor: Hon Walker
Compositor: Chris Gillespie, Happenstance Type-O-Rama
Indexer: Jack Lewis
Cover design: Frances Baca Design and Tolleson Design
Cover images: © Getty Images, Inc. and © Apple Computer, Inc.

Notice of Rights All rights reserved. No part of this book may be reproduced or transmitted in any form by any means, electronic, mechanical, photocopying, recording, or otherwise, without the prior written permission of the publisher. For information on getting permission for reprints and excerpts, contact permissions@peachpit.com.

All videos and photographs are copyright © 2004 Michael Rubin. All rights reserved. Images of Petroglyph Ceramic Lounge—studio, pieces, staff, and customers—are used with permission and may not be distributed or reproduced in public or for commercial applications. Petroglyph name and logo and "Ceramic Lounge" are registered trademarks of Petroglyph, Inc.

Notice of Liability The information in this book is distributed on an "As Is" basis, without warranty. While every precaution has been taken in the preparation of the book, neither the authors nor Peachpit Press shall have any liability to any person or entity with respect to any loss or damage caused or alleged to be caused directly or indirectly by the instructions contained in this book or by the computer software and hardware products described in it.

Trademarks Throughout this book trademarked names are used. Rather than put a trademark symbol in every occurrence of a trademarked name, we state we are using the names only in an editorial fashion and to the benefit of the trademark owner with no intention of infringement of the trademark

ISBN 0-321-25606-9
9 8 7 6 5 4 3 2 1

Printed and bound in the United States of America

Acknowledgments

This book represents a vortex of some of my favorite people whirling around many of my greatest passions. Foremost, I want to thank my friends at Apple—in particular Patricia Montesion, Steve Guttman, and Fred Johnson—for having a vision to enroll people in the digital lifestyle that meshes so well with my own, and for giving me the opportunity to speak directly to the people I want to reach with these media creation tools. Of course, the book was a collaboration with Peachpit Press—thanks to Nancy Ruenzel and Serena Herr for spearheading our efforts. Thank you too for pulling together such a sharp and supportive team: my editor Nancy Peterson, copyeditor Hon Walker, technical reviewers Jay Payne and Steve Martin, compositors Maureen Forys and Chris Gillespie, and production editor Lisa Brazieal. I get a chill even trying to imagine pulling off this book on our radical schedule without the team we had.

While this book reaches into the side of my brain engrossed with things digital and media, it magically embraces the other side of my brain—the Petroglyph side. Thanks to everyone at Petroglyph who tolerates my unusual projects: director of studios Richard Morse, Santa Cruz lounge manager Katy Pagni and her team Rachel Hall and Heather Orr, our shareholders, and most importantly, all our staff and great customers whose ceramics grace these pages and whose passions I hope we captured.

A special thanks to our stars: Chris Hosmer, Fearon Hosmer, Alex Hodgson, Michelle DiBartolomeo, Tess Doud, Lihi Benisty, Steven Carrillo, and my production collaborator on so many of my videos, Lisa Strong-Aufhauser.

Finally, to my family, who encouraged me and supported the unprecedented pace of this book. Jonah and Alina, you were too young to end up in these pages, but you are the most important people in my life. And Jennifer. Do you need words here to acknowledge your contribution to this work? The cofounder of Petroglyph, the creative force of our company, the mother of our children, thank you for playing yourself in these pages and for finally accepting credit for the wonderful business we built together. This book is your book, too. You're in each line and every picture. I love you madly.

Contents at a Glance

Getting Started. xi

Lesson 1   Making a Custom CD from Your Music Collection 1

Lesson 2   DJ a Party with Your iPod 33

Lesson 3   Shooting Digital Snapshots and Putting Them in
Your Mac 43

Lesson 4   Organizing and Refining Your Photos 67

Lesson 5   Printing and Sharing Your Photos 95

Lesson 6   Adding Motion and Effects for a Dynamic Slide Show . . . 119

Lesson 7   Making a Time-Lapse Video 149

Lesson 8   Shooting and Assembling a Very Simple Movie 167

Lesson 9   Adding Narration to Your Dynamic Slide Show 197

Lesson 10   Shooting with Hollywood-Style Techniques
for Better Videos 227

Lesson 11   Editing and Finishing a Professional-Looking Movie 247

Lesson 12   Creating Unique Music for Your Projects 275

Lesson 13   Putting Your Slide Show on the Internet 307

Lesson 14   Burning DVDs of Your Videos and Slide Shows 321

Index 359

Table of Contents

Getting Started xi
What iLife Does for You xii
The Methodology xiii
A Word About the Lesson Content xv
System Requirements xvi
Copying the iLife Lesson Files xvii
About the Apple Training Series xviii
Resources xviii

Lesson 1 Making a Custom CD from
Your Music Collection 1
Starting iTunes 2
Getting Songs from CDs into iTunes 3
Change Infod 11
Browsing and Viewing Your Tunes 19
Make Playlists 23
Play a Playlist and Adjust Song Order 26
Burn a Custom CD 28
What You've Learned 31

Lesson 2 DJ a Party with Your iPod 33
Move Playlists to Your iPod 34
Customizing iPod Playlists 35
Play Your iPod Music Through a Stereo 36
Adding a Playlist to Your iPod without iTunes 39
What You've Learned 41

Lesson 3   Shooting Digital Snapshots and
Putting Them in Your Mac 43
Getting to Know Your Digital Camera 44
Shooting Great Photographs 47
Get Familiar with iPhoto 54
Importing From a Camera 55
What You've Learned 65

Lesson 4   Organizing and Refining Your Photos 67
Organize Your Photos into Albums 69
Reorder Shots 73
Adding Comments, Keywords,
and Ratings to Images 75
Creating Smart Albums 81
Cropping Photos 85
Adjust the Look of Images 90
What You've Learned 93

Lesson 5   Printing and Sharing Your Photos 95
Preparation for Sharing 96
Printing Paper Images 96
Make a Bound Book 99
Make a Quick Slide Show 111
Other Sharing Options 116
What You've Learned 117

Lesson 6   Adding Motion and Effects for a
Dynamic Slide Show 119
Open iMovie and Look Around 120
Accessing and Using Photographs from iPhoto 123
Add Titles to a Video 133
Add Fade In/Fade Out Transitions 139
Simple Adjustments to a Dynamic Slide Show 142
Adding Music from iTunes 145
What You've Learned 147

Lesson 7   Making a Time-Lapse Video 149
Preparation 150
Finding a Project 151
Setting Up the Camera 152
Shaping the Raw Material 153
Using Your iSight Camera Instead of a Tripod 161
What You've Learned 165

Lesson 8   Shooting and Assembling a
Very Simple Movie 167
A New Way to Think About Video 168
Organizing Your Video 169
Getting to Know Your Digital Camcorder 172
Shooting Video 175
Getting Video into iMovie 177
Getting the Right Shots 181
Getting Shots with Relationships 183
What Editing Does to Video 185
What You've Learned 195

Lesson 9   Adding Narration to Your
Dynamic Slide Show 197
Using Your Camcorder as a Microphone 198
Using Audio in iMovie 202
Adding Narration While You're Working in iMovie 219
What You've Learned 224

Lesson 10   Shooting with Hollywood-Style
Techniques for Better Videos 227
How to Approach Shooting a Video 228
Getting Coverage in Your Scene 236
Looking for Story Structure 244
What You've Learned 245

Lesson 11   Editing and Finishing a
Professional-Looking Movie 247
Reviewing Material from the Camcorder 248
Editing a Dialogue Scene 259
Add Background Music 266
Saving Your Video 268
Uploading Your Video to the Web 270
What You've Learned 273

Lesson 12   Creating Unique Music for Your Projects 275
Creating New Music 276
Mixing Your Music 289
Adjusting Your Time Scale and
Working with Real Time 292
Combining Loops from One Family
to Add Variation to Your Songs 294
Getting Your Music into iTunes 300
What You've Learned 304

Lesson 13   Putting Your Slide Show on the Internet 307
Getting Still Photos from Your Video 308
Putting Digital Files into iPhoto 313
What You've Learned 319

Lesson 14   Burning DVDs of Your Videos
and Slide Shows 321
Getting to Know a DVD 322
Getting an iMovie Movie Ready to Burn 324
Building a DVD of Your Movies 327
Previewing Your DVD 354
Burning a DVD 356
What You've Learned 357

Index 359

Getting Started

Welcome to the official Apple training course for the iLife suite of products—iTunes, iPhoto, iMovie, iDVD, and GarageBand. You don't need to have any special background to get started, other than having a Mac (and perhaps a healthy curiosity about what you can really do with it). Learning iLife really means learning to live digitally; you're not so much learning to use new software as learning how to comfortably integrate your Mac into the niches in your home, school, and work. The iLife tools are only part of the picture—and this book is not so much a training manual as it is a way to show you how to enrich your world by weaving digital audio, photos, and videos into many aspects of your life.

Even if you're a longtime Mac user, delving into these interesting and fun applications may be something you've put off, having chosen instead to focus on other, perhaps higher-level software tools. It's time to take a look at these (*deep breath*) life-altering products. Instead of teaching you all the geeky details of these hip tools, I'm going to concentrate on how real people really use them. I may even skip entire areas of functionality, all with an eye to having fun, achieving quick success, and forming a foundation of confidence from which you can build.

What iLife Does for You

There was a time (probably last week) when your photographs were in one part of your house, your music collection somewhere else, VHS videotapes scattered around the television, and, if you have a camcorder, Hi-8 (or some such format) cassettes in a bag. Each medium is tricky to keep organized.

But when all your media is digital—in the form of digital snapshots, digital audio (CDs, MP3s, and so on), and digital video (DVDs and DV cassettes)—keeping them organized is pretty easy, sharing content is streamlined, and using the material interchangeably between formats is both simple and kind of fun.

A Macintosh is designed to sit at the epicenter of your digital home. It's just a computer, but now it's finely tuned to make the management and combining of all this content effortless. Better than that, Apple provides—free on all Macs—software that orchestrates the commingling of all this content. iLife is a family of products made up of programs designed to stand alone but also tuned to work together in remarkable ways.

What iLife teaches you is *media literacy:* the ability to communicate in a variety of powerful ways, different from speaking or writing or even doing page design. Making professional-quality videos and movies, and being able to combine picture and sound together effectively, is a skill that applies throughout your life. Once you have it, you'll be stunned how often you can use it—for personal pleasure or commercial advantage.

It's too simplistic to say that iTunes is the music software and iMovie is the video software. iTunes handles the organization of your music, true, but once your music is there, using it in slide shows and videos is very easy. There's music in iPhoto and iMovie too. You can't build a box around each component of iLife. So while you might want to learn all you can about each product, the truth is it may be more fun to learn a little bit about a bunch of products. Rather than focus on expertise in, say, iTunes, this book will aim to help you create real-world projects. Face it, learning software is no fun. But making movies or promoting your business or building a creative report for school can be. You'll end up learning the software along the way.

The Methodology

This book moves through lessons by progressively increasing the complexity of the media you're using. You start by learning about audio alone, then move to managing still images, printing still images, turning still images into moving (*dynamic*) images, and exploring the possibilities of video. With digital content and the three core iLife applications (iTunes, iPhoto, and iMovie), you can create everything from scrapbook photos to T-shirts, books, DVDs, dynamic content for Web pages, and even a feature film ready for projection on the big screen.

Course Structure

Beyond all, the lessons are meant to be practical: not esoteric projects to show off the software, but rather real-life projects from real-life people, with time constraints, well-worn equipment, and concerns about budget. The lessons cover three general areas: music and sound, still images, and movies.

Lessons 1–2	Mostly music: use iTunes to make a custom CD, and play your music on both an iPod and through a regular stereo system
Lessons 3–6	Mostly still images: use images from your digital camera in iPhoto; print photos; make a slide show; create a professional looking book of prints
Lessons 7–12	Mostly movies: combine still photos with music, special effects, and titles in iMovie; make a time-lapse video; learn to shoot video creatively and edit to maximum effect; add narration to your videos; mix sound with picture; and create original music that you add to videos
Lessons 13–14	All of the above (sharing your projects): upload slide shows and videos to the Web with an Apple .Mac account; email photographs; and burn DVDs of your projects using iDVD

Role Playing

One of the most enjoyable aspects of this book is that you're going to assume the role of three different people, all using iLife, all using the same equipment. One is a parent, Christopher, overseeing his daughter's 12th birthday party. The second is a high school student, Charlie, putting together a report for school. And the third is a small-business owner, Jennifer, using her Mac for a variety of commercial media functions.

Your alter egos: Christopher, Charlie, and Jennifer

All three of them happen to be in the same place at the same time–a contemporary ceramics painting studio. You will see the one place and common event through iLife from three unique vantage points.

The setting: Petroglyph Ceramic Lounge, on a typical January day.

Therefore, you can progress through this book of lessons in a number of ways. You could start at the beginning and work systematically, Lesson 1 to Lesson 14. I recommend this.

I would not recommend the seemingly logical path where you skip from lesson to lesson, focusing on one product, say iPhoto. By the end you'd think you'd have a pretty good set of experiences in iPhoto. But you'll miss the intricate and powerful ways the different products intertwine and build on each other.

I would also encourage you to pass on trying to follow one personality through the iLife suite—for instance, Jennifer, the business owner. Maybe you too own a business and are primarily interested in the ways your Mac and iLife can immediately impact your work. Again, this has its merits, but since all three people are using all the products, being too faithful about following the individual with your agenda will lead you to miss important points that may be the focus of one of the other characters.

A Word About the Lesson Content

Often, training materials are professionally created—using actors, complicated production (with lights, microphones, tripods, and a crew), and so on. The resulting material is of high quality but bears little similarity to the kind of projects you will be working on. In order that this training be as real-world and practical as possible, it was made in precisely the way you would make your own videos—the quality of the shots (for better or worse) is comparable to what you can get with a typical consumer equipment; the sophistication of the projects is precisely what you can achieve using the iLife tools, with settings (and challenges) you will commonly find yourself in. The events depicted here were truly recorded in the way you are being taught to work. Hopefully, this will give you clear and realistic expectations about what you can do with your newfound skills.

System Requirements

This book is written for iLife '04, which comes free with any new Macintosh computer. If you have an older version of iLife, you will need to upgrade to the current iLife version to follow along with every lesson. The upgrade can be purchased online at www.apple.com, and is available from any store that sells Apple software.

Before you begin the lessons in this book, you should have a working knowledge of your Mac and its operating system. You don't need to be an expert, but you do need to know how to use the mouse and standard menus and commands, and how to open, save, and close files. You should have a working understanding of how OS X helps organize files on your computer, and you should also be comfortable launching applications (from the Dock or at least the Applications folder). If you need to review any of these techniques, see the printed or online documentation that came with your computer.

The minimum system requirements for the iLife suite of products are:

- Macintosh computer with a PowerPC G3, G4, or G5 processor and built-in FireWire and

  600 MHz G3 for GarageBand, G4 for GarageBand software instruments

  733 MHz G4 for iDVD

- 256 MB of physical RAM

- Mac OS X v.10.2.6 (Mac OS X v.10.2.8 is recommended)

- QuickTime 6.4

- 1024-by-768-pixel resolution

- 4.3 GB of free disk space to install iTunes, iPhoto, iMovie, iDVD, and GarageBand; 250 MB to install iTunes, iPhoto and iMovie only; an additional 4.2 GB to install all projects and media files on the accompanying training materials DVD

Copying the iLife Lesson Files

The *Apple Training Series: iLife '04* DVD-ROM includes folders containing the lesson files used in this course. Each lesson has its own folder and you should copy these folders to your hard drive to use the files for the lessons.

To install the iLife Lesson files:

1   Insert the *ATS_iLife04* DVD into your DVD drive.

2   Drag the iLife04_Book Files folder from the DVD onto your Desktop. This will copy the folder to your hard drive. Inside this folder is the Lessons folder, which contains all of the files you'll use for this book.

About the Apple Training Series

Apple Training Series: iLife '04 is part of the official training series for Apple applications, developed by experts in the field and certified by Apple Computer. The lessons are designed to let you learn at your own pace. Although each lesson provides step-by-step instructions for creating specific projects, there's room for exploration and experimentation. You can progress through the book from beginning to end, or dive right into the lessons that interest you most. It's up to you.

For those who prefer to learn in an instructor-led setting, Apple also offers training courses at Apple Authorized Training Centers worldwide. These courses are taught by Apple Certified Trainers and balance concepts and lectures with hands-on labs and exercises. Apple Authorized Training Centers have been carefully selected and have met Apple's highest standards in all areas, including facilities, instructors, course delivery, and infrastructure. The goal of the program is to offer Apple customers, from beginners to the most seasoned professionals, the highest quality training experience.

To find an Authorized Training Center near you, go to www.apple.com/training.

Resources

Apple Training Series: iLife '04 is not intended as a comprehensive reference manual, nor does it replace the documentation that comes with the applications. It's designed to be used in conjunction with other comprehensive guides that explain features, functions, and lots of interesting details; for instance:

- Apple's Web site: www.apple.com
- *The Macintosh iLife*, by Jim Heid (Peachpit Press), an accessible and popular reference to all the iLife products.

- *The Little Digital Video Book*, by Michael Rubin (Peachpit Press), a concise resource on how to make your videos have more impact and look professional. While the book is not about the iLife software specifically, it expands on many of the concepts touched on in the lessons on shooting and editing video.

1

Lesson Files	A couple of CDs from your personal CD collection
Tools	iTunes, Internet connection (optional)
Time	Approximately 45 minutes
Goals	Play CDs in iTunes
	Import all or a portion of a CD into the iTunes Library
	Add or adjust CD information about albums or songs
	Browse and search efficiently through your music library
	Create and customize personal playlists of your favorite music
	Make custom CDs

Making a Custom CD from Your Music Collection

Imagine having instant access to songs you have always loved but haven't played in eons (because they were buried on albums you generally didn't like). Imagine setting up what amounts to your own private radio station—playing all your favorite tunes for hours on end (days, even). iTunes makes this possible. CDs, those silvery discs that have become the center of your musical world, are about to become archaic. It's time to start thinking of a CD as an *archive*, a safe backup. To really enjoy your media, you want it readily accessible and malleable as only a digital creation can be.

Although this lesson demonstrates a fundamental aspect of iTunes— that is, getting your CDs into your computer, organizing them, and burning a custom CD of your favorite songs—it has a broader goal. Somewhere near where you're sitting right now are probably dozens, perhaps hundreds of CDs that you've been purchasing for the last many years. The idea of this lesson is to initiate the ambitious project of moving that entire collection from discrete CDs into a single, massive jukebox—an enormous body of acoustic joy!

As discussed in the "Getting Ready" chapter, you're going to follow three characters through their adventures with iLife. In this lesson, let's begin by seeing what Christopher, the father of the birthday girl, is up to. He's working with his daughter to make a special birthday party CD as a gift to her guests. You'll start by working with just a few CDs to get into the groove.

Starting iTunes

As with many Apple programs, you have multiple ways to launch iTunes. You might double-click the application file on your hard drive, located in the Applications folder. You could simply insert a music CD into your drive, which will automatically start iTunes. For the purposes of this lesson, single-click the iTunes icon that resides in the Dock.

First-Time Use

Christopher uses iTunes all the time. But if this is the first time you've launched iTunes, the program's iTunes Setup Assistant will direct you through a series of windows.

1   Click the iTunes icon in the Dock.

2   Click Agree in the software license agreement window. (But only if you mean it.)

Click Next in each window to use iTunes' default settings. These settings, by the way, are pretty smartly selected. The only one you might want to skip is the one asking if you want to go to the Apple Music Store. You don't need to go there now, and can easily go later to download songs when you're ready.

Click Done. This concludes the set up and will take you right into iTunes—a clean empty space where you can begin your lesson.

Getting Songs from CDs into iTunes

There's a lot to look at in the iTunes interface—but perhaps the best way to get familiar with it is simply by putting a CD into your drive and seeing what happens. You can follow along with your own CD as you watch Christopher begin the process of making a CD for the birthday party.

When you insert an audio disc into your Mac's ComboDrive (or SuperDrive; it works for both CDs and DVDs), your CD will show up as a "source" in the left column, and details about it—a list of songs and their durations (among other things)—will appear on the right if you're connected to the Internet. Christopher begins with a little Sheryl Crow:

Source column   CD tracks

Playing Songs and CDs

Once your CD is onscreen, you can use iTunes as a simple CD player. You don't have to do anything fancy with iTunes in order to listen to it. The fast way to play a song is to double-click a line item in the song list. But if you want to see what you're doing, follow these steps.

1   Using your pointer, single-click a song title. A blue bar will highlight it.

8	☑ What I Can Do For You	4:14	Sheryl Crow
9	☑ All I Wanna Do	4:33	Sheryl Crow
10	☑ We Do What We Can	5:39	Sheryl Crow
11	☑ I Shall Believe	5:34	Sheryl Crow

2   Click the Play button. The play and volume controls are together on the top left of the window. While a song is playing, the Play button turns into a Pause button (press it again to pause the song).

NOTE ▶ The spacebar on your keyboard also acts as a play/pause button.

Also, while a song is playing, a speaker icon appears in the leftmost column of the list of songs.

As the song plays, look around at the iTunes window.

At the top of the window is the album and song information, along with a bar representing the length of the song. A little black diamond shows what part of the song is playing. You can grab this diamond and scan backward or forward in the song.

There are also forward and reverse buttons alongside the Play/Pause button. Click either of these to skip to the next (or previous) track. Click and hold to scan through the track you're listening to.

When the song you initially selected is done playing, iTunes moves on to the CD's next track. Notice, however, that the blue selection bar stays where you started, although the speaker icon hops to the next song. This can be confusing at times.

TIP ▶ If you want to know what song you're listening to, look for the speaker icon and ignore the blue bar.

The checkmark next to each song title indicates that you want iTunes to play that song (if the opportunity arises) or import that song (in the event that you're pulling music into your Mac). Uncheck a title, and iTunes will ignore the song—either skipping it when you import or, if it's already in your computer, skipping it when you're playing a list of tunes.

8	☑ What I Can Do For You	4:14
9	☑ All I Wanna Do	4:33
10	☐ We Do What We Can	5:39
11 ◄))	☑ I Shall Believe	5:34

Using Automatic CD Album Information

What if you insert a CD and it shows up on your Desktop merely as "Audio CD?" What if your CD shows up in iTunes but is clearly devoid of key information—namely song and album titles? It surprises many people to learn that the song info you see in iTunes doesn't come from the CD. It comes from somewhere external to your Mac.

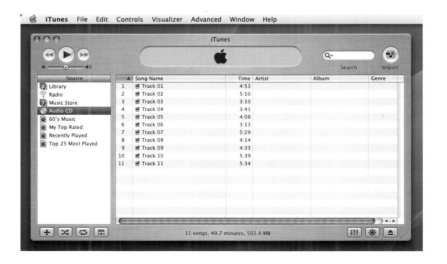

Here's the deal: Although your Mac can certainly tell that this is a music CD, and one that has, say, 11 songs of varying lengths, it doesn't know anything more specific about the album and its contents. And that is why you want to be connected to the Internet. Your Mac alone can't tell you this information, but a wonderful online database (called the Gracenote Compact Disc Database, or CDDB) is available to help. iTunes can gather this information automatically if you set it up to do so (which you did when you went through the Set-Up Assistant the first time you launched iTunes). If you loaded your favorite CD, and the screen looked too blank for you, make sure you are connected to the Internet, and then do the following.

1   Go to iTunes > Preferences.

2   From the General panel that opens, make sure "Connect to Internet when needed" is checked. That will allow iTunes to automatically go online and get disc data when you insert a CD into your Mac.

3   Click OK.

4   Select the Audio CD in the source column.

5   Go to Advanced > Get CD Track Names. This will access the Internet and
    find the information you seek from the CDDB.

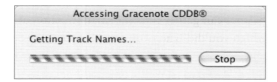

Once the process is complete, the iTunes window should look similar to
before, but with lots of useful data on the screen.

Now that you can play the CD in your Mac using iTunes, it's a good time to
take a closer look at other sources in iTunes and how you work with them.

Understanding iTunes Sources

When you open iTunes the first time you'll see a big, empty table that you'll
use to organize and ultimately play your music.

The organizational structure of iTunes is similar to that of iPhoto; you may even
recognize it as similar to that of the Mac OS. On the left side of the window is
a Source column. Your CD is a source. Choose a source, and details about its
contents appear on the right side (although your other iTunes sources may not
yet have any contents to reveal).

And just as the Mac OS offers a handful of different kinds of sources (hard disks, CDs and DVDs, connected servers, and so on), each with its own distinct icon, iTunes has a few of its own sources as well.

CDs show up in the source column only when you have a CD in your Mac. Eject a CD and it will disappear from this list.

Library is the big container that will hold all of the audio files (songs, albums, downloads) you put on your Mac, including, of course, the songs you import from CDs. You'll make subsets of this potentially enormous collection to make it easy to find the songs you're looking for. When you move songs from CDs into iTunes, you're loading music into your Library.

Music Store is the oft-mentioned Apple iTunes Music Store, where you can download (legally!) songs or albums directly into your iTunes collection—streamlining the process of building your library.

Playlists are malleable, expandable collections of songs that you build yourself. They are the heart and power of iTunes. Since you make them yourself, you won't see any playlists in the Source column when you start up, but soon you'll have many.

NOTE ▶ *There are, of course, other sources, although you can ignore them for the time being.* **Radio** *uses your Internet connection to bring you online music channels for your listening pleasure.* **60's Music, My Top Rated, Recently Played,** *and* **Top 25 Most Played** *are special sources that are built for you automatically; you can disregard them throughout this book. These automatically generated playlists are signified by a small round gear in the Source icon.*

Selecting and Importing Songs and Entire CDs

Getting music from a CD into your Mac is pretty simple. In the parlance of hipsters everywhere, the act of importing songs is called "ripping."

The time it takes to import an album (or song) depends on a few factors—notably the speed of your Mac (a dual-GHz G5 will import an album faster than an 800 MHz G3, for instance). Import speed is measured by how much faster it is to import a song than to play it. A 10X import, for instance, will rip a 5-minute song in 30 seconds, or a 60-minute album in 6 minutes.

> **NOTE ▶** Casual observation indicates that a 300 MHz G3 rips at around 4 times faster than real time; a dual-gigahertz G4 rips at around 10X; and a dual-gigahertz G5 at 20X. For one or two songs, those differences are relatively small. But if you're moving 300 CDs into your music collection, the difference between ripping 4 albums per hour and ripping 20 per hour is significant and will radically impact your productivity and probably your enjoyment of this experience.

1   Select your CD as your Source.

2   Make sure there's a checkmark next to the titles of all of the songs you want to import into iTunes. Uncheck any songs that you don't want to import; those will remain on the CD, never to see the inside of your computer.

3   Click Import. Notice that once a song begins to import, the information bar at the top of the iTunes window indicates the song being imported, the speed of the import, and the time remaining to complete the task.

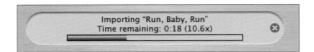

While importing, iTunes places a small orange import icon on the leftmost column of your track list, where the speaker is when you're playing a song.

▲	Song Name	Time
1 🔶 ☑	Run, Baby, Run	4:53
2 ☑	Leaving Las Vegas	5:10
3 ☑	Stong Enough	3:10
4 ☑	Can't Cry Anymore	3:41

By default (as set in the preferences), when you start to import tracks, iTunes will also start to play them. (It can do both simultaneously.)

NOTE ▶ Although playing while importing is generally an okay thing to do, it can be confusing too. The song that's playing is not necessarily the one being imported, and vice versa. Casual importers may find themselves waiting for the album to finish playing, not realizing it finished importing long before. If you want to stop songs from playing, click the Stop button (or the spacebar); this won't affect the importing. Keep an eye on the import icon and the track info at the top of the window to see your progress.

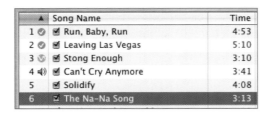

When a song has been completely imported, iTunes changes the import icon into a green checkmark. When the entire CD is done importing, it will "bing" politely.

Now that you've ripped your first CD, eject it and insert another. Rip a few more CDs, and then move on to the next section.

NOTE ▶ iTunes defaults to creating AAC audio files, which are considered an excellent audio format with good sound quality and small file size. Unfortunately, some MP3 players don't support it, and you might want to have MP3 audio files instead. You have control over the method and quality of compression that iTunes uses to copy a song. To adjust the settings, go to Preferences > Importing. From there, you can adjust the Import Using pop-up menu and select an audio format.

AAC is also known as MP4 (the successor to the MP3 format). You might recognize it as the format of the songs that you purchase from the Apple Music Store as well as from streaming music providers such as XM and Sirius. Other formats include AIFF and WAV, which are standard audio formats that provide very high sound quality but generate large files. Commercial CDs tend to contain AIFF sound files.

Change Info

Let's say you've finished ripping a handful of CDs and had no hitches. When iTunes automatically looked up information on the Internet about each CD you placed into your Mac, it loaded a bunch of data into a database it keeps in your iTunes Library. In most cases, you won't need to mess around here, but if the CD data doesn't come up the way you want it to—either because you don't have an Internet connection, because the data doesn't exist for your CD, or you simply don't agree with some of the characterizations the CDDB database offered, you'll need to add or adjust information. It's easy to do, and as you get more advanced with iTunes, you'll learn many interesting ways you can catalog and organize your collection.

NOTE ▶ The Gracenote CDDB is compiled through user submissions and not from record companies. Consequently, there may be some errors or subjective opinions about data included.

Adjusting Information Before Importing

Let's begin by adjusting information for a CD you haven't yet imported into your computer. Follow these steps if you have a CD with "problem" information.

1   Insert a new CD. If the CDDB has info on this album, it will show up in the iTunes window.

In this example, the album is Rock 'n' Roll Gumbo—an album from New Orleans great Professor Longhair. The CDDB has information on the album but considers it to be in the blues genre. As far as I'm concerned, zydeco is a better genre classification. So let's change it.

2   Select the CD Source icon.

3   Choose File > Get Info.

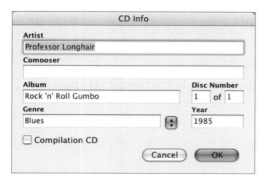

The CD Info window opens and gives you an opportunity to adjust basic info before you import. If you add info prior to importing, the data will follow the songs into iTunes automatically. If the CDDB did its job correctly, all this data should be filled in. In my example, I just want to change the genre.

4   Add or change information in the fields. Christopher changed the "Blues" genre to "Zydeco."

5   Click OK when you're done.

Adjusting Information After Importing

Adjusting information prior to importing is good for data that's related to entire albums, but it's not the end of the process if you still need to add data about individual songs. In particular—say, for a custom CD that a friend has provided or for an arcane CD that isn't yet in the CDDB , you might need to add or change more info for the disc.

To do that, let's import our albums and check out the same Get Info function on albums and songs, this time using it in the Library. It looks similar to the way it did a moment ago, but now there are more fields and options.

Here's the Library after a few albums have been imported. One of them was not recognized by the CDDB, and its tracks were sorted to the bottom of the list of songs.

See the five tracks at the bottom of the list with missing information? Since Christopher didn't input new info prior to importing, he'll have to do it now. First, he's going to add information that is common to all the songs—the album info.

1   Select all five tracks. To do this, click Track 01. Then hold down the Shift key and click Track 05. All the tracks from 01 to 05 will be selected together.

16   Making a Custom CD from Your Music Collection

2   Choose File > Get Info.

Since it's a little unusual to modify information for more than one track, iTunes will pop up a warning to make sure you intend to do this. If you're confident of your Mac skills, you could choose "Do not ask me again"; however, it's a good rule to keep the safety on. Either way, click Yes in the warning window.

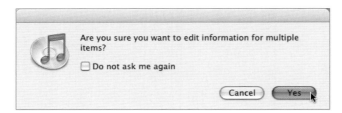

iTunes will now open the information window, in this case entitled Multiple Song Information. If the CDDB didn't recognize the CD, the window will start out blank. Fill in as much data as you can.

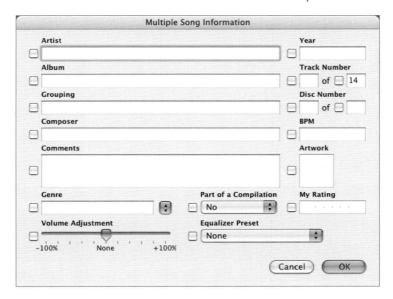

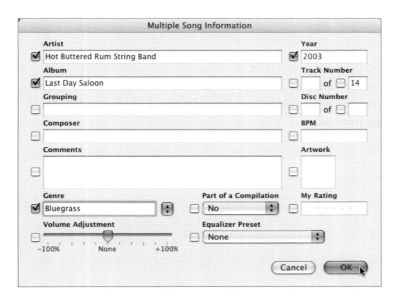

3   Click OK and check out your Library. The songs have been updated, sorted by artist.

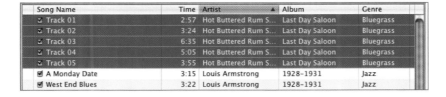

iTunes still doesn't know anything about the individual tracks. For that you'll need to go through song by song.

4   Select Track 01.

5   Choose File > Get Info. Notice this is the third time we've chosen Get Info, and it has behaved slightly differently each time. First it was for a CD prior to importing; then it was for multiple tracks after importing; and now it's for a single track.

What you see initially is the Summary tab of information. Four tabs appear along the top of this window.

6 Select the Info tab, opening up an area in which you can enter a variety of important tidbits about your track.

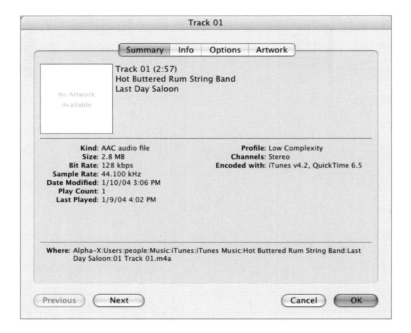

7 Change the name of Track 01 and click OK. Track 1 is really called "Sweet Baby's Arms."

8 Repeat these steps for all unnamed tracks, and before you know it, your Library is complete and looks something like this:

TIP ▶ If you can't see all the information about a track in the window, you can change the width of the column. When you move the pointer over the lines that separate columns, the cursor changes. You can drag the column border to the right or left to enlarge or narrow a column, respectively.

Browsing and Viewing Your Tunes

Pouring all your CDs into iTunes isn't enough. Being able to find songs you're looking for is critical. Clicking any column in the iTunes Browser will sort that column alphabetically. Generally, an alphabetical arrangement by artist is pretty useful.

In the top of the window is a search field; just start typing and iTunes will do its best to find songs that you are describing—whether the letters you type are part of the name of a song, an artist, or an album. One particularly cool aspect of the search feature is that it starts looking as you type so you don't have to type an entire word, and you never need to press Return.

TIP ▶ By default, when you're searching for music, iTunes checks the Artist, Album, Composer, and Song Name fields. You can narrow your search by choosing just one of these fields. To do so, click the search icon (the magnifying glass) to the left of the search field, choose the category you want to search, and then type your criteria in the search field.

After Search, the most useful method of browsing a large collection is the built-in Browser. See that eye in the top corner of the window? Click it. The track info area will rearrange itself into some useful quadrants.

In this view, simply select one of the items in any of the three columns and you can quickly drill down any search through the collection. If you select All in any column, you get the full Library. Browsing by genre creates an experience that is akin to the way you might wander down aisles in a music store. If your tastes are more eclectic, you could skip genre and focus on artist. Click an artist's name, for instance, and only songs by that artist are shown in the window below.

1   Two albums from this artist are displayed together. Select one of the albums, on the right, and the search is narrowed even further:

2   To get back to the full Library, select All Artists (or All Genres) and you'll see all the songs again.

TIP If you don't want to browse with the Genre column visible—say you simply never use this very general criterion—you can make the column invisible in the Browser. Choose iTunes Menu > Preferences > General, uncheck "Show genre when browsing," and then click OK.

Now that you've seen how to import and browse, you're ready for the key feature of iTunes: the capability to pull together songs from different albums and different artists based on whatever criteria you feel are important. It all comes down to playlists.

Make Playlists

In the good ol' days, when you wanted to listen to music, you listened to a whole album. A CD was a nice, functional unit of music. Still, if you had the time, it was generally preferable to make a party tape or disc—a compilation of your favorites. New technologies produce new opportunities; introducing the "playlist." It creates an experience akin to an instant, malleable, best-of CD.

A playlist is a set of songs that you build and sequence yourself. By making a playlist, you are not affecting your iTunes Library at all. The Library is where all the songs live; the playlist is just a convenient way to access some of them. It's also an essential building block if you want to burn a CD of some tracks (as Christopher wants to do for the birthday party), add a bunch of tunes to a slide show in iPhoto, or organize your music collection for your iPod.

1   Click the + button at the bottom of the Source column. This adds an untitled playlist to your Source list.

2   Type a name for the playlist. (Christopher calls his "Jessica's Birthday," which you may also want to do to make it easier to follow the lesson steps.) Click the new playlist in the Source column, and notice that there

is nothing on the right side of the window. It's empty since you haven't added any songs.

3   Click Library. The main window shows the songs you've imported so far.

4   Drag a song from the list of tracks on the right and drop it on Jessica's Birthday.

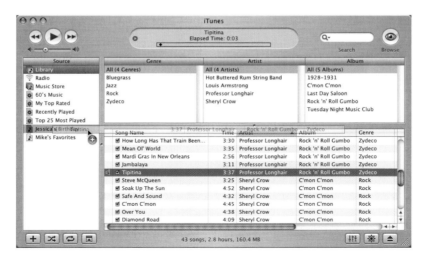

5 It may not look like anything happened, at first, but if you select Jessica's Birthday you'll see your song in that playlist.

6 You can add more than one song at a time. Common to many Macintosh applications is Command-click—which lets you select a series of disconnected items at the same time. Go back to your Library, click one song, then hold down the Command key and click a second song from that list. Both songs will be selected. Drag the pair of songs to your playlist.

NOTE ▸ Shift-clicking works for selecting groups of contiguous songs.

7 Click an album from the Album column and drag it to Jessica's Birthday. All of the songs from that album are added at once.

You can add individual tracks or whole albums in many ways. This represents just the basics. No matter the method you use, before you know it the Jessica's Birthday playlist has a number of songs that you can play back-to-back.

> **TIP** You can include a song in multiple playlists. You can even add songs to one playlist from another simply by dragging songs across the playlists.

Deleting a song from a playlist will not delete it from your Library. Deleting from the Library, however, will remove it from your computer. You'll get a warning dialog, but be careful when you delete.

Play a Playlist and Adjust Song Order

Whenever you select a playlist, iTunes will display some key information at the bottom of the screen: how many songs are in the list, how long it takes to play the entire list straight through, and (in case you care) how many bytes of data it represents. (This last bit of info is most useful when you want to burn the songs in a playlist to a CD.)

Playing the playlist is much like playing a CD. Choose a song, click Play (or just double-click the song), and the rest of the songs follow in the order they appear in the playlist.

Random Play

Sometimes you want to be surprised by a song. Particularly with large playlists (or your Library), you just want iTunes to choose a song for you and play it. The Shuffle button at the bottom of the Source column handles this for you.

1   Select a playlist to play.

2   Click the Shuffle button. It will turn blue when it's shuffling your music.

Clicking Shuffle will reorder the songs in your playlist (temporarily, and randomly). If you don't like the new order, click the Shuffle button again and iTunes will restore the sequence of songs. You can always try again.

Changing Order

But what if you don't like random playing, and you don't like the order in which you've dropped songs into your playlist? It's simple to change the order of your playlist in a more permanent way.

1   Click and drag a song within the playlist.

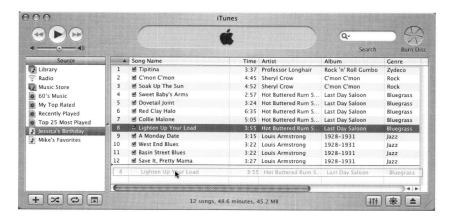

Notice the black line that indicates where the song will go if you release the mouse button.

2   Release the mouse button when the song is where you want it.

Burn a Custom CD

Once you have arranged a playlist, you might want to burn a CD for yourself. Once the Jessica's Birthday playlist is ready, all her father needs to do is alert iTunes he wants to burn a disc.

1   Click Burn Disc icon at the top of the window

The button will transform into a warning icon—alerting you it's ready to go, live and "hot." The information window will direct you to insert a blank CD into your Mac's combo drive.

2   Insert a blank CD. iTunes will check to see if the disc is good and that the
songs on the playlist will fit on it.

The size of the playlist (in megabytes; MB), noted at the bottom of the
screen, is critical. A CD will only hold around 650 MB of music. iTunes
is smart enough to coach you through splitting up your playlist over a
couple CDs if it happens to be too big, or you could do it yourself.

NOTE ► iTunes measures sizes by the actual file size of the audio file.
But when you burn a CD, iTunes converts all your files regardless of their
format to the CD standard format, which may be larger (or smaller) than
what iTunes reports for your playlist. A 650 MB CD holds about 1 hour
and 10 minutes of music regardless of how compressed your MP3 files are.

3 Click the Burn Disc icon. iTunes will begin the process, spinning the Burn Disc icon as it works, and keeping you posted as to the burning status in the info window at the top of the screen. In a few minutes, the disc will be complete, and your Mac will eject it automatically.

The best complement to a custom CD is a custom label. Many software packages are available to streamline the label-making process. Some go so far as to insert photos (from iPhoto) and the list of songs (from your playlist in iTunes). They also provide cover art for your jewel case, as well as a label to affix to your CD.

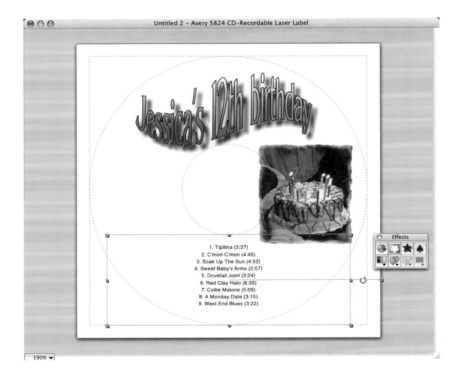

What You've Learned

- Double-click the title of a song on a CD to play the song.

- Click Import to rip CDs to iTunes.

- Uncheck the titles of songs you don't want to import.

- To adjust song and album information, use Get Info either before or after you import.

- Use iTunes' Browser and search field to find songs.

- Create a new playlist with the + button.

- Drag one or multiple songs from the Library to a playlist to add them to that list.

- Drag tracks up or down in a playlist to change their order.

- Click the Burn Disc button visible in each playlist window to record all of those songs to a CD.

2

Lesson Files	No files for this lesson
Tools	iTunes, iPod
Time	If you have an iPod, about 15 minutes (otherwise, much longer)
Goals	Move playlists from iTunes to your iPod
	Keep iTunes and your iPod synced together
	Plug your iPod into a stereo to play music in public

DJ a Party with Your iPod

If you don't have an iPod, skip this lesson. Or go get one.

It's true, an iPod is just a glossy little hard drive that's well-suited for storing, accessing, and (of course) playing music. But if you talk to anyone who uses one, you'll quickly realize it's truly one of the best-designed portable tools you'll see these days. A book like this cannot describe the intense power and joy you will have when you can walk around—or drive, or fly—carrying (hang with me here) not just a few CDs, not just a Discman's worth of songs, but your *entire friggin' music collection* in your pocket.

Plugging in your headphones and enjoying your collection privately is great, but one day you'll want to take advantage of the fact that where ever you go you can hook up to a land-based stereo system and bring your music to a wider audience.

Christopher and the birthday party head out to a ceramics studio for the "big event," and he wants to bring along his iPod to hook into the studio's sound system for a private DJ experience. Since Jennifer, the studio owner, has an iPod, too (sometimes using it in the studio for special occasions), she's accustomed to this set up and is happy to help make the party as comfortable as possible.

Move Playlists to Your iPod

Your Mac and your iPod were made for each other, so moving your music to your iPod is an intuitive affair. When you connect your iPod to your Mac, the iPod automatically checks to make sure that the music on your Mac is also on your iPod. Consequently, if you've added new music to your iTunes Library, the iPod checks to make sure it is up-to-date.

> **NOTE** ▶ Be aware that an iPod is principally made for only one iTunes Music Library. If you have multiple computers with different music on each, your iPod can be a servant to only one of these masters. Moving an iPod around between different Macs can be less efficient than dedicating an iPod to a particular computer's Library.

1   Start by plugging your iPod into your Mac. If your iPod came with a dock, connect it to your Mac with the iPod Dock Connector to FireWire cable.

2   If you're using a dock, place your iPod into it once it's hooked up to your Mac. Notice that iTunes opens automatically when it sees your iPod.

iTunes also begins to transfer all the songs and playlists in your Library to your iPod. The icon representing your iPod in the Source list flashes red during the update. Do not disconnect your iPod while music is being transferred.

> **NOTE** ▶ If this iPod has previously been synced with another Library, you'll get a warning when you hook it up. You'll have the option to override all the music on the iPod and sync it with the new Library, or to cancel the syncing process.

Customizing iPod Playlists

You don't always have to copy every song from your Library to your iPod. If you have 20 GB of music on your Mac but only a 15 GB iPod, it won't even be possible. Consequently, you may want to be selective about which playlists you move to your iPod.

When an iPod is connected to your Mac, you'll see an iPod icon at the bottom of the iTunes screen.

1   Click the icon and you'll bring up the preferences associated with syncing your Mac and iPod.

From the Preferences window, you can see all the iTunes playlists and can choose the ones you'd like on your iPod.

2   Check the playlists you want, and click OK.

Now when you sync your iPod, only the selected playlists will be updated.

> **TIP ▶** Name your playlists with your iPod in mind. This requires you to keep titles short (the iPod displays only 21 characters). Since the iPod alphabetizes titles, you can "trick" it into keeping your favorites at the top by inserting a hyphen (–) or a period (.) as the first character in the name.

Play Your iPod Music Through a Stereo

Because the iPod has such a compact and streamlined form, you might think of it as only an individual, private musical device. With headphones this is, of course, true. But it's very easy to hook an iPod into a more public music system. Whether you connect it to a mini FM broadcaster—so that you can hear your music on any nearby radio—or to speakers for direct playback, an iPod is definitely portable but not necessarily private.

With iPod in hand, and a single cable, Christopher can take his favorite music on the road, ready to hook into any available stereo system for a public music experience.

> **NOTE ▶** The law prohibits the public playing of copyrighted music— whether from CD or iPod or record album. Restaurants and retailers know this and tend not to put their private music collection over loudspeakers. They can be seriously fined. Instead, they often choose licensed collections (from services like Musak, AEI, DMX, and so on), for which they pay a small fee. The only way you can play your iPod over a stereo, legally, is if it's for a private group—yourself, your friends, your home. Christopher gets to play his iPod at the ceramics studio because it's a private party.

At the ceramics studio, Christopher checks with Jennifer, the studio owner, then plugs his iPod into the store's sound system. The cable required is different on each end: a 1/8-inch stereo miniplug to go into the iPod; a pair of RCA phone plugs on the other end, to go into a stereo.

1   Plug the 1/8-inch stereo miniplug into the top of the iPod.

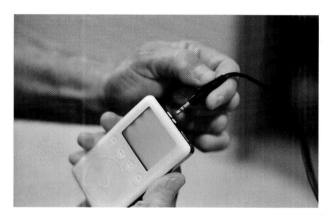

2   Connect the pair of RCA plugs to the stereo. Most stereo receivers have many audio input jacks for a variety of devices (CD players, turntables, and so on). If you find some empty jacks, you can use those, or choose the AUX input jacks usually provided for other assorted audio devices—like your iPod. The two jacks are color coded for stereo sound channels: red for right, white for left.

If your iPod is going to remain connected to the stereo for a while, you might want to use an adapter to plug it into a power source. If you have a dock, you can set it up and hook the FireWire cable into a FireWire-AC adapter (which comes with your iPod). Then you won't have to worry about running out of juice.

NOTE ▶ If you're using an iPod with its dock, the dock sports its own plug for a "Line" connection to the stereo (it looks just like the little hole on the top of the iPod itself). You can select either plug to connect; they work in the same way.

With your iPod hooked up, set the stereo to play from the AUX source (or whichever source you hooked the iPod into) and start playing the music from your party playlist.

Adding a Playlist to Your iPod without iTunes

Christopher planned on using his Birthday Party playlist from iTunes on his iPod. But as the girls painted and talked, they wanted to hear other songs from the iPod that weren't on the Birthday Party playlist. The iPod makes it easy to add any song on the device to a playlist, even without a Mac or iTunes nearby.

With iPod in hand, scroll to the bottom of the Playlists screen and you'll find a playlist that you didn't create: the On-The-Go playlist.

1   Select a song. (You could also select every song by an artist, a whole playlist, or an album.)

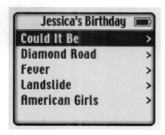

2   Hold down the round Select button in the middle of the iPod dial until the selected item flashes for a moment.

Select button

When the flashing stops, the item has been added to your On-The-Go playlist.

3   Repeat steps 1 and 2 for any other songs, artists, playlists, and albums you want to add.

4   When you're ready to play your selections, select the On-The-Go playlist.

In the On-The-Go screen, you'll see a list of songs you've added to the list in the order in which you added them. (The songs—or items—you selected first will appear at the top of the list.)

5   Press Select to begin playing the playlist.

6   You get only one On-The-Go playlist. You can't remove a song, but you can clear the entire list and start again. To clear the On-The-Go playlist, scroll to the bottom of the playlist, and select Clear Playlist.

In the resulting Clear screen, select Clear Playlist again, confirming that you really do want to wipe that playlist clean.

What You've Learned

- For automatic syncing between your iPod and your Mac, plug your iPod Dock into your Mac, and then set your iPod on the dock.

- iTunes lets you customize sync settings—such as syncing some playlists and not others—in the iPod Preferences window.

- To connect the iPod to any stereo receiver, use a 1/8-inch minijack-to-RCA stereo jack cable. This can plug into the jack on the top of the iPod or to a comparable jack in the iPod Dock.

3

Lesson Files	Lessons > Lesson03 > L3.Student roll 1
Tools	iPhoto
Time	Approximately 45 minutes
Goals	Learn how to use composition and lighting for better photographs
	Import pictures into iPhoto
	Rotate and delete images in iPhoto

Shooting Digital Snapshots and Putting Them in Your Mac

This lesson will demystify the way a computer can talk to (and control) a digital camera. It will give you some basic guidelines for handling your camera and creating impressive snapshots, as well as dealing with less than ideal lighting and subject orientation. It will also introduce you to iPhoto, the iLife tool for moving those photographs from camera to Mac, and ultimately organizing and sharing them.

You'll follow Jennifer, the studio owner, as she looks at her inventory. She might use a camera to help catalog and organize her ceramics, so that staff can identify pieces or vendors can fill a certain order. But as she gets more creative, she sees she can make beautiful photos of her ceramics that could inspire customers, creating not just "mug shots" but advertisements.

To see the process of getting shots into iPhoto, you'll also follow Charlie, the high school student, as he begins to prepare photos for his school project.

Getting to Know Your Digital Camera

It can be daunting to buy a digital camera. The technology changes very quickly, as do the prices and features of the cameras. There are professional-quality cameras with interchangeable lenses, hefty weight, and high-end controls. There are compact consumer cameras with mostly automatic controls, a small zoom lens, and a flash. There are numerous features by which you can compare cameras, but perhaps the most significant is that of image quality. To make image-quality comparisons, all digital cameras are rated by a number of "megapixels." Aside from how the camera feels in your hands, and, of course, its price, mega-pixels are key measurement for digital cameras.

Understanding Your Camera's Resolution

You can't talk about digital cameras without someone mentioning *megapixels.* Pixels are the smallest elements of a picture, like the dots on your TV screen if you look at it up close, or those of a newspaper photograph. Images are made up of these tiny dots of color and shade; the more of them, the higher the res-olution; higher resolution means better-looking images. Of course, high-reso-lution images take up more space on your Mac's hard disk (and your camera's memory card) than low-resolution images do, so for any given memory card or storage device, there's a trade-off between more low-quality images and fewer high-quality images. A megapixel is a million pixels, and it's a pretty good place to start when comparing cameras. All digital cameras use between, say, 1 and 6 megapixels to capture an image. And in many ways this defines how good the camera is.

But how many megapixels is enough? The answer depends on what you plan to do with your photographs. If you want to look at them on a TV set, the resolution can be pretty low, because a television is a very low-resolution display (equivalent to about 1/3 megapixel). Using images on the Internet requires even smaller files—and thus no matter how good your camera, you'll end up squeezing the image down to a radically lower pixel resolution (*way* below 1 megapixel). On the other hand, printing images demands the highest resolution—the larger the print, the higher the resolution you want.

High resolution

Low resolution

High resolution

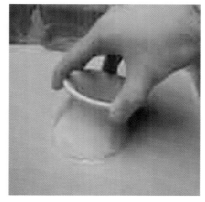
Low resolution

Prints this small make it hard to reveal the difference between resolutions. Still, the image on the left could be blown up to a poster and look pretty good. The one on the right is already suffering even though it's small.

TIP ▶ Images with lots of detail and color will look worse (revealing odd, digital-looking anomalies) with low-resolution cameras. However, images with large areas of solid color, good contrast, and few details—as you often find with close-up shots—tend to look okay with low-resolution cameras, at least better than wider shots.

So, if you have a low-megapixel camera, shoot more close-ups than scenic vistas. If you want more range, or plan to shoot wide, you may need a higher-megapixel camera.

A 2-megapixel image will print with excellent quality at typical snapshot sizes (3.5×5 and 4×6 inches). If you want to make enlargements at, say, 8×10, you may want to move up to 3 or 4 megapixels. And if you're a pro, or you plan to do really high-quality photography, 5 or 6 megapixels will likely do the trick. If you never plan to do anything more than display images on TV or on the Web, you can use the lowest-megapixel cameras available and save yourself some money.

NOTE ▶ This, by the way, is why companies tend to demonstrate their DVDs, photos, and other compressed images using close-ups rather than wide shots. If you want to see how good an image really is, check the stadium crowd shots or the leaves turning on a million New England trees; these are far better indicators of potential problems than the model on the beach is. You really want a combination of both mottled details and solid colors to reveal different kinds of potential problems.

TIP ▶ Some companies offer combo camcorders and still cameras. In general, a camcorder image is of inferior image quality to a still camera; you might be better served by using separate devices, each well tuned for their task. Also keep in mind that you can grab a still frame from digital video any time you want (using iMovie, for instance) and don't have to have a special camcorder or specific feature to provide that function. It may be low resolution, but it's good for small snapshots or Web images.

Shooting Great Photographs

Take Lots of Photos

One of the best qualities of a digital camera is that it takes photos instantly—a 21st-century Polaroid Instamatic. You snap pictures pretty much the way you always have, but you can look immediately to see if the shot came out the way you hoped. And because no film or processing is needed, there's really no additional cost involved in shooting lots of pictures.

> **NOTE ▸** There's no additional cost except for batteries, that is. Digital cameras chew up battery power, and that can get pricey. Some cameras can go through a custom battery pack in less than 100 shots. Keep this in mind as you compare your camera options.

Taking lots of shots gives you the opportunity to work the way professionals do. It used to be that you'd take one shot of something and hope it worked. But now you can shoot 1, 10, even 50 shots if it's important that you get that perfect snapshot. And like a professional, you can peruse all the pictures you took, throw out most of them, and keep the cream. Without changing anything about your photographic abilities, this technique alone will improve your photo collection.

Read Your Camera Manual

It wouldn't be possible for this book to describe the specifics of how your model of digital camera works. Suffice it to say it has a shutter release button (the "snap button"), some automatic and preset exposure controls, and an LCD screen for viewing images. It also has a jack under a flap somewhere that lets you connect the camera to your Mac's USB port with a cable, which usually is included with the camera. Spend some time with the manual that came with your camera to familiarize yourself with the basics of shooting and exposure.

Get the Exposure Right

As a rule of thumb, keep light behind *you* (not your subject) when you're shooting. Backlit subjects can be interesting once in a while (that hip silhouette look is very arty), but you'll probably miss the details you may want in your subject.

There's a fair amount of light in Jennifer's ceramics studio—it comes from skylights, from spot and task lighting pointing at the tables, and it comes in the front window as ambient light. Shooting photos in the studio, can be tricky because if you point the camera towards the front door, anyone you're shooting is going to have the bright daylight from the window behind them. If you can't get the light behind you, and you don't want a silhouette, your only option is to force your camera to flash even though it thinks there's enough light (after all, it sees plenty of light). Using a flash in this way is known as a *fill flash*. Any flash should be considered a last resort in photography—try instead to get a more naturalistic look through proper exposure.

Backlit subject

Backlit subject with fill flash

Autofocus and autoexposure technologies are pretty advanced, and taking pictures in automatic mode will likely produce the best all-around images. As your skill and comfort expand, using more manual controls (like forcing the fill flash) will enhance your range and options as a photographer.

Creating Interesting Photographs Through Composition

Often the only difference between boring photos and stunning ones is the way you frame your subject—what photographers call *composition*. When composing your photos, consider not always centering your subject, a technique that can make your photos more appealing and dynamic. You also may want to move in closer than you normally would, cutting out space around your subject to keep attention from drifting. This technique often reveals more detail and emotion as well.

> **NOTE** ▶ Cameras autofocus by looking at an object placed in the center of the frame. (Your camera may have a little box or marks in your view to indicate this center region.) Problem is this predisposes you to put the object you're shooting right in the middle. Some cameras allow you to *offset* your frame once the camera has taken a focus reading. If your camera has this feature, you can push a button to lock in the focus, then move your view slightly before taking the picture. To create dynamic composition in your photos, this capability is important.

It can be tempting to photograph subjects in rigorous, rather clinical ways. If I say, "Take a photo of these three objects," many people will line them up and shoot them, from eye level, getting all three of the objects completely in frame.

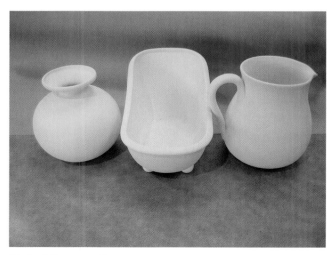

Kinda dull composition

This kind of photo has its place and, once in a while, mixed in with other dynamic snapshots, is fun and important. Still, many people's scrapbook snapshots are always framed like this and are just about this interesting: everyone lined up, looking at the camera, pausing from whatever they were doing for a photo. Giving your subject the freedom to move naturally while you take candid snapshots is important. Composing scenes with some people close to you and others slightly obscured will allow for more naturalistic photos.

A little better composition

Once you're comfortable with a more relaxed style, try changing your vantage point. Taking shots from different angles, including from above and below, is another key to creating interesting photos. Too many pictures are shot from the photographers point-of-view, just standing around with camera to her eye. Using a camera with a flip-out screen (which today's camcorders tend to have) allows a wider range of positions, from holding it over your head to setting it at ground level, without having to keep your head behind the camera.

low angle (left), high angle (right)

Also, try moving closer to your subject, allowing the camera to see only a part of the object or person you're shooting. Letting the camera do some initial cropping like this is a great compositional tool. When you're photographing someone's face and want a very close shot, it doesn't look unusual even if you crop off the top of the head a little—the eyes are the important part.

Tight shot, cropped in the camera

TIP Every one of these guidelines applies both to still photography and video. As you get into video more, keep these shooting rules handy to dramatically improve the photography in your videos.

Getting closer to subjects and cropping tightly as you frame a shot can be very effective in giving your snapshots a professional look. An important rule of composition is called the rule of thirds—which says, in effect, don't put your subjects in the center of the frame, but rather a little off center (up/down or left/right). When you frame a snapshot, mentally create a grid of thirds across the screen, making sure your primary subject is located along one of the imaginary lines.

 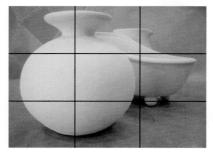

Similarly, feel free to leave objects in the foreground of your shots, probably out of focus, and use them to frame the rest of your image (while still using that rule of thirds). Foreground objects (window frames, door frames, people in profile, and so on) do not need to be immediately recognizable to add to the composition of the frame.

Finally, think about the background behind your subjects: You don't want it to compete with the subject too much. If it is visually "busy" or does not contrast with the subject enough, it can dilute the impact of your image.

Ideally, the background will be simple and will have some basic contrast with the foreground object.

Summary Tips:

- Get close to your subjects.
- Use foreground objects to frame your shot.
- Change your position to shift your point of view.
- Select the right background: less busy and more contrast with your subject. You don't want to have to hunt through a picture to find the subject.

Get Familiar with iPhoto

iPhoto is organized much like iTunes. On the left side of the screen are the sources—in this case, a Photo Library and a bunch of "albums." An album is the equivalent of an iTunes playlist: a collection you create, a subset of your Library that organizes and simplifies viewing.

iPhoto and iTunes are also similar in the way they work. You import content (from a CD in iTunes; from a camera in iPhoto), which is copied onto your hard disk and organized in your Library. Both programs have "smart" albums/playlists; both let you make your own albums/playlists by dragging songs/photos from the Library. Both allow you to share songs/photos with other Mac users in your local network (around your office or home perhaps) with Apple's Rendezvous networks. (In short, if you can print to the same printer, you can probably share photos and music.) Both essentially organize your digital content; in addition to letting you easily burn CDs (from iTunes) and print photos (from iPhoto), both programs show up in other iLife applications. For instance, in iMovie and iDVD you can select content from your Library or albums/playlists to make those applications more dynamic so that your movies are not just cut video, but video integrated with stills, moving stills, live sound, and recorded music.

If you understand the basics of iTunes, you already know much of what you need to know about iPhoto.

Here's the empty iPhoto window. If you weren't paying attention, you could easily mistake it for iTunes.

Even if iPhoto is not open, your Mac is set up to open iPhoto and immediately import photos when you plug a digital camera into your computer.

Importing From a Camera

For this lesson, we'll look at the importing process from the perspective of Charlie, the high school student, and imagine using his camera. This is how he manually imported his images into iPhoto.

Importing may seem challenging at first, but it really couldn't be easier.

1 Plug your camera into your Mac with the cable that came with your camera.

The rest of the process should happen automatically. But if for some reason it doesn't, use this method:

2 In iPhoto, go to the Import pane (click the Import button near the bottom of the iPhoto window). If your camera is turned on, iPhoto will see it and report on it in the bottom portion of iPhoto's main window.

3   It's a good idea to erase photos from your camera after you import them, both to free up space on the memory card so you can take more pictures, and to keep from having to deal with duplicate photos later. You can do it yourself with your camera, but a really easy way is to have iPhoto erase photos automatically when it's done importing. If you want iPhoto to handle this, check the blue box near the Import button on the right.

4   Click Import. And iPhoto will manage the rest.

Of course, you don't have a camera loaded with Charlie's photographs, so to mimic his experience, you're going to add photos to your Library in the other way photos end up in iPhoto—copied from your hard disk.

Preparing for the Lesson

You will begin by dragging a folder full of photos to iPhoto.

1   Launch iPhoto. If you've never used the application before, the window will be empty. Make sure the Organize tab at the bottom of the window is selected (and light blue). iPhoto is ready for your "roll" of film.

2   Open the Lessons folder that you copied to your hard disk from the enclosed DVD.

3   Open the Lesson03 folder, and drag the entire folder called **L3.Student roll 1** into your open iPhoto window.

iPhoto will go into Import mode and start taking in the folder of photographs.

Notice that at the bottom of the window, iPhoto is providing information about this import. If you had a camera attached, you would see it named here. At this point, iPhoto will indicate that no camera is connected, but will still show the photos importing. It runs through the photos in thumbnail view as they are copied into your Library, and it also shows how many images remain to be imported.

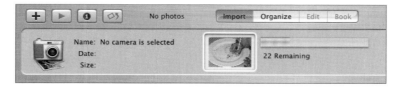

When all of the photos have been imported, the iPhoto window will start to fill with images, which are the pictures Charlie took in the studio as part of his report on the ceramic process.

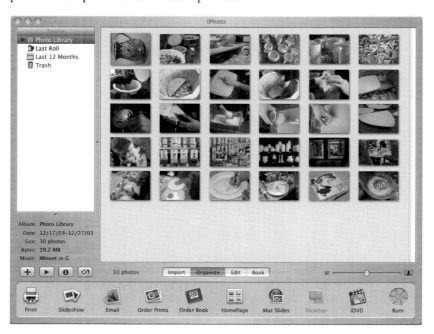

Whenever you import new photos into iPhoto, they end up in the iPhoto Library. There are two ways you may want to view photos in the Library. The first is in one giant stack, the way it looks by default. The second is by *film roll*, which is by batches of photos that you've imported. (The first batch of photos you import is one film roll, the second batch is another film roll, and so on.)

Make sure you are in the Organize panel of iPhoto (as opposed to Import, Edit, or Book). This is the screen from which you manage most organizational attributes of your photos. For instance, you can orient them right side up, toss bad or redundant snaps, and add titles and other key text information.

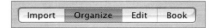

4 Go to View > Film Rolls. While it may be a little hard to understand the use of this when you have only one roll, this is an extremely good method to browse and view your growing Library.

Now the photos in the Library are organized by roll in order of date imported.

The small triangle next to the roll icon allows you to open and close the roll. When you have many rolls, this top line serves as the roll label even if the pictures aren't visible, and it makes browsing much easier.

Change Roll Information

iPhoto automatically names each of your rolls of film and dates it with the time and date of your import. Roll names come from the camera and tend to be gibberish and pretty useless. If you dragged a folder in, as you just did, the roll name is the folder name, and the date is the date the folder was created, not when it was dragged into iPhoto. Now is a good time to see how to adjust this information.

1   Click a roll. iPhoto places blue squares around the roll name and each photo in the roll.

Notice the information fields on the left side of the window, beneath the sources.

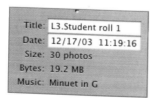

2   Type new text in the data fields in the lower left. Remove the "L3" and change the date to today (the day you imported the roll). The fields are not adjusted globally for every shot in the roll—only for the roll itself. (This is similar to the Get Info work you did with iTunes in Lesson 1.)

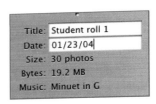

Title:	Student roll 1
Date:	01/23/04
Size:	30 photos
Bytes:	19.2 MB
Music:	Minuet in G

NOTE ▶ In this digital age, the concept of film rolls may not really be the best fundamental unit of picture organization. iPhoto4 lets you drag pictures from one roll to another and even create new rolls made up of pictures previously in other rolls (Command-click a bunch of images to select them, and then choose File > New Film Roll from Selection). This way your "rolls" can be more like "events," regardless of how you originally input them.

Delete Photos

If a picture didn't come out, waste little time leaving it around to clog the pathways of productivity. Delete it. Select a photograph and press the Delete key on your keyboard. If you delete a photo from your Library, it's removed from your hard disk permanently. Make sure this is a move you want to make.

There are a few shots in Charlie's photo shoot that he wants to weed out immediately.

1   Scroll through the roll, looking at the photos.

If the photos are hard to see, it's time to put the Size Slider to use. You can slide the knob (at the lower right part of the iPhoto window) left and right, to grow and shrink the size of the images in your display. You're not changing the photos, mind you, just zooming in to look around. Tiny pictures tend to be too small for all but the most general kind of visual searching; try a medium size where they are large enough to recognize— all the better for adjusting them a little. The good news is that you can

change this whenever you want, for whatever kind of searching you are doing at the given moment.

2   Find the photo of the painters that looks like this, and select it. A blue box should outline the photo.

3   Press Delete on your keyboard. The shot will disappear. It's gone from your hard disk.

Delete anything else you find particularly bad or redundant.

Rotate Photos

Perhaps the most frequent adjustment you'll make to photographs, particularly right after you import them, is to reorient them so they are all right side up.

On the lower left of the window, below the sources, is a button that rotates photographs counterclockwise (or, if you hold the Option key, clockwise). The first time you go through a roll of film, it's a good idea to delete bad pictures and rotate the remainder so they are oriented correctly.

1   The first photo in Charlie's roll is sideways. Select it.

2   Click the Rotate Photo button. The default is counterclockwise. You could click the button three times to get the photo upright, or you could simply hold down the Option key to toggle the rotation to a clockwise direction.

If you want to change the direction in which this button rotates photos, go to iPhoto Preferences and change the Rotate option. Most people tend to hold the camera in the vertical position one specific way all the time. You'll see in your own photos whether or not the default is right for you.

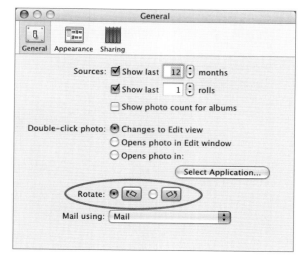

Once the images are rotated, iPhoto repositions them in the Library so each row accommodates the tallest image.

Continue through Charlie's roll of film until you have properly oriented all the images in the roll.

TIP To select multiple shots at once, click a photo, then hold down the Shift key before clicking another one; all of the photos from the first to the last you clicked will be selected. To select shots that aren't next to one another, use Command-click for the second (and subsequent) photos.

When you're done with this lesson, all the photos should be oriented properly and look like this in your iPhoto Library.

Now you're ready to do more subtle refinements on your rolls of film.

> **NOTE** ► Once you're more familiar with iPhoto, there is a more stream-lined way to review and orient your photos (among other functions available). It involves using the Slideshow controls, which you'll work with in Lesson 5.

What You've Learned

- Composition is important to good photography.

- When you're shooting, it's best to keep light behind *you*, not your subject.

- For more natural photos, try to avoid using the flash.

- Move closer to subjects, crop freely in the camera, and adjust your position to get a distinctive point of view.

- The rule of thirds says to keep subjects out of the center of the image; instead, move them to the sides or up and down a little in the frame.

- To import photos, you just plug your digital camera into your Mac, go to the Import pane in iPhoto, and click the Import button.

- To move folders of photos into iPhoto from other locations on your hard disk, you just drag the folder into the iPhoto window.

- An important step right after you import photos is to do a quick adjustment from the Organization pane, deleting bad images and rotating the remaining images to be oriented properly.

4

Lesson Files

Lessons > Lesson04 > L4.Biz roll 1

Lessons > Lesson04 > L4.Biz roll 2

Lessons > Lesson04 > L4.Biz roll 3

Lessons > Lesson04 > L4.Dad roll 1

Tools iPhoto

Time Approximately 60 minutes

Goals Learn how to make custom albums of photographs

Organize your photographs within albums

Improve and adjust the look of your photographs

Lesson **4**

Organizing and Refining Your Photos

When you start taking lots of digital photos of all the different events in your life, you'll want to keep them organized. Just like with traditional photography you can create albums. One important difference is that digital albums are a lot more powerful. In this lesson, you'll learn the basics of organizing your collection into albums and making those photos look as good as can be, ultimately leading up to sharing them with friends and family.

As you move through this lesson, you'll become familiar with each of the photography projects going on at the studio. Charlie, for instance, was busy in the back room mostly, illustrating a report he wants to make for his class on the ceramic process. Consequently, he's shooting steps in the journey from a plain white object to a finished piece. Christopher, the father, is busy shooting his daughter's birthday party. Meanwhile, Jennifer, the studio owner, takes only a few shots, combining these images with those she's been collecting over the prior weeks and months. She's always looking to shoot images of inspiring customers pieces and interesting events around her studio, and from time to time she illustrates a particular technique to help educate other customers.

Regardless of their individual agendas, all three characters will go through similar processes to organize their photographs.

Preparing for the Lesson

Your first task will be to get the Lesson 4 media into iPhoto. Here's how to do it.

1   If it isn't already open, launch iPhoto. You should see Lesson 3's Student roll 1 in the iPhoto window—if it's not, follow the steps in "Preparing for the Lesson" in Lesson 3 to bring in that material and prepare it. Make sure the Organize tab at the bottom of the window is selected (and light blue). iPhoto is ready for your next rolls of film.

2   Open the Lessons folder that you copied to your hard disk from the enclosed DVD.

3   Open the Lesson04 folder; and drag **L4.Biz roll 1**, **L4.Biz roll 2**, **L4.Biz roll 3**, and **L4.Dad roll 1** into your open iPhoto window.

When these four rolls are added to Student roll 1, your Library should look like this:

By default, iPhoto adds rolls to your Library and sorts them by roll date. To make viewing easier at this point, collapse the rolls into a single line each by clicking the black triangle on the left side of each roll icon. Before moving on, put your screen in this state:

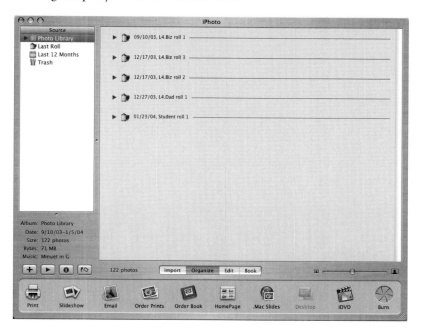

Organize Your Photos into Albums

Regardless of whether you're playing the part of the parent, the student, or the studio owner, the primary method for organizing photos in iPhoto is to create "albums." As I mentioned earlier, an album in iPhoto is virtually the same as a playlist in iTunes. Let's prove it by first working with Christopher, Jessica's dad, as he begins to organize his party pictures. In the steps that follow, you'll also prepare albums for the other characters.

1 Click the + button to add a new album to the Source list.

2   Type the name *Birthday Party* for this album in the New Album window, and click OK.

3   Drag the entire roll of film called **L4.Dad roll 1** from your Library onto the Birthday Party album icon in the Source list; this will add all 29 snapshots that Christopher shot at his daughter's birthday party.

4   Click the album name to see the shots that you've moved into this subset of your Library.

5   Make three more albums. Jennifer, the studio owner, needs an album called *Company Press* and one called *Sgraffito*. And for Charlie, create one called *Ceramic Process*.

6   Go back to the Library and drag the entire roll called Student roll 1 to the album entitled Ceramic Process.

7   From the Library, click the black triangle to open **L4.Biz roll 1**. Make the images small enough that you can see the entire roll at once.

The business owner is looking through her recent shots and pulling together a bunch that illustrate the painting technique called "Sgraffito" (a process of scratching through one color to get to another). She also happens to have captured pictures of a few pieces customers have done that utilize the technique. All of these will be aggregated in her Sgraffito album.

8   Find the following shots and move them into the Sgraffito album

TIP You could select and move one photo at a time, or move the whole roll to the album and then toss out the extraneous images from the album (select them and press the Delete key)—whichever method feels more efficient.

9   Open the **L4.Biz roll 2** and **L4.Biz roll 3** albums, so all Jennifer's snapshots are visible in the Library.

For the Company Press album, the studio owner is pulling together particularly interesting shots of her business—the look of her studios, a little bit
about what happens there, some projects in the community, as well as
some nice finished pieces by customers.

10 Find the following shots and move them into the Company Press album
(some of the shots are included in L4.Biz roll 1):

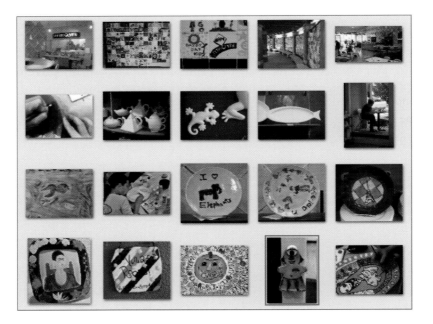

Remember, you don't always have to select and move one shot at a time.
Just as in iTunes, if you want to select a group of shots that are continuous, you can select the first, then Shift-select the last, and drag the entire
batch to the appropriate album. Before you drop the shots on the album,
notice that the number of images you're adding shows up in a red circle.
Also, if you are comfortable with selecting a discontinuous set of shots
(clicking the first shot and Command-clicking additional shots), keep that
method in mind, too.

This is the essence of manual album creation. Christopher has an album of
pictures from the birthday party; Charlie has an album of shots illustrating the

ceramic process for school; and Jennifer has a few albums for various projects associated with her business.

Click each of the albums you now have in your Source list, and make sure they contain all of the right images. These four albums will play an important role in a number of upcoming lessons.

Reorder Shots

The photos are placed in your album in the order you dragged them there. But odds are this isn't the order you ultimately want to see them. You have the opportunity to rearrange them in ways appropriate for viewing—maybe chronologically (Christopher's birthday party), or perhaps based on some theme (such as Jennifer's Sgraffito shots). Or you could group them by similar content with no concern for specific order. Whatever your strategy, it's easy to move photos to a new location within the album.

1   Open the Ceramic Process album by clicking on it. Charlie is doing a report on ceramics for his class and has shot a number of excellent photos for the purpose.

    Part of the preparation of his report, however, is getting the shots into some kind of logical sequence. The order in which he shot them (and the order in which they appear in the album) does not correspond with a logical narration of the process.

2   Move the shot of the finished ceramic piece from the beginning of the album to the end. To move it, just click and drag it to the new position. A black bar pops up within the sequence of thumbnail images to indicate where the photo will be placed when you release the mouse button.

3 Organize the rest of the shots so they tell a story. For instance, the shots of raw bisque (clay that has been fired until it's hard and white) should come toward the beginning of the album. This is about what the shots should look like when you're done:

4 Before you're done with this album, go through it and delete any shots that are too similar. Remember, Charlie is going to make a presentation and he wants it to be as concise as possible. It's pretty easy to whittle the 29 shots on his roll down to a respectable 17, which should really illustrate what he has learned about ceramics:

Adding Comments, Keywords, and Ratings to Images

Including information, such as comments and keywords, with your photographs is not only useful in keeping organized, but a great memory jogger when years have passed and you're not quite sure where a picture was taken or who the guy was standing on your left. iPhoto provides a number of methods to help you catalog pictures.

Adding a comment to a photo is the most basic, the most detailed, but perhaps the least useful since iPhoto can show you this information, but can't do much with it. Selecting one or a few keywords to attach to an image is exceptionally powerful, even though it provides less information than a comment. Selecting a rating is also easy, and can be used by iPhoto in interesting ways, especially when combined with keywords.

Going through your rolls of film and adding information for each picture may be beyond your commitment to your photo collection. Regardless of whether you add notes, keywords, or ratings to one photo or all of them, iPhoto does its best to simplify the work involved, and it offers powerful organizational features if you're willing to do the work.

Adding Comments

When you select an individual photo in either the Library or a particular album, regardless of whether you're in the Organize or Edit pane, you'll see a list of shot information on the left side of the window, beneath the Source list.

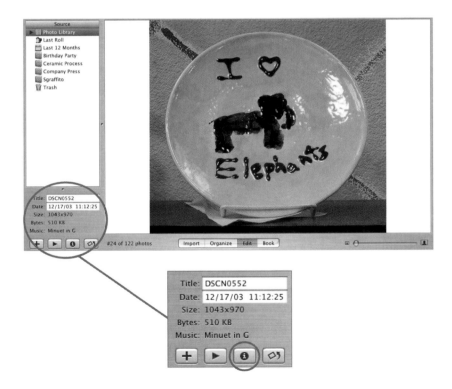

Clicking the Information button opens a small window in which you can type additional information about an image in a comments field. (In fact, clicking that button gives you one of three different results: add a comments field, make the comments field disappear, or make the entire information section disappear.)

Adding notes to the comments field is a good way to include a detailed description that might be useful down the road (like who is in a picture or where a shot was taken).

Adding Keywords

For general organization, iPhoto offers a keywords feature.

A *keyword* is a preset word or phrase that you can assign to any image. By assigning keywords, it'll make it easy to find specific kinds of photos in your collection. You can select a keyword from a preset list, which forces you to catalog shots and helps avoid that age-old organizational problem of having different labels—as in dog, dogs, pets, our dog—for the same type of photo. Each variation on a label would only make it a little more difficult to keep all the dog shots together.

You can also create your own keywords if the ones provided with the program aren't enough.

Helping one of our characters use keywords will make the process even clearer:

1   To see the preset keywords in iPhoto, choose Photos > Show Keywords. This will display the Keywords menu options.

These keyword options are a good start, but studio owner Jennifer needs some specific keywords related to the way she plans to organize her photos.

2   Click the Keywords pull-down menu at the top of the window, and select New. This lets you add your own keyword to the list. (As you can see, a keyword can be either a word or short phrase.)

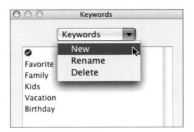

3   Add a new keyword: *Customer Pieces*.

Now you've created a new keyword that you can assign to one or more photos.

4   Go back to the Library of photos from Jennifer (L4.Biz roll 3). Go through the images until you find one of a finished customer piece, and select it.

5   Keep the Keyword menu onscreen. Once you've selected a shot, select the appropriate keyword—in this case, Customer Pieces—and then click Assign.

This adds the keyword to the stored data about this photo.

6   Select a group of shots of finished pieces.

7 Go back to the keyword window (which should be open) and assign Customer Pieces to those shots as well. Notice that assigning works just as well with one photo as with a group.

If you're unsure of the keywords you have used, or you simply want to see what you've done, turn on the View > Keywords option; the Organize pane will show your progress.

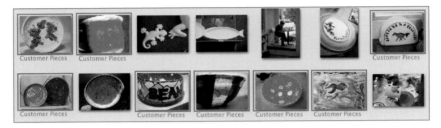

NOTE ▶ You can assign more than one keyword to a photo.

8 Go through all the business owner's photographs and assign the keyword Customer Pieces to all images of finished, glazed ceramic objects.

Adding Ratings

In addition to assigning keywords to your photos, you can categorize your shots even further by using ratings. iPhoto provides a scale of one to five stars (five stars being the best) that you can assign to any image. It can be too much work to rate everything, but sometimes rating—or rating selectively—is useful. Take Jennifer's shots of customer pieces, for instance. By definition, everything labeled with the keyword Customer Pieces is a customer's finished piece. But Jennifer is more interested in the really good photos of customers' pieces—and the keyword alone doesn't communicate this information. By going through the pieces and rating each one, she can store a little more valuable information with each photo.

1 Select one of the customer piece shots.

2 Choose View > My Rating. This will reveal any ratings you give. Otherwise, you can't see your ratings.

3   Rate a number of images, based on your own preferences. With one (or a number) of images selected, go to Photos > My Rating and pick one to five stars.

4   While Control- and Command-key functions can be confusing when you're getting used to a program, you can save a lot of time if you use them for image rating. Instead of going to the My Rating menu, simply press Command-1 (for one star), Command–2 (for two stars), and so on, to Command-5. It's much more efficient.

Once you have rated all the customer pieces, you're ready to use one of the most powerful organizational tools in iPhoto.

> **TIP** You can also rate images and make a few other useful adjustments while watching the images in a slide show (discussed in Lesson 5). It is often a faster way to rate multiple photos.

Creating Smart Albums

While it's easy to add a regular album to iPhoto, a Smart Album is a great tool for creatively organizing your collection. This type of album can be set up to automatically pull certain shots into it without you having to manually put them there. It's like making and always updating an album without requiring you to do any manual work.

For instance, you could let iPhoto aggregate all images taken between November 27 and December 31 of every year. This would create a holiday album that would continue to fill up with holiday photos for years. Or you might choose to collect only your favorite images of your kids in a single album. Assign the Kids keyword to those new photos, rate the images, and iPhoto adds to the Smart Album indefinitely.

Jennifer wants an album that stores only the best photos of the top customer pieces—she wants to use them to inspire other customers and also show the incredible range of creativity that flows through her studio.

1   Choose File > New Smart Album.

A window pops up, prompting you to name the Smart Album and set the criteria by which it will automatically gather images.

2 Type *Cool Pieces* as the name of the Smart Album.

3 Click each of the window's three pull-down menus to set up the conditions. You can create many permutations from these options, allowing for a large quantity of creative assortments of your photographs. For Jennifer, set the condition to select photos whose keyword is Customer Pieces.

When you're done, the window should look like this. The condition will pull together all the photos marked by keyword as Customer Pieces.

TIP If you haven't yet rated all your Customer Pieces, you could make this Smart Album with only one condition. Then, working from inside the Smart Album you can rate them, which would be easier than working from the disparate rolls in the Library. Whether you're rating images during a slide show or going at it from the Organization tab, working from the Smart Album is a good first step to streamlining your rating process.

4   Click the + button to add a new condition. Because the photos are already rated, you can set this one to look for ratings of four stars or better (this means you need to select "is greater than" three stars; the search will not include three-star ratings).

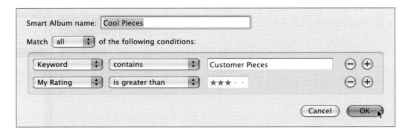

5   Click OK, and a new album is created in your Source list; this one has a little gear icon by its title, denoting that the contents are generated automatically.

6   Select your new Cool Pieces Smart Album, which should show you the best pieces that customers have painted.

Cropping Photos

Perhaps the most important control you have as a photographer is selecting the composition and framing of your photos. And while you do your best when shooting the camera, you may want to cut out parts of an image that are distracting, or reshape the frame to highlight some aspect of the photo. Since it's all too easy to shoot from a little too far away, tightly cropping a photograph is a way to increase the impact and sophistication of many shots.

To augment a picture in iPhoto, double-click the image. This will take you to the edit pane. (Or you could select an image and click the Edit Pane button.)

1   Double-click the photo that looks like this in the Company Press album.

Double-clicking will open up the shot in the Edit pane, which will look like this:

2   Click the cursor anywhere in the image, and drag a rectangle across your image. When you let go, the rectangle remains visible. If you missed the framing you were looking for, you can drag each side of the rectangle in or out to refine your frame.

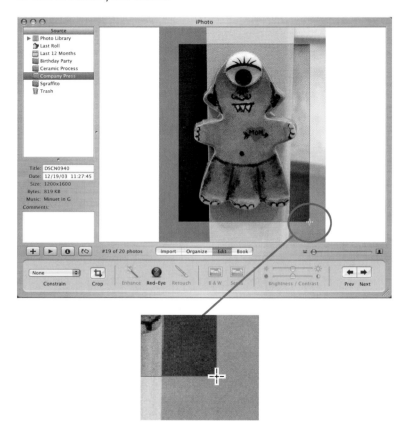

3   Once you have the photograph set up with the frame and shape you prefer, click the Crop button. This disposes of the edges you don't want and redraws the new image in your window.

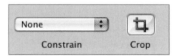

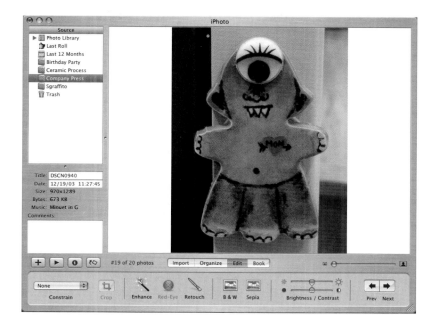

Cropping to Fit a Frame

Sometimes you crop not only to cut out bad stuff, but also to guarantee your photograph will fit in a picture frame (or CD case, or TV set). In these cases, you want to force the shape of your cropping to match the length and width ratios of your frame—known as the "aspect ratio."

1   Double-click this photo:

2   Next to the Crop button is the Constrain pop-up menu. Click on the menu and choose 8 x 10.

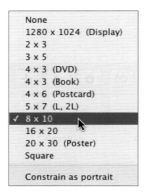

This will preselect a cropping frame that is in the ratio of 8:10—effectively allowing your image to fit into an 8-by-10-inch frame. By clicking within the cropping frame, and dragging to a new position, you are able to move this 8:10 rectangle around over your photo prior to cropping.

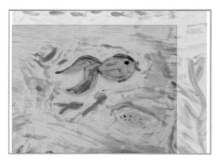 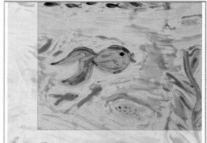

TIP ▸ Even if you centered your subject when you shot your photograph, cropping gives you another chance to offset your subject and create an aesthetically pleasing composition (using the rule of thirds).

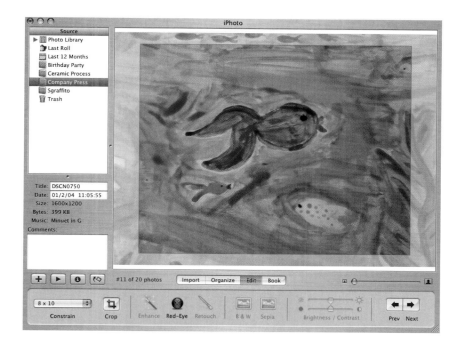

3 Click the Crop button when you have positioned the frame aesthetically.

This technique gives you prints whose proportions fit perfectly in a picture frame or a CD jewel case. It's worth noting that cropping a photo in an album, like changing a name or date, affects the original photo in the Library.

> **TIP** If you don't want to alter your original photo, make a copy of it first and then crop the copy. Select the image, then choose Photos > Duplicate and a copy will be placed in your Library.

> **TIP** Don't forget that you can always undo a bad crop, and virtually anything else you accidently apply to a photo. Command-Z is the keyboard shortcut to Undo.

Adjust the Look of Images

iPhoto comes with some simple but powerful tools for tweaking the images you took with your camera. In the Edit pane, below the image, is a set of tools for automatically and manually adjusting images. On the right side are manual controls for adjusting brightness and contrast. On the left are buttons for one-click "magic" image controls.

The most useful and impressive of these is the power of Enhance.

Enhance

Let's go back to the fish image we just cropped. It's a little dark, and not quite as crisp as it could be.

1   Double-click the image to bring it into the Edit pane.

2   Click Enhance. iPhoto does a quick analysis of your image and determines the best way to adjust brightness, contrast, color balance, and white balance in order to improve your image.

It doesn't always work perfectly, but it's pretty good, and most images benefit. If you don't like the results of Enhance, press Command-Z to undo it.

TIP If Enhance didn't help, you can try your hand at using the manual image adjustment tools located to the right of the automated ones. Brightness and contrast sliders can sometimes help where Enhance is too much. If your image needs considerable image manipulation, it's probably best to tweak it in dedicated image-manipulation software.

Go through all the images in all four albums and crop or enhance until you are satisfied with them.

Red-Eye

If you're using a flash, it's not uncommon to end up with that satanic-looking red-eye—the bane of photographers everywhere. It's caused when the flash reflects off the subject's retina and creates that characteristic glow. Some cameras minimize red-eye by shining a light for a moment before the actual photo is taken; this causes the pupil to constrict before the flash goes off and therefore reduces the retina reflection. Not all cameras have this feature, and even if they do, they don't catch every incident. If you don't get rid of red-eye when you shoot, you can do it on your Mac. iPhoto simply does a little color correction on your subject's eyes—taking that which was red and making it black.

1   Open Christopher's Birthday Party album. There's one shot of a party guest with that eerie red-eye.

2   Double-click the photo.

3   Click and drag a rectangle around the eyes (the way you would if you were cropping the photo—but don't crop it).

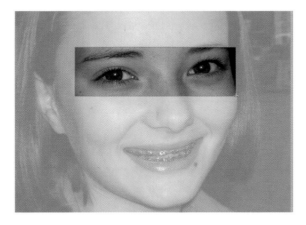

4   Click the Red-Eye tool.

And, like magic, the devil eyes are gone.

What You've Learned

- The + button lets you add new albums.

- You can put photos in a specific album by dragging and dropping an image (or groups of them) from the Library to the chosen album.

- You can rearrange the sequence of images within an album by dragging and dropping them.

- Use the Crop tool to reframe an image to fit in a frame or to improve composition.

- Constraining the Crop tool will perfectly reframe an image in a proportion you specify, for use in a variety of output formats, such as picture frames or CD cases.

- The Enhance feature can automatically improve image problems in some photos.

- The Red-Eye feature can correct that eerie red glow that your flash sometimes creates.

5

Lesson Files	No files for this lesson
Tools	iPhoto, color printer (optional), .Mac account (optional)
Time	Approximately 45 minutes
Goals	Print photos from iPhoto
	Make a book using iPhoto's connection to high-quality publication services
	Create a quick and easy slide show of photos with music

Printing and Sharing Your Photos

Importing and organizing collections are important, but the value of a good collection is being able to share it with other people. Thanks to all of the resources at hand today, you have many ways you can do that. Back in the old days, a photo collection was sometimes handed to a visitor as a thick stack of pictures to be flipped through. Or a few special shots were reproduced from negatives and mailed to family. Or an unsuspecting guest was sat down on a sofa and handed a tome of family adventures to view page after page and examine mindfully. Moving photos into the digital domain still allows for each of these methods, but also adds considerable flexibility for creativity and ingenuity.

In this lesson, you'll examine three methods our subjects chose to share the fruits of their digital labor. Because Charlie is in a relatively low-tech environment at school (no projectors, no DVD players, few computers), he will print glossy paper copies for cutting and pasting on posterboard. Jennifer's project is part of her business operations and will be printed on a high-quality, linen-bound book for her discerning audience. And Christopher, to have some fun himself while entertaining his daughter and her pals, will make a quick slide show to display on his Mac during the birthday party.

Preparation for Sharing

No matter what your intended output for your photos, the creation of an album in iPhoto is an important first step. While it's certainly not required, it makes all the effort that follows far simpler and the process more enjoyable. In each part of this lesson, you'll use a different album from among the albums you created in Lesson 4.

No matter what project you're creating, whether following along with the lessons in this book or working independently on your own projects, take the time to go through your albums several times, checking that the order of images is appropriate, making sure you don't want to add or delete any, and doing last-minute tweaks to orientation, framing, image quality, and so on.

Printing Paper Images

Charlie, the high school student, is creating a class presentation about the ceramic process. Since the hardware at his school is limited, he has chosen to make a poster to present in the classroom to accompany a small lecture he will give. As with all projects, it starts with albums of photos, in this case the album called Ceramic Process.

Once he's opened the album, he's going to print 4-by-6-inch copies of each image using the Print Photos option at the bottom of the screen.

1   Select an album. If you don't select any photos, iPhoto by default will print all the images in the album. If you select one or more photos from within an album, it's those photos that will be prepared for printing.

2 Click Print. The Print button is located in the bar of output options along the bottom of the iPhoto window.

Clicking Print brings up a printing window that allows you to choose a printer, set the margins and, of course, choose the number of copies you want. There are also advanced options you can access from this window, if you have specific printing requirements.

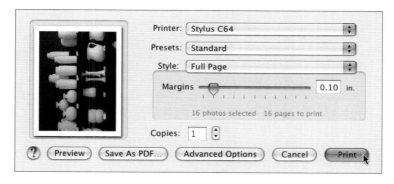

NOTE ▸ Advanced options include Print Settings (picking a type of paper, printing with draft quality or photo quality) and iPhoto settings (printing smaller than 8 1/2 by 11 paper, printing multiple copies of a single print on each page, printing contact sheets)

3 Print a copy of the first photo. Charlie, of course, printed all the photos in the album. High-quality prints tend to take longer to come out of the printer than those of lower quality. Using the Advanced options, Charlie set the print quality to correspond to the type (and quality) of paper he's printing on—plain white paper. For a high school report, the image quality doesn't need to be professional caliber.

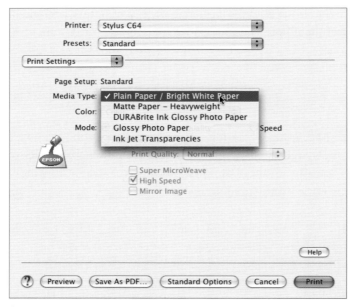

Charlie's advanced options are specific to his printer.

4   Use scissors or a paper cutter to cleanly chop up the print (if required) or trim borders for a clean, report-ready style.

Charlie integrated his photographs with some information he researched about the ceramic process, which he turned into captions for the images. He used a word-processing program to type up the captions, set the width of the columns to that of the photos, and use a font that looked legible and academic. Probably the most challenging part of his process was manually assembling the poster.

Make a Bound Book

Jennifer, the studio owner, is interested in investing in a number of glossy, linen-covered portfolio books of ideas and examples of customers' pieces to distribute to her studios. She also wants to create a special expanded version of the album that includes her home made publicity photos of the ceramic process and of projects the studio has contributed to the community, and nice shots of each of her studio locations. These special books will be holiday presents for key staff members and some of her best customers.

In general, Jennifer shoots video in her studio, using the footage to make training tapes and also to generate still images for her Web site. Occasionally she takes digital still images, which she loads into iPhoto. Over the years she has taken hundreds of photos, and she has aggregated the best pictures in albums based on some basic themes: images of bisque (the inventory of her studios), shots of her studios in action, shots of finished customer pieces that might inspire other customers, and shots of techniques that illustrate and demystify the process.

iPhoto is designed to make, among other things, a good quality hardback book of images. The software helps you put photos on pages, and then lets you automatically access a Web site where you can order the book you designed. While it's an impressive product, it's not inexpensive. A 16-page book of, say, 25 photographs might cost around $45, although prices will vary. Although you might not use it as a replacement for scrapbooking, it's a fine way to deliver special sets of photographs for important occasions.

The quality of Jennifer's photos varies greatly: sometimes 3 megapixels from the still cameras in the studios, sometimes 1 megapixel from a digital camera she used many years ago, and sometimes 1/3 megapixel as frame grabs from a videotape (which you will do in Lesson 13). Keep in mind the image differences when you print photos—if you try making an image larger than its resolution will support, it will look lousy, perhaps compromising the overall impact of the book.

The first step is deciding what the book will be for, what photos to include, and in what order they should show up in the book (and therefore, the iPhoto album).

1 Open the Company Press album. This will reveal images that Jennifer wants to put in her picture book.

The photos appear in the order in which they were dragged into the album. Jennifer needs to group them, at least in a preliminary way, with some kind of logical flow.

The first photo in the album is going to appear on the cover of the book, so it's of particular significance. After looking through the photos a few times (by double-clicking the first one, which opens the Edit window, and then using the forward arrow button to move through them), she comes up with a few themes and a general order to them:

- Cover
- Studio "tour"
- Activity/people at work
- Community
- Bisque
- Finished pieces

2   Take a few moments to drag images around and move them into an order that satisfies the sequence outlined above. When you're done, the order should be something like Jennifer's:

The order may change or evolve over the bookmaking process. But this is a fine start. It's time to visit the Book window.

3   Click the Book tab.

The window changes into a special workspace where you can organize and lay out your book.

NOTE ▶   iPhoto is always looking at the resolution (remember those megapixels?) of your images and determining if photos of a given quality will reproduce well at the size they are in the book. If it finds a quality problem, it will insert a small yellow yield sign (with an exclamation point in it) over the problem picture. Until you're in the page design part of this process, you can ignore these, but ultimately you may not want photos in your book that won't reproduce at the selected size. (Making them smaller often helps.)

Thumbnails of each page   A preview of how the page looks

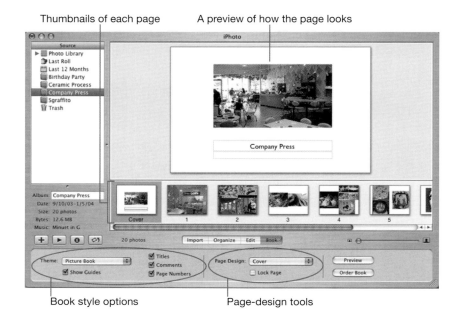

Book style options   Page-design tools

By default, iPhoto gives your book the album's name. It also takes a guess as to the theme (such as a picture book versus a portfolio) and the design of your book, although it's very easy to change both of those.

The Theme pull-down menu offers a number of book styles. It's located in the lower-left part of the window.

4   Click and hold on the word Picture Book to reveal the other options for Theme.

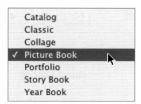

5   Check out what happens to your book as you dial through each option, but when you're done, leave the setting at Picture Book. Once the theme is set, you probably won't need to change it again. Move your focus to the right, to the Page Design controls, where you build the layout of each page of your book.

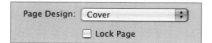

The process of designing the pages will likely be iterative—that is, you will adjust the page photo layout (using the Page Design pull-down menu) and then possibly return to the Organize tab to change the order of some images, maybe delete or add a few to the album's pictures, and then return to the Book tab to continue to work on the page design. Through this back-and-forth, you will sculpt a book.

6   If it's not still selected, select the first page of the book (the first photo in your album, which goes on the cover).

The cover page design allows for a photograph and a title. By clicking the title and typing your own text, you can change it.

7   Change this book's title to *Petroglyph Ceramic Lounge*. This is the name of Jennifer's company. Add a subtitle that says *The First Ten Years*.

When you click one of the thumbnails below the enlarged page, iPhoto will move to that page and present the larger image of it above. You can always click on any of the thumbnails to view a given page.

8 Click the first page in the thumbnails. This will be the cover.

Before you click on the next page, it feels like something is missing right after the cover. Jennifer would like to include a message to the people to whom she's giving the book. An introduction. It turns out that you can add an introduction page, through an option in the Page Design pull-down menu.

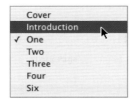

9 Set the Page Design option to Introduction. A new page is inserted, the thumbnails are updated, and default information is plugged into the text fields on the introduction page.

10 Click the fields and type to add your own text.

Also notice that the layout of all the following pages has been changed. It's good to work from the front of the book toward the end, building pages as you go (although, as you will see in a moment, there is a special tool provided that facilitates working out of order).

Jennifer types a letter to her readers. While she's typing, iPhoto enlarges the workspace so it's easier for her to see what she's writing. This text isn't a photograph and consequently isn't going to be visible on any of the iPhoto organization/edit tabs, but it *is* connected to this particular album. You can review it only in this Book view.

11 Click page 2. These photos don't go together. Make this a one-photo page using the Page Design pull-down. Then lock the page.

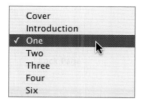

12 Click page 3. These images do go together—they're all shots of a large public installation of tiles made by grade school students and sponsored by Jennifer's company. But there are three images (all in a row in the album) that should be grouped for this page.

13 Change the layout to display the three photos. If you like how this page looks, lock it too.

Notice how the completed pages in the thumbnails have locks on them, meaning that no matter how the rest of the album is changed or images reordered, the images on these pages will be held in place. It's a convenient and important feature. If you don't use it, you may have to keep rebuilding pages that get messed up as you revisit earlier pages. Locking allows you to work more fluidly, a little out of order, if necessary.

14 Click page 4. Make it look like this, and lock it:

But on second thought, this page should really appear before the page of the community tile wall. Changing the order of pages is as easy as dragging them around and dropping them where you want them.

15 In the thumbnails, grab page 4 and drag it before page 3.

The pages themselves are locked, but their order is not. It can be adjusted easily. Notice that as you drag the page to a different location in the book, the other pages shift around to reflect the position. There's no black bar that shows position (the way moving images are handled in the Organize tab), but it's very easy to know where the page is going to go.

16 Make page 5 the bisque page—exclusively for images of the white, unfinished ceramic shapes.

17 Make page 6 a layout with two photos, one that shows a girl painting a plate, and next to it a detail of how the plate looked when it was finished, glazed, and fired.

18 Pages 7 through 10 are all about finished pieces. Experiment with one- to four-picture pages. If you don't like the order and position, click the Organize tab and reposition some of the images, then return to the Book tab to fix the layout.

In particular, because of the way iPhoto automatically fits photos onto a page, some images get cropped slightly, and others clearly are of different proportions and look odd together. It can take some experimentation and some back and forth with the Organize tab to arrange shots so that the layouts look their best.

19 Whatever you do, keep this book to a cover plus 10 pages; thus if a picture is spilling over to an eleventh page, change the design of prior pages to shorten the book. You can make these books any length you want, but the price increases by number of pages (not number of photos). So you need to have control over the length of your product.

NOTE ▸ The book printing service requires that books be a minimum of 10 pages; if your book is shorter, it will add blank pages to fill out the number.

When you've finished the book, locked all the pages, and reviewed the text to your liking, the book is ready to print. You can choose from a couple of methods. To make a printout of your custom book on your own printer, use the File > Print command. From there, you can select your printer, the number of copies, and, if you are so inclined, the option to generate a PDF file of your book.

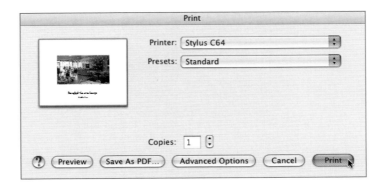

NOTE ▶ The PDF file will be an exceptionally large one, but for some kinds of paperless distribution, like posting on the Web or emailing, it might be desirable.

The most interesting option is to use iPhoto's built-in high-quality book production. iPhoto will contact an outside service to create linen-bound hardback books for you, which are printed and shipped to you in a few days. This is the process Jennifer uses for her picture book. Two buttons are dedicated to this process; find them on the bottom right of the iPhoto window when you're in Book view.

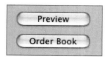

In all honesty, the Preview function—which opens a little window with your book in its final state that you can flip through—shows you a view that's not all that different from what you've seen while working on the book. It's a good idea to preview your work, particularly before ordering the book, but as you've seen, you have a number of ways to do that.

Once you're sure the book looks the way you want it to, click Order Book. iPhoto takes a few moments to assemble the book and prepare a file of information, and then it connects to the bookmaking service, where you can select a color for the cover and the quantity of books.

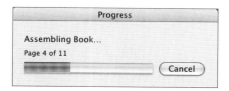

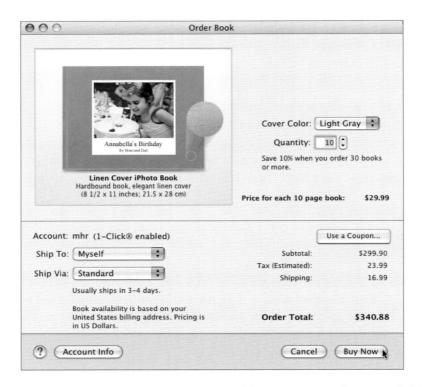

The book service will give you a price (roughly $3 per page, plus tax and shipping), at which point you can choose whether to place your order. Jennifer ordered 10 books.

Make a Quick Slide Show

One of the things iPhoto does best is generate an automatic slide show from all or some of the photos in your collection. A slide show is a good way to review a new roll of film, and tools in iPhoto let you instantly rate images and adjust their orientation, similar to tools found in the Organize tab.

Christopher, the father, takes snapshots during his daughter's birthday party; to amuse himself while she and her friends are working, he decides to make a slide show of images from the party—a little instant nostalgia. Before the kids leave the party and head home, they can enjoy fun moments from the day and have a good laugh.

Christopher's first step is to hook up his still camera to the computer (as described in Lesson 3).

Then he imports the images into iPhoto. He makes a Birthday Party album and drags the whole roll to it. Finally, he does some quick weeding out, reorienting, and enhancing of photos. In all, it takes about five minutes.

When you click on the Birthday Party album, you'll see what Christopher sees.

1   Click Slideshow, a button on the menu of output options at the bottom of the iPhoto window.

This opens the Slideshow settings window. The key considerations now are (1) whether the order of images is important, (2) how long you want each slide to be displayed, and (3) the music that should play during the show.

For many slide shows, it's OK to display photos in random order, but if you want your photos to appear in a short slide show in the order you've arranged them, be sure the "Present slides in random order" and "Repeat slideshow" options are not used. A presentation—like Charlie's school project—would have to display images in a specific order to make sense, if he were going to show them as a slide show. Anything chronological, like photos that recount a trip or tell a story, would also necessitate a pre-selected order. But whimsical slide shows, images shown for fun, or collections in which the element of surprise is important can benefit from being presented in random order.

NOTE ▶ A random-order slide show repeats images, by definition. Random-order often plays the same images repeatedly, even before it has played all the slides (and some might never seem to show up). There is just no telling what you're going to see, or how often it will show, when it's random. You can also have a nonrandom slide show repeat after it has run through all the slides, and thus run on indefinitely. Sometimes this is preferable to absolute randomness.

For Christopher's quick slide show, he decides to display images in the order he shot them. It could be fun to run them randomly, but here—while the kids are still painting—he wants the show to have a definite end point.

2   Set the slide show to play in the order of the album and not to repeat. This requires unchecking the "Present slides in random order" and "Repeat slide-show" options.

3   Play each slide for three seconds. It's a little on the long side, but for kids who might be distracted—maybe laughing at each other or turning away in embarrassment—it's appropriate.

4   Leave the transition setting (at the top of the menu) set to Dissolve. You could alter the way one slide changes into the next. Experiment with various options, and change how fast or slowly the transition occurs (with the slider beneath the setting) if you want, but when you're done, return the setting to Dissolve. A dissolve is a classic transition that isn't distracting and suits almost any situation.

NOTE ▶ Direction is an attribute of some kinds of transitions—such as Cube and Wipe—where you can determine whether slides should replace each other from left to right or right to left. It doesn't apply to Dissolve.

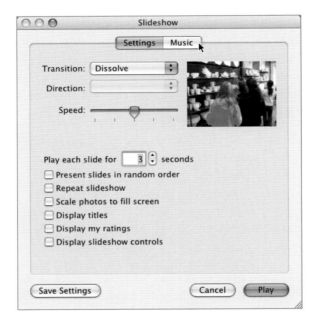

5   Click the Music tab, now that the slide show is set up.

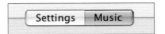

This is where you'd tell iPhoto whether you want to have music with your slide show. If you don't, uncheck the music option and you're ready to play. But Christopher wants music to accompany the show, and the music he'd like is in his iTunes playlist called Jessica's Favs (which he made in Lesson 1). You can select any of your available playlist preferences.

6   iPhoto defaults to Sample Music—in case you don't use (or haven't set up) iTunes with a Library or playlists. Click the pull-down menu to reveal other iTunes playlists that may be more appropriate.

You can select one song (which will repeat endlessly if given the chance) or a single playlist. (To use an entire playlist, make sure you do *not* select a song, or just that song will play.) Once you click a playlist, its contents become visible.

Here, the entire playlist is selected. Once everything is ready, assemble your audience and click Play. This will play the slide show—now—right from your Mac. It's about the smallest amount of work you'll ever need to make a custom and personal slide show.

A moment after you click Play, iPhoto will fade out your Mac's display, start the music, and then begin the slide show. To stop the show at any point, press the spacebar to pause on a given slide or click your mouse to exit the slide show entirely.

Other Sharing Options

When you look along the bottom of iPhoto's Organize window, you'll notice other options besides Print, Slideshow, and Order Book.

Email gives you a simple way to attach photos to an email. Select the photos you want and click Email in the toolbar at the bottom of the window. iPhoto will ask you to select a compression size (Do your friends want photos as large as you can make them? Do you have a dial-up connection, which necessitates small, highly compressed, images?) and then it will attach the images to a blank email in your default email program when you click Compose.

Order Prints, like Order Book, connects you to an online printing service where you can select sizes and quantities of individual prints and have them billed and shipped to you.

HomePage and .Mac Slides are related to your .Mac account, and will be discussed in some detail in Lesson 13. **iDVD** is related to burning a DVD of your slideshows, and will be discussed in Lesson 14.

Desktop instantly changes the Desktop picture on your Mac to the selected photo (usually controlled via your Mac's Preferences > Desktop pictures). A cool feature but not easy to undo.

What You've Learned

- Once you've organized albums from your photos, any number of output options are available.

- Printing one photo or an album of shots is easy using the Print command.

- Formal books can be created for professional printing using various pre-designed themes.

- Setting up a book requires going page by page through the Book tab thumbnails, and selecting a design for each page. By balancing the order of images and the number of images on a page, a book can be customized quickly.

- Assembling a slide show is a very fast project with minimal effort and great payback.

- A slide show can display images randomly from an album (or the Library) or in an order you pick. You can set the duration of each image; two to three seconds is probably ideal.

- Selecting music to accompany a slide show in iPhoto is easy since the program automatically connects to your playlists in iTunes. iPhoto can play one song or an entire iTunes playlist to accompany a slide show.

6

Lesson Files   Lessons > Lesson06 > Start_Birthday_Project6

Lessons > Lesson06 > Sgraffito Script.txt

Tools   iMovie

Time   Approximately 90 minutes

Goals   Get familiar with iMovie

Bring still photos into iMovie

Add photos to a movie as either still or moving images

Add music to your dynamic slide show

Adjust durations of shots in the slide show

Add dissolves and other transition effects between shots

Adding Motion and Effects for a Dynamic Slide Show

iPhoto is great for the quick-and-clean slide show. But it's largely automated. What if you want more control over the show? Now is the time to look at iMovie and see how it manages photographs and music differently than iPhoto and iTunes.

Christopher made a quick slide show for his daughter Jessica and her friends at the birthday party, which was fun and easy. But now that he's home and has a little more time over the weekend, he wants to make a more interesting-looking slide show for the grandparents to watch. iMovie can help him do this. Jennifer used a slide show as a way to generate automatic in-store presentations of customers' pieces (see Lesson 4), but she also wants to use her photos to educate customers in interesting painting techniques. The type of slide show that you create in iPhoto won't work well for her purposes: Some images need to be onscreen longer than others; text and titles need to be integrated with the images; and some parts of images are more important for the audience to focus on than others. Jennifer can make the best training presentation through iMovie.

Here's your chance to see how to use iMovie to create slide shows. We'll follow both Jennifer and Christopher through this process but will focus mostly on Jennifer's project since it demonstrates a greater range of techniques. You'll open iMovie and see how to use it to make dynamic presentations, home movies, documentaries, or training videos, all without using a video camera.

Open iMovie and Look Around

Although iTunes and iPhoto have a consistent interface—similar, in fact, to the Mac OS itself—iMovie is unique. The nature of creating motion pictures dictates some different tools in the interface and some pretty interesting capabilities.

1   Launch iMovie.

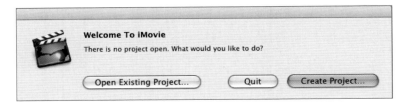

2   Click Create Project. This will prepare a workspace for your movies.

3   Name the project. Since you'll be working on a customer training video (as if you were Jennifer, the studio owner), name this project *Sgraffito Technique.*

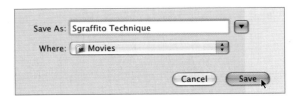

4   Click Save to let iMovie keep your work files in the Movies folder, which is the default in the pull-down menu (the one labeled "Where"). Use this default unless you really want to put the files somewhere else (like on the Desktop).

Viewer   Clip pane

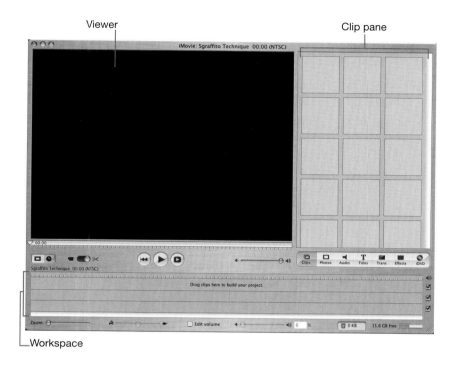

Workspace

Take a look at the iMovie interface. Over the next few lessons, you'll explore this tool in more detail, but for the moment let's focus on a few key regions.

- Viewer – The big, black empty part is your Viewer, a television set of sorts, where you will watch all the video you are manipulating—either raw material still in your camera, or the pieces of video you're editing.

- Clip pane – The grid of small squares to the right of the Viewer is your Clip pane, a storage area that holds bits of video that you import into iMovie from your camera (or other sources, as you'll see). But this area isn't only for video clips. The buttons underneath these squares can change the region into a toolbox with an array of other specific functions.

Raw material starts in this part of the screen (whether from the Clip pane or other menu), and then moves to the bottom of the screen as you work with it.

- Workspace – The long, horizontal area under the Clip pane is your video workspace. It's in this area that, clip by clip, you'll assemble a video. You can adjust your view of what you're building in this workspace. You might want to see your video as a series of representative slides (Clip view); or see the video tracks in lengths relative to their duration (Timeline view). Each viewing option will be useful at some point. In truth, while you're working, you'll find yourself toggling back and forth between views.

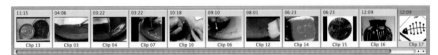

The Clip View button (above) and the workspace presented in the Clip view (below). This is a good way to visualize the pieces of your project as you assemble them. It also notes the name and duration of each clip.

The Timeline View button (above) and the same workspace shown in the Timeline view (below). You can still see the clips, but the duration of each is represented by the size of the box. In this graphical view, it's easy to see how long a shot will play, or where you are watching within a given shot, both key aspects of moving images versus still ones.

In the Timeline view is a vertical line called the *playhead*, which shows the frame in your sequence that you are seeing in the Viewer. A good way to play your sequence is to drag the playhead to the beginning of your project and click the Play button under the Viewer.

For many projects, the video camera is your primary source for material. In this lesson, however since you're not working with video, all your raw material is going to be accessed via the row of buttons beneath the Clip pane. These are particularly important for accessing raw material from the other iLife applications as well as for providing key tools in the construction of your video.

Accessing and Using Photographs from iPhoto

Jennifer's project is a quick one—turning some still photos of a painting technique (called sgraffito) into an easy lesson for customers. The video will run on a large display in the studio.

She wants to build the video mainly from six photographs. Beyond that, she'll add some shots of finished pieces made with this technique to the beginning and end. She has also dashed off a simple script that she wants to use in the slide show for a little clearer explanation.

The script is included in the folder for Lesson 6, called **Sgraffito Script.txt**.

While there are more advanced ways to integrate the script—using voice-over narration, for instance—she wants to do a video with no dialogue, so the movie could play in a busy, noisy studio with sound off and still make sense.

iMovie connects to iPhoto so effortlessly, it's impressive even to someone used to more professional video software. From inside iMovie, you have direct access to your iPhoto Library and (better still) all of your albums.

1   Click the Photos button.

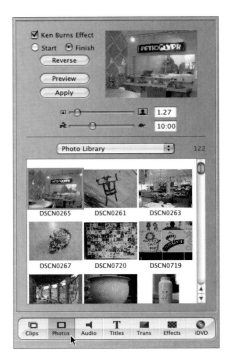

The Clip pane disappears and the Photo tools take its place. At the top of the region are tools for adding motion to still photos (called the Ken Burns Effect), and at the bottom is a window into your iPhoto Library.

2   Click the Photo Library pulldown menu above the photos and select the Sgraffito album, rather than browsing through the entire Library (which could be somewhat inefficient). Recognize the other items here? That's right: It's the source lineup from iPhoto.

When you select an album, it will immediately appear in the scrollable window below, with the first image selected and shown in the window above, ready for modification (if you so choose) and ultimately introduction into your growing video project.

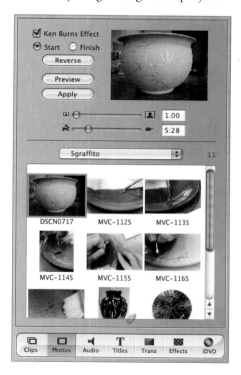

iMovie defaults to turning a still image from iPhoto into a dynamic moving image—using the Ken Burns Effect tools. Notice the Ken Burns Effect is checked, and the image in the window is moving slightly. You'll experiment with this in a moment, but at this point, don't use the Ken Burns Effect.

NOTE ▶ Ken Burns is an innovative documentary filmmaker who has created a number of popular movies (*The Civil War, Baseball, Jazz*). He often uses the visual effect of moving the camera slowly across still images to tell stories. He didn't invent it, but he sure is good at it, and has excited many young filmmakers about movies in general and documentaries in particular.

3   Uncheck the box at the top of the Photo tools area to turn off the Ken Burns Effect. The picture in the little adjacent window will stop moving. Notice that the Start, Finish, Reverse, and Preview options are grayed out. When you place a still photo into a video project, you have only a couple of options: size and position (framing).

4   Click and drag the photo. Drag left. Drag right. Notice your power over this photo.

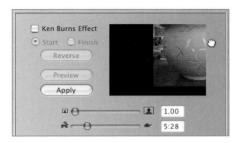

Moving the photo around isn't very interesting unless the photo is much larger than the TV screen. Beneath the photo is a Zoom slider—from "normal" size (the actual image size, represented by 1.00) on the left to "huge" (five times the actual image size, 5.00) on the right.

5 Slide the Zoom slider around to experiment with the image size.

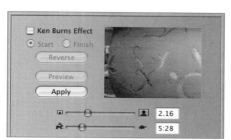

Once you've got the still photo looking the way you want it to, move on to the second slider beneath the first, which controls the duration of a shot (how long it will remain on the screen).

Remember, this is a still image—it has no intrinsic duration. Show someone your real-world scrapbook and they may glance at an image for a moment or sit with it for 20 seconds or more. But slide shows and movies take this power away from viewers and give it to you—the media creator. You have the challenge of making sure that your audience gets to see the image long enough without getting bored.

How long should a photo be? There's no simple answer; trust your instincts. Good filmmakers understand that different images may require different amounts of time to be "read." Close-up shots may be easily read and enjoyed in a second or two. Wide shots and images with lots of interesting details may need longer, four or five seconds perhaps, for the audience to feel satisfied and not rushed.

6 Whatever answer you arrive at for an image, use the Duration slider with the rabbit and turtle to control the length of a shot. The box on the right gives you the actual seconds and frames of the shot, which you control. No decision, by the way, is permanent. If you make a shot too short, it's always simple to adjust it later.

NOTE ▶ Units of video are called frames. Video plays at 30 frames per second, which means that one frame is 1/30 second long. It doesn't seem like a long time (and it's not), but for filmmakers it's enough to make a difference.

7   Set the duration of the shot to 8 seconds. If you can't get exactly 8 seconds by moving the slider, you can also click the box to the right, type in *8:00*, and press Return. Now you're ready to put the shot into your movie.

8   Click Apply. This converts the still image into a video snippet of the duration you specified and places it in the timeline.

Now you see how to take a still image from iPhoto, put it into iMovie, and move it around a little bit. You might be thinking, "So what?"

The power of iMovie is not in the insertion of still photos but rather in giving those still images some life. You do this by slowly moving the image around, as if a camera were looking the image over. For this you need to turn on the Ken Burns Effect.

9   Check the Ken Burns Effect check box. Notice that the Start and Finish buttons are now available.

The Ken Burns Effect works very simply: You decide how you want your shot to look at the beginning (Start) and at the end (Finish), and choose how long it should take to move from Start to Finish.

10 Select the detailed image of the sgraffito technique (MVC 110S) from the scrollable photos in the album presented in the Library.

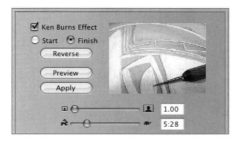

11 Click the Start button. Now you're ready to set up the starting position for your shot.

12 Use the Zoom slider to enlarge the shot slightly, to around two times the image size (2.00).

13 Using the hand cursor, click and drag the image around until you like its position. This is where Jennifer started her shot.

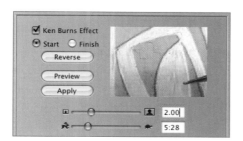

TIP If you want to zoom in by a precise amount rather than just sliding the slider and eyeballing it, you can type a number into the box to the right of the slider for an exact enlargement multiple.

14 Click the Finish button once you've found the starting point. Do what you did before: Using the size and drag functions, position the frame the way you want it to end. Jennifer wants the shot to pull back until it's zoomed out to "normal" size.

Shots don't have to zoom. You could just move the frame slowly from left to right. Or you could choose to zoom in rather than out—a shot could start wide (a multiple of 1.00) and zoom in. Different shots lend themselves to different methods. It all depends on what you want the audience to see and when.

15 Click Preview to see how your move will look once you've set it up.

Jennifer finds the move interesting, but it's too fast. This is a common problem with the Ken Burns Effect—people want to move their shots too quickly. A nice, slow, steady move is easier and far more interesting to watch.

16 To slow down the move, slide the Duration slider to the right, toward the turtle. The length of the shot will be displayed in the box on the right (in seconds and frames). Make the duration approximately 10 seconds.

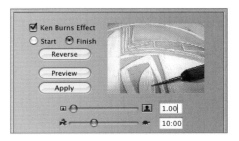

You can go back and forth, adjusting the Start and Finish points as well as the duration until you're satisfied with the preview.

17 Click Apply. This moves your shot down into your workspace. The longer the shot, the longer your Mac will take to prepare it for viewing. Computers need to do a lot of work to generate special effects such as the Ken Burns Effect.

Now this shot will be appended to the first shot you placed in your project.

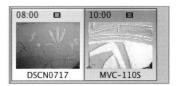

Using the Ken Burns Effect, you can go step by step through a project, selecting shots in the order you want them (or at least the order you think you want them—you might rearrange shots later), applying this camera move, and placing them into your timeline.

TIP Zooms and moves do not need to be very large to be effective. Small shifts left and right or small pushes in or out are plenty. If the move is going to be more substantial, the duration of the shot must be increased so that the move takes place over a longer time span. Remember: slow moves.

Another tip: Not every shot needs to move! Smart juxtapositions of moving shots and nonmoving stills can be very effective (and a little faster to work with).

18 Play your video and see what you've got so far. There are a few ways to do this, and it can be a little confusing. If you just click the Play button under the Viewer, only the selected shot plays, which probably is less than your entire sequence. For the greatest clarity, deselect the clips in the Clip view by clicking a blank area of the workspace, then change to Timeline view by clicking on the little clock button on the top left of the workspace. Click in the timescale along the top of the timeline to pop the playhead to your pointer, drag the playhead back to where you want to play from (the beginning, if that's what you want), and click Play.

TIP You should practice changing the view of your workspace from Timeline view to Clip view and back until you get comfortable with it. Some functions are more suited to one view and some to another, but in any event it's important to be able to move back and forth easily.

19 Add the next six album shots that show the progression of painting and then scratching the design into the plate. On each one, use the Ken Burns Effect and try a different method of moving the image—from close up to zoomed out, from left to right, from zoomed out to pushing in close, and so on.

TIP After using the Ken Burns effect, when you select the next image to work on, the window retains the same setting it just used. This makes applying the same effect to a number of shots quick. There is also a Reverse button that switches the settings so that it does the opposite (a zoom in becomes a zoom out). An easy and interesting effect is to zoom in on one shot and then pull back on the next. Reverse makes this easy.

When you add a shot that contains a special effect, your Mac must *render* the shot—build it frame by frame—before you can see it play. The process of rendering is dependent on your Mac's CPU—faster processors take less time to render. You can see a red bar in a shot denoting the rendering process and how far along it is. When the bar disappears, the shot is rendered and can be played.

NOTE ▶ While your shots are being rendered, the playback of your sequence will be hindered.

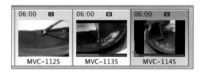

The red bar shows shots that are being rendered.

iMovie makes it easy to add a series of shots to your sequence, all with the same settings for zoom and duration. Once you've got one set up, iMovie will default to those settings for the next shot you bring up. Assuming you want shots to move similarly, this is great.

Unfortunately, decisions about how to move and position the shot are often particular to the individual shot. The good news: Once you've added a shot to your sequence, you can always select it in your timeline and revise any aspect of it—zoom, position, and speed. (I'll address this a little later in the lesson.) You can even select multiple shots and revise them together, the same way.

When you're done, the backbone of the video is done. It should look something like this in Clip view:

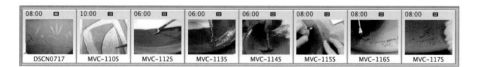

It's only the backbone because the addition of the narrative—using titles and effects—may necessitate lengthening, shortening, or shifting bits.

Add Titles to a Video

1   Open the text document **Sgraffito Script.txt**. This is the narrative that Jennifer needs to incorporate into the dynamic slide show. You're going to start with the title.

2   Click the Titles button.

This opens a window where you can build and preview text and titles to add to your sequence.

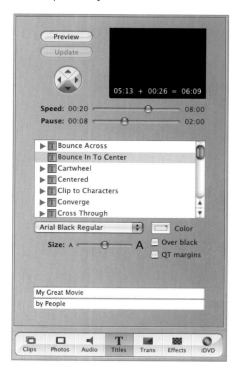

3   Click the first shot in the sequence (always on the far left of the work-space)—the still shot of the pink sgraffito vase. A still shot is a good choice for an opening title. By selecting a shot in the timeline, you are indicating to iMovie that this image is the one to which you want to add a title.

> **TIP** ▶   Any time you have text onscreen for viewers to read, it's important to make it as legible as possible. This means keeping the text from competing with the background. There are many techniques to keep titles legible, from making the letters as large as possible to putting white titles over a neutral or dark background. Moving video tends to compete with titles for attention and can make reading titles a little harder.

4   Select a style of title. Fancy can be fun, but simple and clear is often the fastest and easiest choice. Clicking a title style from the list will start a preview of the style in the small video window at the top of the column.

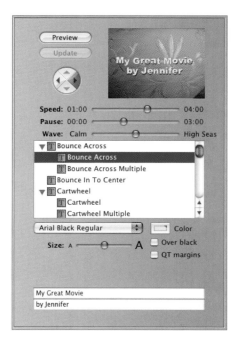

Check out a few, then select Centered Title. Many title styles have two variations: the basic kind, usually with fields for one or two lines of text, and the "multiple," which provides for additional fields that appear sequentially. You can create fields for additional lines in the multiple title by pressing the plus button (+), which is visible when the option is available.

5   Change the text for the title from the default text to Jennifer's actual title—The Sgraffito Technique—by typing it into the field at the bottom of the Titles window. There's the option for a subtitle also. Add *"Scratching your Designs"*.

6   Adjust the size of the text on the screen with the Size slider. You should make titles as large as possible without reaching the edges of the screen. You can also change the font and color here, but for now, leave them as is.

With each adjustment, click the Preview button. You will see your title in the large display, where it is easier to judge its size and timing.

7 Use the Speed and Pause sliders to adjust the timing of your titles and effects.

The Speed slider controls how long a title takes to generate—to move in and perform its little dance, as it were. It's best to think of speed as the duration of the title effect. More important, in many cases, is how long you let the title remain onscreen after it appears. You control this with the Pause slider. For guaranteed readability, leave the title onscreen for as long as the slider will allow—at least 3 or 4 seconds.

iMovie will present the total duration of your title as the sum of two values: the length of the title generation (the speed) and how long it sits there onscreen (the pause).

8 When you're satisfied with the preview, drag the title effect to the beginning of the shot where you want it. Once you've dropped the title onto the shot, iMovie begins to render the effect.

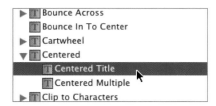

NOTE ▶ iMovie will effectively break your clip into two parts: the part with the title over it (with the duration you specified) and the remaining part, without the title.

Adding Titles over Black

Adding titles over still images or moving video produces exciting results, but for maximum clarity it's often best simply to insert title "cards" (as they did in silent movies). In iMovie this means adding titles over black, and it's as easy as clicking a check box.

For the next title, Jennifer wants a simple card explaining briefly what sgraffito means. Using the same techniques you just learned, she adds text from her script over a black background.

1   Select a different title style: Scrolling Block.

2   Check the check box that says you want the title Over black.

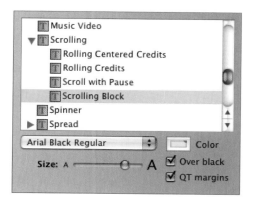

TIP ▶ Checking QT Margins adjusts your title for better visibility if you plan to export your movie to QuickTime for emailing to friends or publishing to the Web. Uncheck this box if you plan to show your movie full size on a television set or if you are going to burn to a DVD for TV viewing.

3   In the empty text field below, type in the first section of text from the script. You might need to experiment with where to place line breaks (returns) to cause the text to read smoothly onscreen.

The text block should read: *Sgraffito is an ancient art form. The word literally means "to scratch."*

4   Adjust the generation of the title by moving the Speed slider and previewing the results. You want a long block of scrolling text to move slowly and be easily readable. About 20 seconds is good.

5   Drag the scrolling block of text to the timeline and drop it between the title shot and the first shot of the blue and white piece.

6   Now, without changing any of the settings, change the text block to include the next section of text. Change it to read: *You probably tried something like this when you were a kid. With crayons. It's easy.*

NOTE ▶ If you wanted the first title card to say this instead of what you wrote in step 3, you could now press the Update button, which would revise the existing title.

7   Preview the new block of text. Adjust the duration to fit.

8   When you like this new scrolling block title, drag it down to the timeline and drop it after the blue and white sgraffito piece.

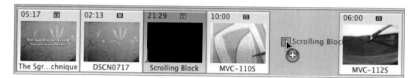

Through this method, Jennifer can continue to add title cards or rolling text blocks throughout her training video. But titles are not enough. To build a truly sophisticated video, particularly a dynamic presentation from still images, some basic transition effects are required. Fades and dissolves are the key.

Add Fade In/Fade Out Transitions

Effects tend to be way overused by those who are new to making videos. Because iMovie makes it so easy to add effects and provides so many interesting options (as, in fact, all professional video tools do), it's tempting to play with them and cobble together a visual oddity for your video projects.

A *transition effect* is a special effect that alters the way you move from one shot to the next. The classic transition effect is the *dissolve*—where one shot disappears and is replaced by the next shot. But just as important is the *fade out* (where one shot disappears to black) and the *fade in* (where the next shot changes from black into an image). Slightly more hokey, but no less important, are *wipes*: geometric patterns that mediate the transition from one shot to the next. iMovie provides a series of different kinds of wipes as well.

In truth, transition effects are used very sparingly in Hollywood movies and television programming. Almost all shows begin with a quick fade in, and they end (at commercial breaks, for instance) with a quick fade out. Dissolves are relatively rare, occurring only to show the passage of time or perhaps a change of location. You hardly ever see wipes. Oddly enough, almost all transitions from one shot to another are just plain cuts—exactly what you now have in your sequence.

But in this particular kind of sequence—a video invented from still images— transition effects would help. You're going to add a series of them, one after another, and then preview the results when you're done with the set of them.

As with adding shots from iPhoto or the Titles window, you begin by selecting the menu button for Transition effects.

1   Click the Trans button, short for transition effects.

2   Click Fade Out.

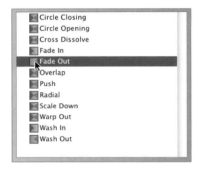

3   Using the Speed slider, set the speed of the fade out to *:20*. This is 20 frames, which is ⅔ second. It wouldn't be a problem if your fade out were 1 second. But whether it's ⅔ second or 1 second, it should be fast. And for visual consistency, all the fades you use within a project should be the same speed.

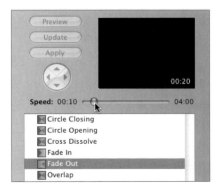

4   Drag the fade out to the end of the shot before the first scrolling title. This means the first image will fade to black, and then the titles will start to scroll.

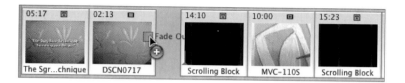

If you were using this transition between two video clips, you would fade in on the other side, but since it's transitioning to a title over black, it's not necessary.

5   Fade in on the head of the blue and white sgraffito clip (MVC-110S), then fade out on the end.

6   Drop a fade-in on the very beginning of the first shot for good measure. Every video project should begin with a nice little fade in.

In this way, titles and video clips can transition back and forth smoothly.

7   Finish adding titles to the video, either over black or over the clips (as you feel appropriate). Instructions and steps are effective as subtitles (or subtitle multiples, depending on how much you have to add).

TIP   If you don't want a title to start at the beginning of the shot, "fake" a beginning by breaking a clip a moment after the start, then apply the effect to the second part of the clip. Lesson 7 will explore this and other ways to break up your clips.

8 Add some "beauty" shots of finished pieces that exhibit the sgraffito technique. These are in the photo album you accessed through the Photos tab.

And that's it. Because this video will be shown in a busy studio, Jennifer doesn't
want narration or music to accompany the images—it would compete with
the store ambience. A QuickTime movie of Jennifer's finished video project is
in your Lesson 6 lessons folder.

Simple Adjustments to a Dynamic Slide Show

Christopher's dynamic video is much simpler than Jennifer's. His objective is
only to create a fun home video from the stills he shot at the party. He's happy
to drag shots from his Birthday Party album into iMovie and use pretty much
the same Ken Burns Effect move in each, with some slight variations. He wants
only a basic title at the start; after that, simple dissolves between some of the
shots are more than adequate. All of this is already in place in the iMovie project you'll work with in this part of the lesson. But Christopher wants to do a
couple of quick tweaks, such as adjusting slide duration, which will give you a
chance to see how to re-edit a project. You'll also add music to Christopher's
slide show.

1 Open the file **Birthday Party**, which is in the Start_Birthday_Project6
folder (in the Lesson6 folder).

As you can see, most of the still shots have been converted to video clips
and are already assembled in the workspace. Notice that the opening title
is in place at the start. The Clip view is good for reviewing and arranging
still images and slide shows (which is why it's very clear and similar, in
fact, to the way shots are represented in iPhoto).

Kind of like in iPhoto, if you don't like the order of any shots, you can
move them around by clicking and dragging them to a new location in
the workspace when you're in Clip view.

2   For this project, however, change to the Timeline view of the workspace. Click on the little clock on the top left of the workspace. This kind of view is good for dealing with issues typical of moving video—the length of shots, the positions of moments relative to running time, relative durations, and, of course, music.

Additional controls are available when you're in this view. In particular, the Zoom slider appears, which controls how much of the sequence you can see at one time in the workspace. Push the Zoom slider all the way to the left, and all your shots are reduced so they fit in the window. Adjust this slider as needed to see your shots.

3   Christopher doesn't like the second shot (the first one after the title). Select it and press Delete to delete it.

4   The move is too fast on shot 4. Select the shot.

Click the Photos button. The shot will reappear in the small window in the upper part of the window ready for adjustments.

5 Change the duration of the Ken Burns Effect. It should be much longer for such a long pan—try 6 or 7 seconds.

6 Click Update. The new duration will re-render.

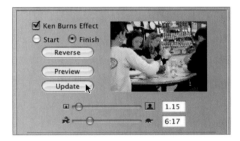

7 Except for this updated shot, every transition has a transition effect across it—mostly cross dissolves, but a few fade out/fade in pairs. Add 20-frame cross dissolves to the beginning and end of this updated shot.

iMovie always tells you the total length of your video (called the total running time). At this point in your re-edit, the running time of the sequence should be around 1:20, give or take. It's displayed above the timeline, next to the project name.

Adding Music from iTunes

For Jennifer, it's no problem that her still photos have no intrinsic sounds. They're just photographs, after all. But Christopher wants sound with his dynamic slide show. For this, he wants to add music.

To add music to your video, you never need to leave iMovie. Just as you accessed your iTunes library and playlists from iPhoto, you can do the same from iMovie.

1   Click the Audio button.

This opens the Audio window—a view into iTunes (as well as a few other tools, which you'll use later).

2   From here, select the playlist you wish to access, or just leave it pointing at the Library, and find the song you want to add to your movie.

NOTE ▸ You can also use the Search field to find what you are looking for.

3   Click and drag the song to your timeline.

iMovie will import the song to your file and place it wherever your play-head is parked. (Or you could place the song at the start of your movie by dragging it there.)

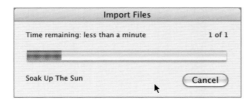

And that's it! You'll see the long purple track of audio underneath all your video clips, likely extending long past the end of your video if it's short. You can slide the song around to begin at any point you choose (although starting at the beginning is always a good idea).

And most importantly, now that the music is in place, you can make adjustments to the durations of your clips to better fit with musical cues in the song.

What You've Learned

- You can access your iPhoto albums from within iMovie.

- Add motion to still photos using the Ken Burns Effect; just set the Start and Finish points of the move, select a duration, and apply them to each photo.

- Change the arrangement of your workspace using Clip view and Timeline view.

- Drag shots around while in Clip view to reorder them.

- To delete a shot, select it and press Delete.

- You can change an existing shot through the Photo window by making adjustments and selecting Update.

- You can access iTunes and drag songs to your timeline from within iMovie.

7

Lesson Files	Lessons > Lesson07 > Start_Timelapse_Project7
	Lessons > Lesson07 > Finished_Timelapse_Project7
Tools	iMovie, camcorder (optional), iSight (optional)
Time	Approximately 90 minutes
Goals	Learn how to set up and shoot a time-lapse video
	Edit the video in iMovie
	Learn how to use an iSight camera to get video you can use in iMovie

Lesson 7
Making a Time-Lapse Video

While it sounds like a film you'd see in a seventh-grade science class, a time-lapse video is just a small variation on what you do anyway with a video camera: that is, to compress real time into something more convenient and interesting. Officially, a time-lapse video is one shot of a slowly changing event, such as a flower blooming, that you speed up through photographic or editing tricks. This lesson will show you the elements involved in making a cool-looking time-lapse video, which can be applied to the most unscientific kinds of personal projects.

Studio owner Jennifer uses the time-lapse video technique all the time. There's nothing more satisfying than seeing a blank canvas (a ceramic piece) evolve over an hour or so into a finished product. Whenever a familiar customer pops into the store—one who she happens to know paints in an interesting style—Jennifer makes a time-lapse video for the in-store display, for the fun and education of other customers.

Charlie creates another variation on the time-lapse theme. He uses an iSight camera to keep a daily video journal for a class project. Because the iSight is attached to the Mac, it works nicely for doing time-lapse photography as well as other projects, as you'll see in the second part of this lesson.

Preparation

The key to a successful time-lapse project is simple: Set up the camera some-place interesting, and then don't move it. Not a smidgen. Not a breath. While this sounds easy, you might be surprised at just how much you bump into your camcorder in the rigors of using the thing. Even if you set the camera on a table or use a tripod, just touching the record button to turn it on and off is too much contact. So part of preparing for a time-lapse shoot is finding the remote control that (hopefully) came with your digital camcorder. You may have thought the remote control was only for playing back tapes, but the control also has a red record button, and this is what you should use to start and stop your camera when you create a time-lapse project.

With camera and remote control, you're ready to find a subject and get set up.

NOTE ▶ Your tripod needn't be a fancy, pricey model designed for video; it can be an inexpensive, old still-photography tripod. The difference is in the "head"—the top part of the tripod that holds the camera and swivels around. For video, the swiveling must be slow and smooth, and the mechanics to execute this (usually involving what is known as a *fluid head*) are expensive. A still-photography tripod just needs to lock the camera down and hold it stationary—much more affordable. Jennifer uses a tripod that's about 25 years old but works like a charm.

Finding a Project

Anything that moves or evolves slowly, over a long period of time, is an appropriate potential subject for time-lapse video. The span of time needs to be long enough, though, that you might otherwise miss the event because of the sheer boredom or impracticality involved in watching for it. On the other end of the spectrum, the time span can't be too long or you increase the chances of bumping (or needing to move) the camera while you create your video. Needless to say, a multiple-day project can be challenging to execute. For now, let's focus on the kinds of events whose time span is 30 minutes to 3 hours.

For Charlie, and other students interested in science projects, this may be limiting. The really good scientific stuff—like plants growing or butterflies emerging from cocoons tends to happen over days or weeks. But social science—watching people—can be a good project, too. Parents like Christopher can capture whole meals with their young kids (I've seen videos of a dirtying floor beneath an infant having dinner; when cut to 30 seconds it can be reasonably amusing) or the slow, delightful process of their child waking up on a Saturday morning. A time-lapse of a teen's room, going from clean to messy, is similarly amusing. Around the house, it's a fun and memorable way to document building a model, making a quilt, or remodeling a room. As long as the camera doesn't move, these video projects work. Business owners can demystify many parts of their company's workings. (Jennifer has made time-lapse videos of kiln loading, the glazing process, and painting methods.) Time-lapse is an interesting technique for training tapes and can be attractive for customers. Customer education can be provided in many ways—pamphlets and instructional booklets are two—but little can replace watching the process over an expert's shoulder.

TIP ▶ Integrating a short time-lapse sequence into a longer project of still or moving video creates an interesting element.

Setting Up the Camera

Find a camera position with a good vantage point of what you want to shoot. In some cases, it works to set the camera on a table or chair and zoom out wide. In all cases, a tripod will help. Using a tripod increases the kinds of positions in which you can hold the camera: It can be at eye level or higher; it can be up in a corner somewhere. It can be right in the middle of things, zoomed in tight on the activity you've chosen.

Before you start, set up the tripod; load a new, clean digital tape into your camera; lock it into the tripod; and check the focus and exposure. (And, if the project is long or important, maybe do a little test or rehearsal.) Then, turn on your camera and get hold of the remote. Using the remote only—never touching the camera—start recording.

Depending on the event's actual length, you may try one of two options. For shorter events (say, under an hour), you will let the tape roll, undisturbed, until it runs out. Later you can carefully select the best parts. For longer events, turn on the camcorder for shorter periods of time—say, a few minutes—then off again. And then, a little bit later (how much later depends on how long the event is), do it again. For a two-hour event, you might try shooting five minutes then stopping for five minutes repeatedly. Or you could just improvise. Jennifer's plan is to shoot Richard painting a plate in the Italian brushstroke style, something she's seen him do in about 30 minutes.

Shaping the Raw Material

When you're done, you have a long, probably pretty boring clip of video. Congrats! The key to improving it is removing most of it and building a short (say, 60-second) version of the events of the day. To do this, you need to use video-editing software like iMovie.

1 Open the iMovie project Start_Timelapse_Project7 in the Lesson07 folder.

Start_Timelapse_Project7

Inside all iMovie project folders lie three important items. Ignore the Media folder and the .mov file here, and focus on the iMovie project file (a document with a little star on it).

Media   Start_Timelapse_Project7

Start_Timelapse_Project7.
mov

2 Double-click the project file **Start_Timelapse_Project7**. The iMovie project included with this book will open. Unlike in the earlier iMovie lessons that used iPhoto for source material, your Clip pane will have a clip of video.

3   Click the clip in the Clip pane. It will appear in the Viewer.

You can play the clip by clicking the Play button, or you can scan over the entire clip by dragging the playhead around in the scrubber bar—the blue, horizontal segment beneath the Viewer window. This is an important region of the iMovie display—which you will explore in Lesson 8—but for now, just check it out from time to time.

4   Drag the clip to the workspace at the bottom of the screen. The clip should pop into view. The way shots are currently presented in your workspace is called Clip view. While Clip view is quite useful for some projects, it is less useful for this time-lapse project.

5   Change to Timeline view. Click the clock, and the workspace morphs into a timeline display of your video, with a ruler running across the top of the window to measure passing time. The clips are represented by rectangular boxes underneath the ruler. The clip lengths are relative to each other— the longer the box, the longer the clip takes to play.

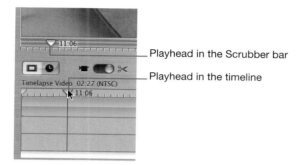

Playhead in the Scrubber bar

Playhead in the timeline

6   To scan through the clip, grab the playhead and drag it around in the time-line. Notice that this also moves a playhead in the scrubber bar under the Viewer. If you don't see a playhead, click in the ruler area to make it appear.

This gives you a relatively interesting vantage point from which to observe your time-lapse event: As you drag the playhead, the event zooms by before your eyes, the painting being created and erased as you move to the right and left.

7   Drag the Speed slider from the midway point toward the hare's side. Without making a single edit, you can easily squeeze this 2-minute, 27-second video. With the slider pushed all the way to the left, the video will play in just 29 seconds.

Watch the video. Pretty funny. Very Keystone Kops.

8   Now, put it back to normal speed (the slider's middle position). A comical look has its place, but not here; that isn't the kind of video Jennifer wants to make for her customers.

9 Turn off the sound. For most time-lapse videos, sound is not useful. Sound increases the reality of video, but this project is more surreal. Uncheck the sound check box, which is to the right of the timeline. The audio is still part of the video, but it doesn't play.

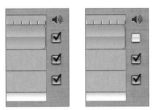

sound on (left); sound muted (right)

Making Your First Cut

You're now going to experience the most basic, fundamental way to edit video: You're going to chop up a clip of video and toss out the parts you don't want.

As a business owner, Jennifer doesn't have a lot of time for editing video. *Editing* is the art of cutting up video and making something interesting out of the pieces. Far simpler, and better suited to Jennifer's schedule, is simply cutting up video and throwing out the bits that aren't good. This isn't really editing; it's called *culling*. Jennifer culls all her video material. It's fast and easy. Making a time-lapse video is really just a specific method of culling videotape and looking for good bits.

Before you begin to cull Jennifer's video, here's a quick editing lesson: Whenever you chop up a piece of video, you should think of each cut you make as actually two cuts—the first indicates where a segment of the video will begin, and the second indicates where it will end. When you do this, you will have cut the original clip into three pieces (in order, left to right in the timeline): the material ahead of the section you liked, the section you liked, and the material after the section you liked.

But you don't always want to throw out the bits you don't use. There's plenty of good video in those "trimmings." Keep that in mind over the next few steps.

1   Start playing the time-lapse clip from the very beginning. Don't think of this as watching your video, but rather as looking for where you want your video to start. If you want your video to start at the beginning of this clip (which makes sense with this video), then pretend you already made a chop right at the beginning and threw away the material you didn't need.

2   Look for a nice frame on which to end the first "shot." You can stop any-where in the clip by pressing the spacebar. You can advance forward or backward with the precision of one frame at a time by using the arrow keys on your keyboard.

> **NOTE ▶** When you make the transition from video consumer to video producer, one of the first skills you develop is the ability to separate your-self from your material. It may be video of your family, your company, or your vacation, but when you sit down to edit, you need to stop "watch-ing" your video and start "looking at" it. You're looking for things in it, and observing how subjects on the screen move around. It's very different from watching (and enjoying) a video.

3   Choose Edit > Split Video Clip at Playhead when you've got the playhead at the spot where you want the video to end, and you can see the frame in the Viewer.

When you chop your video into pieces, you'll see that although none of them moves, the timeline shows that what had been one clip is now two.

And while this book doesn't delve into most keyboard shortcuts, the Split Video Clip at Playhead command is such an elemental part of cutting your video that its shortcut is critical to learn: Command-T. It's an important tool—perhaps the most important you will learn in this lesson. With this excellent chopper, you can cut, delete, and rearrange video with the power of a professional. You are going to see more sophisticated tools for editing—in iMovie as well as in professional-level software like Final Cut Express and Pro—but not much beats a good digital razor blade to simplify editing down to the basics.

Each time Jennifer pressed record (the material between the jumps), she recorded for 10 or 20 seconds. As you roll through each segment she recorded, you're looking for one three to six second clip.

Let's recap: Your video starts at the beginning of the big clip. You rolled a few seconds in and found a good place for the first shot to end, and you chopped it there. That defines the first shot.

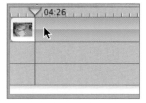

NOTE ▶ In time-lapse video projects, you will find a rhythm between how long a shot is and how much time you cut out before the next shot. For this video, each shot seems to work when it is three to six seconds long. If shots are much longer, you start to lose the momentum in the time-lapse effect.

4   Keep rolling through your video from this point and look for where you want the second shot to begin. You will pass a *jump*—a place where Jennifer stopped the camera and then started it a little bit later. You don't want to see any of Jennifer's jumps in your finished project.

5   When you find a good starting place for the next shot, make another chop (Command-T).

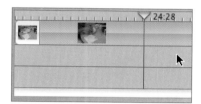

Now you have created three pieces of video: The first is the first shot; the middle one is basically garbage that you've decided you don't need; and the third is the remainder of the video.

6   Select the middle piece (the one you don't want) and delete it.

It's a little hard to see in an illustration, but you just created a good jump. You threw out a snippet of video and have begun the process to reduce the 2 minutes, 30 seconds of video into something shorter and more interesting.

7   Continue this process: From here, keep rolling through and find a good frame with which to end the second shot. Again, keep it between three and six seconds long.

NOTE ▶ About two-thirds of the way through the video, Jennifer repositioned the camera—she zoomed in tighter. During a shoot, it's generally never a good idea to move or zoom the camera in any way, but on long projects it can sometimes work if you do it once (and only once).

Snip, snip, delete. Snip, snip, delete. Work through the whole source clip until you reach the end. Your sequence should be about 60 seconds long, with 13 individual shots.

One addition that makes time-lapse video effect particularly striking is to drop cross dissolves over every transition.

8   Add one-second cross dissolves between every pair of shots. As described in Lesson 6, open the Trans window, select Cross Dissolves, set the duration to :30, and then drag the Cross Dissolve icon onto each transition in the timeline.

You'll have to zoom out to see the transitions.

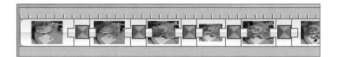

NOTE ▶ Once you've set the duration of the Cross Dissolve (or any transition effect), iMovie will default to this setting next time the effect is selected. Since in general you want to have consistent durations for these kinds of transitions, it's a great feature.

9   Add a title card. To do this, as you learned in Lesson 6, click the Title button. From the Title workspace make a simple, centered title card over black as the first shot in the sequence. Jennifer's title reads *The Italian Brushstroke Technique.* (If you really want to have fun, you can try some of the other title methods now and see what each one does. But remember, particularly for Jennifer—who uses her video in her business—simple is usually better.)

And now you (and Jennifer) have created a time-lapse video. If you'd like to see Jennifer's finished project, check out `Finished_Timelapse_Project7` in the Lesson07 folder. The setup and editing method you just practiced works for any topic, not just painting ceramics. With a digital video camera and without any complicated tricks in iMovie, you now know enough to cull any video as well as a professional. In addition, you understand the fundamentals of iMovie and editing well enough that expanding your skills will be easy.

Using Your iSight Camera Instead of a Tripod

Time-lapse videos are really nothing more than a video created from a single camera shot, coming from a camcorder that is completely unmoving. If you don't have a camcorder and a tripod, but do have an iSight camera on your Mac, technically speaking, you have the same set-up. If the iSight camera is affixed to a laptop, you can shoot anywhere your Mac can go. Point it out a window, at a construction site, whatever and wherever.

But even sitting at a desk, you can use an iSight camera combined with iMovie and the techniques you learned to build a time-lapse video to create other kinds of projects.

When Jennifer started her company a decade ago, she often set up a tripod and camcorder and recorded her thoughts, her process, the set-backs and accomplishments. If she had an iSight camera and iMovie, the process would have been considerably easier (not scattered among dozens of old VHS tapes). Charlie has decided to use his parents' set-up to make a video journal for a class project.

Because iMovie works with Apple's iSight camera as easily as it does with iPhoto and iTunes, you can use this videoconferencing camera as a typical video camera: record the video and edit the results into a compelling document.

> **NOTE ▶** A growing body of funsters are using iMovie and the iSight camera to shoot movies. Unlike recording to tape, the material you shoot with the camera goes right into the editing software in one step.

Charlie uses his parents' iSight setup on the family computer to keep a private series of thoughts on school and life.

1   Make sure your iSight camera is set up and working. If you don't know how to use the iSight camera, use the Set-Up Assistant in iChat AV to establish the connections and make sure the camera is communicating properly. This isn't a required step for working with iMovie, but iChat is nicely equipped to walk you through the iSight connection.

If you use iChat to make the connection, make sure you turn off iChat before you launch iMovie. You may have to quit iMovie and relaunch it, if you're already in that program. iMovie may not see the camera if you have iChat turned on.

iMovie has a switch that toggles between the input and editing of video. Whichever source is selected, the Viewer in iMovie displays video of that source.

2   The video-editing setting is the scissors, and this has been the setting for the past few lessons. Now drag the switch to the left side—the camera— for inputting video.

If only the iSight camera is connected to your Mac, your one option with this mode will be to enable the camera—and you'll see just one option in the camera pull-down menu. You can access the option from the triangle on the left of the little camera icon.

NOTE ▶ If, in addition to your iSight camera, a camcorder is connected to your Mac with a FireWire cable (and the camera is turned on and set to play back video), there will be a pair of options in the pull-down menu. Regardless, choose iSight.

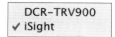

3   Once you've selected iSight, iMovie gets its raw material feed from a new source—and the video from the camera shows up in the Viewer. To record the image you see, click the Record With iSight button above the grayed-out video shuttle controls.

Immediately, iMovie will go into recording mode, placing a new clip in the Clip pane and displaying the count in seconds along the bottom of the clip while it records.

No need to panic that you're being recorded: the great thing about the mastering of editing techniques is that you now can get rid of video you don't like (particularly if you find it unflattering).

4 When you're done recording, click Record With iSight again. This ends the recording and begins the automatic conversion of the low-resolution clip into a video format that iMovie can manipulate.

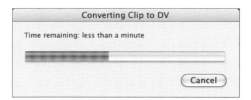

5 When the conversion is done, you have a clip in iMovie that is ready to edit like any video clip.

Charlie kept a daily journal about the events in his home; he also used stills and video he shot around his house and neighborhood to intercut with this journal material. After a few weeks of recording and a day of editing, he presented a short documentary to his class.

What You've Learned

- To set up a camera for a time-lapse video, you need a tripod and a remote control.

- Use Command-T to chop up a clip in iMovie.

- When you chop up a piece of video, always think of it as creating three pieces with two cuts—the piece ahead of the clip you like, the clip you like, and the piece that trails the clip you like.

- To create the time-lapse effect, simply delete the pieces you don't like.

- The time-lapse effect works best with one-second cross dissolves between clips.

- Use your iSight camera as a source for making videos; if the camera is attached to your Mac, then the video is comparable to the time-lapse video in terms of how you might edit it.

8

Lesson Files   Lessons > Lesson08 > Start_QuickVideo_Project8

Lessons > Lesson08 > Example_BizOwnerVideo.alias

Tools   iMovie

Time   Approximately 60 minutes

Goals   Learn how shooting video and editing video are part of
a single process

Learn basic camera functions and how to shoot properly

Learn to recognize video material that's suited for editing

Understand how to get video from a camcorder into iMovie

Trim and arrange shots in iMovie

See how to make a very basic video

Shooting and Assembling a Very Simple Movie

You started working with still images in the early lessons of this book, moved on to dynamic still images, and then explored culling video. Now you'll make an important transition to *editing* video.

Up to this point, you used the editing tools in iMovie to cut up raw material and throw out parts you didn't want, but you maintained shots in the timeline according to the order in which you shot them. You also treated the segments you liked as if they were slides—discrete elements to be shortened or lengthened, but ultimately almost like still images. Now you will see how an editor uses different portions of a single video shot to build structure. To tell a story, you will rearrange the order of video clips, which will likely have no relationship to the order in which they were shot. This is the essence of editing, and it's important to understand before digging deeper into Hollywood-style shooting (as you'll do in Lesson 10) and editing (Lesson 11).

Having built a slide show from a series of static shots with Christopher, and then following along with Jennifer as she turned her still images into a more dynamic presentation using iMovie, you might start to wonder if it's worth the extra effort to use video. But video has properties you just can't get from a dynamic slide show. Partly because of the power of sound, a video is more "real" and possibly more personal. Also, video allows you to see the way people behave and interact with more subtlety. Finally, by using cinematic techniques to gather elements and put them together, you have more power to convey emotion and direct the viewer's experience.

Once you have command over both stills and video, using iPhoto *and* iMovie, you'll become a far more sophisticated media creator—with a range of options for any given project.

This lesson is a quick introduction by Christopher to the language of Hollywood filmmaking. By seeing how shooting and editing work together, and how you can impart emotion to the viewer through your work as a director and editor, a world of high-quality personal videos opens up. Then, in subsequent lessons, you'll be ready to acquire skills that can be applied to everything from your first school project to a feature film debuting at a prestigious festival.

A New Way to Think About Video

There's an important distinction between the video that you *shoot* and a video that you *make*. You probably don't need a lesson to shoot with your camcorder. But making videos is an entirely different beast. Jennifer tends to shoot with her camcorder as if it were a still camera. Her video looks good, but she'd be hard-pressed to *make* something out of it. Christopher understands that shooting is his opportunity to get some raw materials with which to build. And like building a house, it's not enough to have lots of materials; rather, you need the right pieces to fit together.

Think of making a video as the union of two distinct tasks: shooting and editing. Camera plus computer. Professionals call this duo *production* and *postproduction*. Any way you slice it, a video is both of these in tandem.

Everything you do—before, during, and after shooting—needs to all fit together. For instance, a video recording of 30 minutes will require 6 GB of free hard disk space on your Mac. It's hard to think of the video you shoot without considering the consequences on your computer. And if you have only a few hours to dedicate to a project, small increases in how much you record explode into considerably more work when you edit. Labeling tapes properly and keeping records of what's on each one is work you do long before you get to your computer, but ultimately it will save hours when you're ready to make a video.

Consequently, "video" is a process—a series of interlocking activities. Until you have some perspective on the entire arc, it's hard to focus on any one part.

Organizing Your Video

Following the most basic rules of organization will make everything else you do in video streamlined and manageable. Nothing is worse than knowing you shot something important but being utterly stumped when you try to find it. Not remembering what tape has that that perfect sunrise shot, for instance, or shuttling aimlessly back and forth between tapes trying to guess, is enough to keep anyone from enjoying the process.

Label your tapes. Period. There is no substitute for this rule. Label them, and, after they are shot, sit down for an enjoyable romp watching them. While watching, make notes about what's on the tape using a paper *log sheet*, one for each videocassette. Labeling your cassettes and keeping log sheets is important if you ever hope to find material you shoot.

Right after you buy a digital videocassette, take it out of the wrapper, put the enclosed blank label on the cassette, and number it—starting with 1 and counting from there. You can add other info if you'd like, but the unique tape number is critical. You don't want three cassettes labeled *24*.

TIP ▶ You could use just a number (1, 2, 3…), but if you plan on doing lots of video editing, you may want to differentiate between the tapes you shoot in your camera and the tapes onto which you record finished video from your Mac. In that case, use a letter before the number: *S* for a tape you shoot and *F* for a tape containing final video. (Alternately, you could pick any logical letters; professionals use *M* for the master tape that final videos go onto.)

Then print out a blank tape log sheet (a version is online at www.nonlinear. info/dv/log.pdf) and write the tape number at the top and information about what's on the tape below. If you keep all your tape log sheets together in a folder or binder, you'll never lose track of a great shot—and even if you never edit your tapes, you'll be able to grab one on a whim and watch something you know you'll enjoy.

Good tape-logging style

Without this organization strategy, in no time you'll have a dusty box of unlabeled or poorly identified cassettes with nary a clue as to what's on most of them.

TIP The numbers that keep track of the frames on a videotape are called *timecode* and are important in keeping accurate log sheets. If no number is already on the tape when you start recording, the camera starts at 00 and adds numbers while you shoot. Then the number increases incrementally, 30 frames every second, ultimately counting seconds, minutes, and hours.

Timecode is almost always presented in the top-right corner of your video-tape. Camcorders can turn the display of the timecode on or off, but even if you can't see it, every frame has a number. As you get more comfortable with video and your camcorder, you will learn how to keep that number from ever jumping back to 00 in the middle of a tape. If you can keep this timecode continuous, ascending, and unbroken for an entire tape, a world of easy organization opens up to you. You can work without timecode, but if you do lots of video, it's a valuable reference, allowing you to jot down the number on your log sheet along with a description of the shot. It will greatly help you find shots quickly. For more information on video organization, check out *The Little Digital Video Book* (Peachpit Press, 2001).

Getting to Know Your Digital Camcorder

For this section of the lesson, break out your camcorder. Get a cassette, label it, and load it. Now you're ready to shoot. Put the camcorder in your hand and notice where your fingers naturally fall on the body of the device. There are three primary controls on the camcorder that you'll rely on almost exclusively while shooting video: the shooting/playback switch, the Record button, and Zoom. Follow along to get familiar with these controls.

1   Turn on your camcorder. This may not be as straightforward as it sounds. There generally isn't going to be an on/off button, but rather a swivel switch that powers up the camera and engages one of a number of selected settings. There's probably not a single name for this thing, but we'll call it the shooting/playback switch. This toggles the camcorder from video recording to video playback. (It may do a few other things, but ignore those for now.) The switch is usually very near the red Record button.

2   Find the Record button. It's almost always a little red button under your thumb. When you press it once, it starts recording. Press it again and it stops.

TIP ▶ The camera may beep when it starts and stops recording. There may also be a small red light near the lens that flashes while recording. Both of these features are great when you're starting out but may be distracting later on. Most camcorders let you turn off these features, but the method is usually buried in the onscreen menus. Check your manual if you want to adjust them.

3   Find the zoom control. On smaller camcorders it's sometimes a little knobby thing on the side or top edge; on larger camcorders it might be a rocker switch. Either way, the control is (or should be) under your index finger.

4   Adjust the straps on your camera to put your fingers in as natural a position as possible for recording and zooming. You don't want to have to look for either of these functions. Finding the shooting/playback switch does not need to be as quick, although you do want to be able to turn your camera on (by switching to shooting) with little trouble.

In addition to these three controls, there's always an LCD screen, hinged to the left side of the camcorder and ranging from tiny (1.5″ diagonally) to *grande* (3.5″ diagonally). Larger is more useful, perhaps, but it makes for a larger and heavier camera, and tends to demand more battery power to use—so find the trade-off that works for you.

Using a camcorder is usually a two-handed affair. One hand, your right, goes through the strap and is poised over the Record button and the zoom control. Your left hand is purely for stabilization. This is not a minor task. Use your left hand to steady the camera, either by lightly holding the extended LCD or gripping the camera body. Keep your elbows pulled in tight, and for heaven's sake, don't move.

Shooting Video

Now you have a camcorder in your hands and under control. You need to shoot something. At this stage it doesn't matter what you shoot; you just need to get some footage on tape.

A good starting point that will illustrate some shooting basics is a simple personal portrait.

1   Record five seconds of black. Before you start any project, it is good form to record a few seconds of black—of nothing (the floor, the lens cap, your hand). With a new videocassette, this gets the tape to roll away from the head; for a variety of technical reasons, material at the very beginning of a tape is hard to use. This trick has the added benefit of providing a very clear demarcation of where a particular scene begins. When you're watching the videotape on fast-forward, the black gap gives you a cue that something new is about to start.

2   Record three shots of where you are right now. Each should be about five seconds long. The first shot should show the audience where you are located. In a classroom? At home at a desk? Lying in bed? The second shot should tell us something about who you are. What personal items are with you? What sets you apart from the next person? And the third shot should represent what you're doing at the moment. Reading a book? Snacking?

Make the shots very different from each other. Each should be unique. Practice holding still while you shoot. Practice using the composition rules you learned from still photography.

3   When you're done with your shots, record another few seconds of black.

4   Switch your camcorder from camera mode to playback mode (sometimes labeled VCR or VTR). Shuttle controls—those familiar play, fast-forward, and rewind buttons—should appear on your camera somewhere (maybe on the LCD, maybe on the body).

5   Rewind the tape to the beginning.

6   Play the tape and watch it on the LCD screen. Notice the counting number on the top right of the LCD. That is your timecode number. It starts at 00:00 and counts seconds and frames. Timecode is really useful for locating shots on your tape.

7   Stop the camera when your last shot concludes and the black rolls into view. You always want to stop your camera on the black and never let it roll into the "blue" area. If you do this consistently, the timecode counter on the tape will never reset to zero, and every shot on the tape will have a unique (and thus useful) number.

Now that you've got some video recorded, it's time to put it into iMovie. You can follow along with your video, but I'll use Christopher's video to demonstrate.

Keep Video Short

The example you're about to see from Christopher, and probably the video you just shot, is quite short. When you create your own videos independently of this book, keep in mind that digital video consumes a lot of hard disk space even though the image quality is actually inferior to that of the poorest digital still-camera image. The reason video requires so much space is that it comprises many quickly moving still frames (just like film). A second of video is made of 30 discrete frames; even at low quality, that's an awful lot of images to be stored. A video clip of five minutes takes up a gigabyte on your hard disk. In other words, that 60-minute tape you shot at the party, if copied into your Mac, is going to fill up 12 GB of space.

Because of this (and other factors), start by keeping your video projects limited: Shoot less than 20 minutes of video for anything you intend to edit. This not only will save precious hard disk space, but also will keep the project relatively short and manageable.

Getting Video into iMovie

Unlike iPhoto, iMovie doesn't automatically import your video when you plug in your camcorder. Still, it's pretty easy. In Lesson 7, you saw how iMovie can get video from the iSight camera; it's just as easy to get video from your digital camcorder.

1   Plug your camcorder into your Mac with a FireWire cable.

FireWire is the standard type of computer connection for digital video (and other high-bandwidth computer connections). Its technical name is IEEE 1394, but it's also referred to as i.Link, Sony's brand name.

FireWire jacks: A 4-pin jack on a digital camcorder (left); and a 6-pin jack on the back of a Mac (right)

At each end of your FireWire cable is a different type of connector. The tiny one, which tends to plug into a camcorder, is a *4-pin connector*. The big one is shaped like a D and is called a *6-pin connector*. A 4-pin-to-6-pin FireWire cable, then, is the essential link between camcorder and Mac.

FireWire connectors: The smaller 4-pin side (left) and the D-shaped 6-pin side (right)

NOTE ▶ The common connector between a Mac and an external hard drive is a 6-pin-to-6-pin FireWire cable.

2   Make sure your camcorder is turned on and set to play back your tape. That setting is probably labeled something like VCR; it's often a switch located near the red Record button on the back of the camera.

3   In iMovie, change the mode from editing (the scissors) to capturing video (the camera). If you have an iSight camera plugged in, you'll need to select

your camcorder from the pull-down menu under the camera icon. If not, just switch it to the left.

Now iMovie is looking at, and controlling, your camcorder.

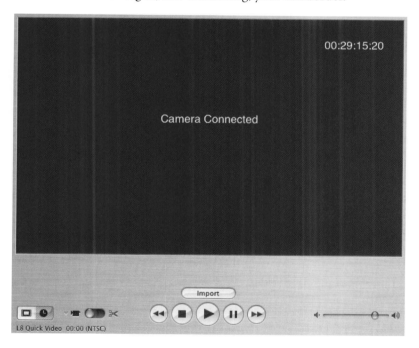

4   If you click the big Play arrow under the display, your tape will start rolling and you can watch it on your Mac.

5   Click Stop (the square), and the tape will stop and the screen will go blue.

6   Click the Rewind button onscreen, and the camera will go into a fast
     rewind. (If you click Play and then hold down the Rewind button, it
     will go into slow rewind, and you can watch the video onscreen.)

You'll also see a number on the top of the display in iMovie—this matches
the timecode number on the videotape and should help you locate where
you want to be, provided you're using timecode to keep yourself organized.

Christopher got home after the party and rewound his tape just to the
point where he started recording that morning. Then he clicked Play to
watch it. Of course, if you're going to take the time to watch a tape, you've
got the time to import it.

7   When the tape is rolling and you find the beginning of the material you
     want to put in your Mac, click Import.

TIP ▶ For most video you shoot, import the entire bunch of material you will use for editing, and avoid starting and stopping the import process to find small bits you think you want to edit. By grabbing all the video in one big chunk (or at one time) you save a great deal of wear and tear on rather fragile consumer camcorders. Getting everything in the computer has the additional benefit of sometimes revealing small gems of video that you might have missed if you imported discrete moments from your tapes.

Again, as you saw in Lesson 7, the video you import immediately shows up in the Clip pane. iMovie is pretty smart about video playing from a tape. Whenever it "sees" that you stopped the camera and started recording again—even though there is no discernible break in the picture on the tape—it ends one clip and starts making another. (This only works if you have already set the date and time on your camcorder.) This is usually very useful (although in Lesson 11, you'll learn when it's not as useful). For Christopher's video—just like yours—he started and stopped his camcorder three times, and so there are three clips in the Clip pane.

NOTE ▶ Funny thing: Getting digital content into a given application is generally known as *importing*. Still, tradition tends to confer other names to this process. Getting songs into a computer is sometimes called *ripping*. Getting video into a computer is often called *capturing*. Truth is, the words all mean the same thing.

Getting the Right Shots

For this part of the lesson, close the iMovie project you created to import your clips. You're going to use material Christopher and Jennifer have shot to explore principles of shooting and editing.

The bits of video you need for movie editing are called *coverage*. You need a certain minimum of coverage to have video elements you can edit. There is also such a thing as too much coverage—dozens of shots from dozens of angles. It can be too much to manage and makes for hard-to-watch videos.

Simple shooting not only makes sense, but it's also pretty much the most professional approach to a video project. In this lesson, you'll witness the minimum of necessary coverage and see how potent it is for editing.

1   Open Lesson08 > **Example_BizOwnerVideo.alias**. (The alias is linked to the project in Lesson13 > Start_BizVideo_Lesson13 > **BizOwnerVideo**.)

Some still images from Jennifer's studio videotape

2   Click on the shot in the Clip pane and watch the few minutes of video that Jennifer shot in her studio.

She used her camcorder with good technique. She framed shots with nice composition in mind. She followed good videography rules—she held the camera steady and didn't use the zoom (much). But the shots are little more than moving stills. Each is nice, but few have any relationship to each other. And while they might be assembled in some clever way to give you the feeling of being in the studio (with the sound adding an important element), they're not the right pieces for editing.

The problem with Jennifer's video is that she had no agenda when she shot it. She just pointed the camera at whatever interested her. So, what she ended up with is a slide show of moving pictures. You'll need to go further and gather specific *kinds* of shots, shots that will go together neatly when you edit the video.

The secret, then, of making videos good and creating them easily does not lie in knowing how to edit, and it doesn't lie in good videography. The secret is in shooting *holistically*, which means always keeping the eventual editing in mind.

In Hollywood, a scene is set up, and the director shoots it a number of times from a number of angles. By having different shots of the same subjects doing the same things, an editor can assemble that material in ways that have great impact. It doesn't take too many shots to get the material you need to do this. And you don't need to have actors with scripts. Almost any event in the real world has a natural kind of repetitiveness to it, and you can leverage this by moving decisively into specific positions, gathering up the bits of video you need to make the video.

Getting Shots with Relationships

Instead of shooting a series of interesting shots with your camcorder, think of every shot as having some kind of relationship to at least one other shot. If you shoot someone from far off, your next shot should be the same person from closer. If you shoot someone from the front, think about also shooting them from the back. If you show someone reading a book, show the audience what they are reading. Whatever you do, get a minimum of two shots that relate; you will use these when you go to edit.

Having relationships between shots highlights one the most significant differences between video projects and still-image projects. With a still camera, you pick it up and shoot once in a while. You might shoot bits and pieces throughout an event. With video, you want to pick the camcorder up and shoot one scene, getting proper coverage from multiple angles, and then be done with it. You're not going to try to shoot many bits of lots of different scenes, but lots of shots of one scene.

Have a look at the video for this lesson, Start_QuickVideo_Project8 > **L8 Quick Video**, in the Lesson08 folder. This is an iMovie project that Christopher is working on. He shot a couple of minutes of the girls trying to find the ceramics they wanted to paint.

If he were using a still camera, this moment might have been condensed to a single shot, probably not even an interesting shot. But in video he can expand the moment and begin to show their interactions, moods, and dynamics. For the audience, he can also make it compelling by creating bits of interest, maybe even suspense. Video makes this possible.

Notice there are three shots in iMovie, three distinct vantage points of the same event. More than anything else, this is the key to making videos.

What Editing Does to Video

Even though you have only three clips in your Clip pane, you have ample coverage to make a short movie. (Actually, it will be less a movie and more what is called a sketch.) The traditional way to approach iMovie is largely clip-based, meaning the program is designed for you to drop clips of video into your workspace, drag them around until they are in the right order, and trim their length so they don't bore people. While this is a perfectly legitimate way to approach your video, it misses both the power and fun of editing, so you won't do that here. You will take three shots and cut them up into lots of smaller pieces. By arranging the pieces, you can control the viewer's experience.

As you look at Christopher's video, instead of seeing three clips in the Clip pane that need shortening and organizing, recognize his video as two minutes of raw footage taken from three vantage points.

Trimming and Arranging Your Footage

The methods Christopher uses to edit his short video are precisely the same ones Jennifer used when she edited the time-lapse video. In short, use the Command-T function to chop the shots into pieces, and then select the pieces you like and put them in order. The difference here is that the order of shots is highly subjective. (The time-lapse material presumably has to appear in the order in which it was shot.)

How do you start? With a wide shot, to establish where the girls are?

Wide shot, back view

Or the close-up shot, showing some odd activity but not yet revealing who is there or where they are?

Close-up shot of hands and ceramics

Or the medium shot, clearly showing what the girls are doing, full of personality but in some ways ordinary?

Medium shot, side view

Your role as a director is to get the bits of coverage you need. But your role as the editor of this video is to make the hard decisions about how to tell the story.

We'll see how Christopher made his choices—but you should realize there are no right or wrong answers. The problems you face here have many solutions.

1   Start with the wide shot. It serves to establish where the scene is taking place, and has the benefit of creating a little mystery: Here's where they are, but what are they doing? Select the wide shot and begin watching it in the Viewer.

2   Use the scrubber bar region and drag the playhead forward and backward until you see the moment you like. When you come to a 3- or 4-second region where it seems the action is interesting and the camera is steady, back up and find a good place for the clip to start.

Christopher found a spot around nine seconds into the clip. The actual count, in seconds and frames, is inscribed in the scrubber bar near the playhead.

3   Use Command-T to break the clip, once you're stopped on the place you want your shot to start.

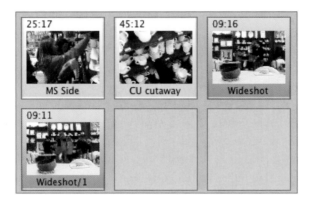

Notice what happens in the Clip pane when you use Command-T before you've added the shot to your workspace: The original clip is split into two pieces, and both remain in the Clip pane (and are highlighted in blue). The first segment has the original name; the second has the original name with an appended *1*: Wideshot/1.

4   Keep playing the Wideshot clip until you find a good ending point. (With both shots still selected, they play together in the Viewer as if they weren't chopped up, although you can see the split point if you look carefully.) Use your best judgment as to where to end the clip, but the completed shot should be only a few seconds long. Christopher's is about four seconds.

5   Use Command-T to break the Wideshot clip again. The first part, then, is the trimmed-off bit at the head end. The second part (Wideshot/1) is the "good" bit. And the third part (Wideshot/2) is the trimming at the tail. You don't want to delete these pieces yet, since you might need them later.

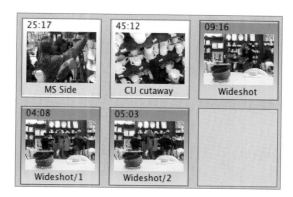

NOTE ▶ Be careful when you drag clips from the Clip pane to the workspace—particularly after you've chopped them up with Command-T. All the bits are still selected (highlighted in blue), and when you click and drag one, you may be inadvertently dragging them all. One of the greatest challenges when starting out in iMovie is keeping an eye on what shots are selected—both in the Clip pane and in the workspace—as you play, delete, and rearrange.

If one clip is highlighted in the workspace and you click Play, only that clip will play. If you want to play an entire sequence, you need to select either all the clips or none of them.

TIP▶ Wide shots generally need to be onscreen a little longer than close-up shots in order for the audience to have time to "read" the image. There's a lot of detail in a wide shot, and it takes a few moments to look the frame over and satiate that need to know where you are, who is here, what is happening. A length of four or five seconds is usually better than one to three seconds.

6   Now that you've diced up the wide shot into a good piece and some trimmings, drag the good piece into your workspace. This will be the first shot in your sequence.

It doesn't matter if your workspace is set to Clip view or Timeline view; you'll see the clip there (highlighted in blue). For now, set the workspace to Clip view.

7   Perform the same technique on the MS Side clip, finding a good few seconds in the middle—where you like the action and the camera work feels solid.

8   And finally, do it again with the CU Cutaway clip. There's lots of visually interesting images of hands and activity in this 45-second shot. Find a nice three seconds and place it after the MS Side clip by dragging it from the Clip pane to the workspace.

In Clip view, the three shots look like this. Watch them in the Viewer.

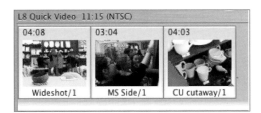

Sometimes it is easier to watch clips and orient yourself in a video by switching to Timeline view and dragging the playhead around to watch a video. You can immediately cue to the first frame of your sequence by clicking the Cue to Head button before you click Play. You can also choose to watch your video full-screen (rather than in the Viewer) by clicking the Play Fullscreen button (to the right of Play).

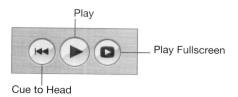

Play

Play Fullscreen

Cue to Head

In a way, you're done. You've taken your three shots, found the best moments, and assembled them. If you wanted to, you could click and drag the shots around in Clip view to see if you could improve their order—perhaps starting with the close-up shot, then going to the medium shot, and finally ending with the wide shot. iMovie makes it very simple to shuffle shots in this way. But as you now know, this isn't really the heart of editing. To edit, you must listen to your gut, and Christopher's gut is saying, "The moment I witnessed was much more than this 11 seconds reveals. The moment I was shooting was sillier, stranger, longer…"

To accomplish this, you must go back to the raw material—the trimmed-off bits that you didn't use at first, and find more interesting moments. For instance:

9   Go back to the Clip pane, and start watching the MS Side/2 clip. There are lots of interesting interactions between the girls there. Christopher found another moment he likes around five seconds in. Using Command-T again, chop out this bit (iMovie creates more new bits—MS Side/3 and MS Side/4; MS Side/3 is the one you want) and move it to the workspace.

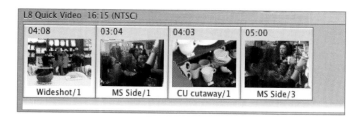

10 Similarly, there were other good moments in the CU Cutaway shot. Review the pair of trims in the Clip pane and find a few more seconds of nice

material. Using Command-T, chop up the piece you like and drag the "moment" to the workspace after the last shot.

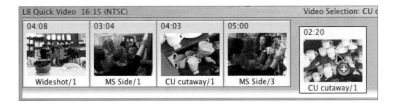

So now the sequence is about 20 seconds long. It begins wide, to establish where the girls are, then has a typical Hollywood A-B-A-B back-and-forth rhythm, which comes up often in editing. (You'll explore this in detail in Lesson 11.) But it needs an ending. This A-B-A-B thing could go on all day, or at least until you run out of material.

A good way to end a short scene like this is with another wide shot, to let the audience back away from the action and take it all in. But after watching this sequence a few times, Christopher decides that the opening is weak. Preferring to keep the viewer in suspense a little bit, he decides to move the first shot to the end.

11 Drag the first shot to the end of the sequence of shots. Notice that when you move it, all the other shots slide around to accommodate the change.

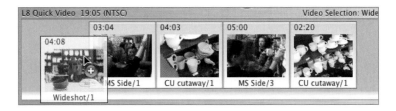

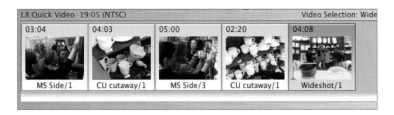

This is better, but Christopher experiments with some other arrangements of these shots, as should you. Opening, for instance, with the close-up (that is, moving the fourth shot to the beginning) is another interesting way to organize it. Truly there is no right answer.

What becomes apparent is that the opening shot must be much longer than the others. Whether close-up or wide or medium, it needs to play long enough for the viewers to settle in, get some kind of orientation for themselves, and be able to look around at what is happening. A few seconds (even three) isn't enough for this. Five seconds is more appropriate.

Modifying Shots in Your Timeline

For much of your editing work, you will alternate between the Clip view and the Timeline view of your sequence. Moving shots around is easy in Clip view; seeing relative lengths and playing from some spot in the middle of the sequence is easier in Timeline view. Modifying shots is accessible only from within Timeline view. When you're in this view, your pointer turns into a special (and powerful) trimming tool that allows you to adjust where shots begin and end, even after they're in the timeline. The Trim tool lets you not only shorten shots but also lengthen them.

In the present configuration of shots (medium, close-up, medium, close-up, wide) Christopher wants to make the first shot—the medium shot—longer. The Clip view says it's 3 seconds, 4 frames long. The timeline shows it to be roughly the same length as the others. The timeline isn't as pretty a view of your work, but it's exceptionally functional.

> **TIP** If you want to see your whole sequence but can't, don't forget that you can use the Zoom slider to change the scale of the timeline. When it's all the way to the left, you will see your entire sequence, regardless of how long it is or how many clips you have. If you need to zoom in closer in order to work, use the scroll bar along the bottom of the timeline.

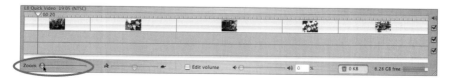

NOTE ▶ You might be interested to learn that the Timeline view is the *only* view that professionals use when working in Final Cut Pro and Final Cut Express (more on why in Lesson 11).

1   Select the first shot. It will be highlighted in blue.

2   Move your pointer to the end of the first shot. It will turn into a bar with arrows on both sides—this is the Trim tool.

3   Click and drag to the right. This will extend the selected shot until you let go. The new duration of the shot is displayed in the ruler portion of the timeline.

Watch the frames you are adding in the Viewer above. Use the Viewer to help identify the frame on which you want to end this shot.

Using the Trim tool, you can extend or shorten any shot in your sequence. It is just the tool for tweaking those extra few frames from a piece that is too long, or clipping out a blip of something you don't want to see. It's a new feature in iMovie that radically changes the power and ease of this editing software.

NOTE ▶ In the language of editors, this is called *nondestructive* editing. It means that when you cut up material and move the bits around, you aren't really cutting up or throwing out anything—you're only looking at a select piece of a larger whole, as if you were viewing the original video clip through a small window. Because of this, iMovie gives you instant access to the material you didn't use in your clips without having to go "get" it from somewhere else. It's always magically hanging around the edges of your clips in the timeline.

Christopher's sequence is about 20 seconds long. He added a one-second fade in at the start and a one-second fade out at the end, and is ready to move on to more challenging scenes with more complicated kinds of coverage. You can watch a QuickTime movie of Christopher's short sketch called **Finished_QuickVideo.mov** in the Lesson08 folder.

What You've Learned

*   Shooting and editing are interwoven, and they work together to make videos.
*   Connect your camcorder to your Mac with a 4-pin-to-6-pin FireWire cable.
*   Use the camera/scissors toggle switch to move from controlling a camcorder—for importing or just playing—to manipulating shots within iMovie.
*   When your camcorder is in playback mode, you can control it from inside iMovie—playing, rewinding, and reviewing using the shuttle controls.
*   When you want to move video from a tape in the camcorder into iMovie, click Import. The resulting clip or clips will end up in the Clip pane.
*   You need to shoot at least two different angles on any action you are videotaping if you intend to edit it. This material is called *coverage*.
*   The two angles should have a special relationship to each other—close-up/far off; in front/behind; someone looking at something/the object they are looking at.
*   With even a minimum of coverage, you can use basic editing techniques to build a small story in iMovie.
*   Command-T chops up bits of raw material in the Clip pane.
*   Drag clips to the workspace to arrange them in the order you want.
*   Use the Trim tool to extend or shorten shots in the timeline.

9

Lesson Files Lessons > Lesson09 > Start_Birthday_Project9

Tools iMovie, camcorder (optional)

Time Approximately 90 minutes

Goals Use your camcorder as a microphone to record audio interviews

Think of a finished video as having two distinct elements—pictures and sound—that can be managed independently

Separate the sound portion from the picture of a video clip in iMovie, and work with sound on a separate track

Use the Mac's built-in microphone to record narration while you're editing your iMovie

Adding Narration to Your Dynamic Slide Show

Part of what makes projects interesting is using sound creatively. This might mean adding music to a slide show in iPhoto or sound effects and narration to a video in iMovie. There are many kinds of sounds (often categorized by professionals as dialogue, music, and effects) that combine to make a finished sound track. Like photography, sound is a specialty unto itself.

Unfortunately, sound can be really difficult to manage on your camcorder if you try to do it while you're shooting video. The built-in microphone is *omnidirectional*, which means it picks up sounds from everywhere around you while you record, resulting in a lot of unwanted noises. Also, because you shoot from a number of different positions—moving close to and far away from your subjects, starting and stopping the camera between shots—getting a consistent stream of audio is almost impossible.

If these challenges weren't bad enough, the results of poor audio make for really poor videos. For some psychophysical reason, bad-quality video looks better with good sound, and, amazingly, good-quality video looks worse with bad sound. Many factors go into what constitutes good sound: clear voices that are distinct from background noises; proper relative volume of speech and other elements of the picture; a rich tapestry of sounds to add texture and emotion to the video.

Because it's so hard to get good-quality sound from the camera's microphone while you shoot video, the fastest way to get good sound in your finished projects is to ignore most of the audio from your shoot and instead use music from a professionally created CD. Your video will benefit from the great production value of someone else's work. But if you want *production sound*—that is, the sound that's going on while you're shooting the video—it takes more effort. You need to use additional microphones and have someone carefully monitor how everything sounds while it's being recorded. For people like Charlie, Jennifer, and Christopher, this adds too much complexity, demands too much equipment, and probably requires too much work.

There are alternatives. You can use your camcorder not only as a digital video recorder but also as a digital audio recorder. And your Mac itself has a built-in microphone. With these handy audio tools and a little basic information, you can add professional-quality sound (and thus professional-quality production values) to your dynamic slide shows and, ultimately, your videos.

In this lesson, you'll revisit Christopher's dynamic slide show from the birthday party. Adding music as you originally did was an excellent option to create a sound track. Now you will take interviews Christopher recorded during the party and make a narration track with them. Later you'll check in with Charlie and see other narration alternatives that iMovie provides for his simple school report.

Using Your Camcorder as a Microphone

Put the lens cap on your digital video camcorder. For the moment, forget that this small gadget shoots video. Instead, look around the body of the device and find the microphone. Every camcorder has one. While it may be hard to find, it should look something like the classic microphones you've seen before; maybe it's got a black or silver mesh over a little area toward the top or front of the camcorder. If you can't find it, check your manual.

Now, instead of shooting video, hold the camera in such a way that you can press the Record button while holding the microphone a few inches from the sound or person you want to record.

TIP ▶ If you're having difficulty knowing whether you're recording, you can keep the LCD flip screen open so you can see the red dot indicating that recording is under way.

Recording audio while you're shooting video can be extremely challenging for at least a couple of reasons. One is that every time you move to get a different shot, your distance to the source of sound changes significantly. When you record audio while shooting video, the microphone tends to take a backseat to the lens. The problem isn't the technology; it's just the nature of shooting video. Move away for a wide shot, and the microphone can't pick up any talking. Move close for a detail shot, and the voices boom. Using this sound is exceptionally difficult for technical reasons.

Another reason that it's quite challenging to record sound and video at the same time is because it's no small feat to record interesting conversation. When you really listen to it dispassionately, even enjoyable conversations are unbearably dull. You might have expected to record a fun bit of conversation, but it goes on and on, with no beginning and no end, and only a long stream of sound. Our brain fools us into thinking conversations are discrete and finite—when in truth they are very slow, very repetitive, and often missing key words or using half thoughts. Even with great tools and lots of practice, when you try to record one, you still end up missing parts; it's hard to capture the entire thing.

To circumvent the challenges of recording a conversation in video and audio at the same time, shoot video for the picture part first, and later record audio. That way you can focus specifically on the goal of getting good sound, and you have a better chance of getting the raw materials required to make high-quality product.

Christopher wants to record some of the endearing things his daughter and her friends are talking about at her 12th birthday party. But instead of shooting video and concentrating on the sound at the same time, Christopher concentrates solely on getting the images he needs to edit. Then, at some later point in the event, he makes a mental shift—using the camcorder only as a microphone to interview the girls, asking questions, eavesdropping a little, intently listening to the sounds of the event.

Using the camcorder as a microphone has many advantages, in addition to those just described. In the first place, there is something far less invasive about a microphone than a camcorder. People act differently when a lens is pointed at them. While they still might be a little uptight with you holding out a microphone (even one shaped like a camera!), they do tend to relax once you're making eye contact and standing closer—both possible now that the camera isn't in front of your face.

> **TIP** Keeping the lens cap on the camera tends to help disarm your subjects, for some reason. Anything you can do to help your subject relax will result in a better recording (audio as well as video).

Christopher holds the microphone about an inch or two from the mouth of whoever is speaking. This guarantees the voice will be very clear and much louder than any of the background sounds in the room. While it's always challenging to record people (as luck would have it, people always seem to be their funniest when you're talking to someone else, and the microphone is so far away you can barely hear them), holding a camcorder like a microphone is a direct and easy way to get live sound.

Using Audio in iMovie

Once Christopher has recorded a few minutes of interviews, he could go back to shooting video or consider himself done. But Christopher isn't going to be making a video at all; instead, he wants to use the camcorder to get a few minutes of audio to add to his dynamic slide show.

1   Open the **Birthday Party** file in the Lesson09 > Start_Birthday_Project09 folder.

You may recognize this as the finished state of the dynamic slide show Christopher created in Lesson 6. In that project, it was easy to add music from a CD to give the video a finished feeling. But that outcome is very different from the result he gets by using the sound from the real event.

NOTE ▶ With interviews instead of music, a product changes from a "music video" into a "documentary."

2   Delete the music in the audio track by selecting it and pressing Delete on your keyboard. The sound was fine before, but it's not required now.

> **NOTE ▸** You could just mute the music track by unchecking the audio box on the far right of the timeline. But visualizing the work you'll be doing here is a little easier if the music is gone. So, the lesson will proceed with the music deleted even if you decide you'd like to keep it and mix it at the end.

Look at the Clip pane. In the pane are seven audio segments. Christopher imported the video from his camcorder precisely as he did with video and audio in Lesson 8. The screen is black, but this does not mean there is no video. The video is black. (It's the back of the lens cap, actually.)

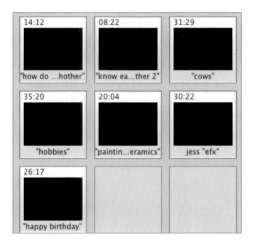

> **NOTE ▸** When there is no video image to help identify the clips, adding labels to each is more important. These clips are labeled, but you could adjust them to your liking.

And although these clips may not look like much, each contains a snippet of conversation on a given topic. They can be chopped up with Command-T to find small gems of dialogue, but for now we're going to treat them as good interview clips in their entirety.

Separating Picture from Sound

Before you can work with sound alone, you must be comfortable splitting the sound from the video you shot. Imported clips in the Clip pane consist of merged picture and sound, even when the picture is black. Your first task, then, is learning to separate each shot into its components.

1   Set the workspace to present the Clip view.

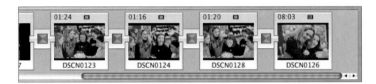

2   Go back to the Clip pane. In the order the shots appear in the Clip pane (starting at the top left and moving through them as if you were reading), drag them to the end of the clips in the workspace. In this case, video clips already appear in the workspace (albeit clips with pictures and no sound!), but disregard them for a moment. You're going to be working in the space *following* the video made in Lesson 6.

You may need to readjust the slider to the right after each clip is added, to reveal the last clip, before you add the next.

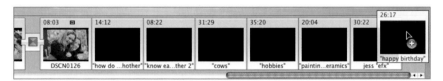

3   Once all seven clips are in, change the view to Timeline. Remember to slide the Zoom slider all the way to the left so that you can see the entire sequence.

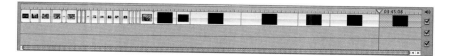

Notice the dynamic slide show (which was built back in Lesson 6) at the beginning of the timeline, to the left, and the big (black) audio clips at the tail, to the right. Also notice that there are two empty tracks underneath the pictures. You'll explore these in a moment.

4   Choose the first interview clip.

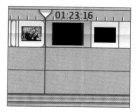

5   Choose Extract Audio from the Advanced pull-down menu at the top of the screen.

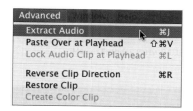

This will split the clip from the union of picture and sound into two tracks: the picture in one track (above) pinned to its sound in a second track (below).

There's no discernible difference when you play it now compared with before, except that now you can manipulate the sound independently of its picture. The picture in this case is just black, but the Extract Audio function works with any video source clip.

6   Go ahead and extract audio from all the interview clips. You can do one at a time or select multiple clips.

It takes a moment for each clip to be "extracted."

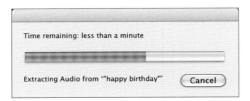

iMovie splits the picture from the sound and places the sound alone in the track below the picture.

NOTE ▶ While the distinction may be a subtle one, it may help to know that in iMovie, extracting audio doesn't really split the audio from the video and move the audio to the new track. In truth, it *copies* the audio to a new track and *mutes* the playing of the audio in the main (top) track.

Pause for a moment to examine the timeline. There are three tracks running together. The top one holds the video clips, picture, and sound together, as imported from your camcorder. The next two are for solo audio—music from iTunes, narration (which we'll create later in this lesson), or extracted audio clips. iMovie places audio clips where there is room. If you want to mute a particular track, uncheck the box on the far right of the timeline. Unchecking the box for the top track, for instance, plays your video without the production sound.

iMovie recognizes these audio clips as having a relationship with the video clips they accompanied when they arrived. That's what those yellow pins represent. While the picture and sound are now separated, you need to take it one step further—you need to unlock their relationship.

7   Select all the interview sound clips by Shift-clicking each one.

8   Choose Advanced > Unlock Audio Clip. The pins go away, and the sounds are set free from the (useless) black images.

9   Select all the black picture clips and press Delete on your keyboard.

Now you have what you need: free-floating clips of audio alone. You're ready to start integrating them with the video (alone) at the beginning of this timeline.

NOTE ▸ If you happen to glance at your workspace in Clip view, you might be surprised that none of these interview clips are shown. The clip view presents only clips with video; music, narration, and other sound-only clips are effectively invisible. One more reason to stay in the Timeline view while working on sound.

Just by glancing at the timeline, you should clearly see that the aggregate length of audio interview material is longer than that of the video. Some of your work, then, is going to be to get the two tracks more in line: by shortening the sound part or lengthening the picture part. You can do this through a combination of making some of the dynamic slides longer and deleting some audio—either whole clips (using Delete) or parts of clips (using Command-T, then Delete).

Although much of the interview material is fun, it's best to stay focused on the goal of creating a dynamic and rich slide show.

10 Listen to all seven audio clips in the timeline again. What material is superfluous? It cannot be said enough: as an editor, your job is not only to remove bad stuff, but to remove good stuff when it's just too much.

11 Delete audio clips 4, 5, and 6 (counting from the left). Christopher felt that the most applicable and interesting interview material is the "cows" dialogue and the "Happy Birthday" audio segment. Using this material alone would make the audio too short. Consequently, Christopher chose to keep the interview answers about how the girls know each other. It's actually a pretty good introduction.

Unlike with video clips, when you delete these audio clips, the later clips don't automatically slide down to fill the gaps you create. You get to move each clip to the position you want it. (In fact, you could even overlap them as you work and move them around. It wouldn't hurt anything.)

12 Drag the remaining four audio clips to begin at the far left, under the dynamic slides, one after another.

Notice the snap and the sound effects that cue you to a boundary between two clips. It's helpful to know when you're correctly positioned at the head of a clip.

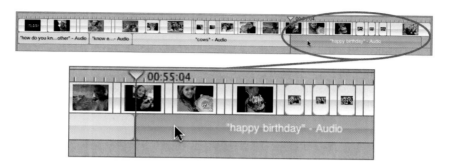

iMovie resizes the timeline to present the entire sequence, effectively stretching everything out to be larger and clearer in the space provided.

13 Play the entire sequence in this rough state to get a feeling for the audio and the video. Always ask yourself questions: *Where do they work together well? What misses?*

One good way to keep an audio track moving along is to clear out the extraneous pauses in the interview; there are moments of stalling while people are thinking. To an audience, these are uncomfortable and often sound like mistakes. Christopher wants to remove them to improve the flow. He does this with Command-T and Delete.

14 Zoom in on the section you plan to edit. Select the first audio clip and then choose View > Zoom to Selection.

To make the audio clearer visually, you can turn on a display format for sound, called *waveform*, when necessary.

15 Choose iMovie > Preferences and check "Show audio track waveforms."

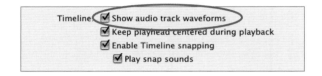

This adds a graphical representation of your sound's volume to the track.

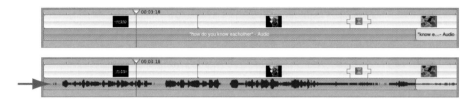

Now it's much easier to see where lines of audio start and stop, which in turn improves your accuracy while editing out bits you don't like.

There is one more technique that takes audio editing to the professional level: *scrubbing*.

16 Grab the playhead and slide it back and forth over some part of your timeline. iMovie mutes the sound when you do this. But press and hold the Option key on the keyboard *first* and then drag the playhead around, and you hear the sound, playing forward and backward at nonplay speeds. It sounds like an old record. It may be unusual, but this is the best way, along with the waveform, to precisely locate where to make cuts so as not to clip someone saying a word or making a sound that would otherwise make your track jarring to hear.

Now you have the required tools to do fine audio editing.

17 Find the pause at the end of the first audio clip. The last words the girl says before the pause are "and now we go to school together."

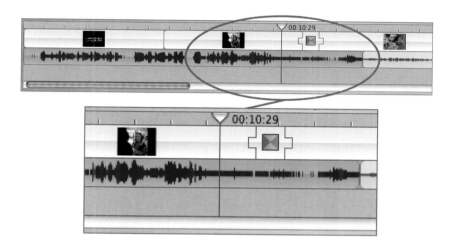

18 You could chop the clip here (Break Clip at Playhead) and delete the trimming. But instead, for a variation, use the Trim tool to pull the end of the clip to the place where the playhead is parked.

iMovie snaps the end of the clip into the spot where the playhead is parked—with that distinctive "snapping" sound—which makes this trimming easy to do and remarkably satisfying because of the crisp precision.

19 How to deal with the gap? You could slide the first clip down to fill it in, or you could pull all the following clips up. It's good to work on just one part of the video at a time, solve the problems you find there, and move on. In this case, Christopher doesn't want the interview to start right at the beginning, so slide the first clip down to fill the gap—it solves two problems at once.

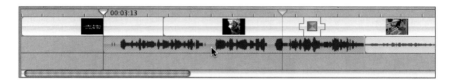

20 Do the same thing for the second audio clip. There's a bit of dead air at the end of the answer. Make the clip end after "like, three years."

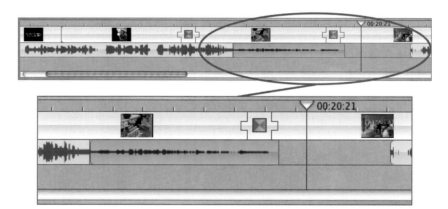

You'll learn a lot about sound and the acoustics of language when you focus on conversations at this level. Sometimes it's hard to know exactly when a word ends. You may make an edit and feel like you've clipped a word. But when you add a frame to the shot, it sounds like the next word is already starting. You just have to trust your ears and make the best edits you can without spending all day messing with frames.

21 Slide the "cows" shot to fill the gap.

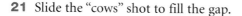

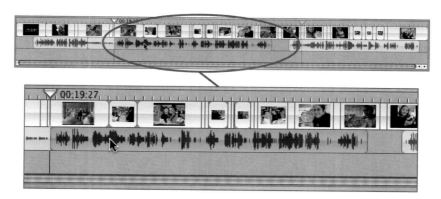

NOTE ▶ It's possible to drag shots from one track to another if you have a creative need to overlap sounds or a functional need to set something aside while you work on an audio issue.

And now Christopher comes to a creative snag. The "cows" interview ends, there's a gap, and then the "birthday" interview begins. But he wants the birthday material exclusively to accompany the images of the birthday cake and candle ceremony and conclude with the end of the last shot. Just from glancing at the timeline, he can see that the birthday audio material is far longer than the image sequence that includes the cake.

Sliding the birthday audio clip earlier to fill the gap only makes the problem worse. He could slide it down to end where he wants it to end, but that will only reveal the problem, not solve it.

22 Drag the birthday clip so that it finishes at then end of the last shot.

The gap between the two audio clips isn't the only problem; the birthday audio clip is too long. (Or, conversely, the accompanying images run too short.) The solution lies in adjusting the picture track. By pushing and pulling images (and deleting some if required), it's possible to align the two tracks to synchronize a little better, with the goal of not having any blank spots in the audio track.

23 Before you resolve the problems by changing the pictures, some uncomfortable pauses in the "Happy Birthday" clip still need to be removed. After the first "Happy birthday, Jessica" is a long pause. Use Command-T to chop up the clip and remove the silence.

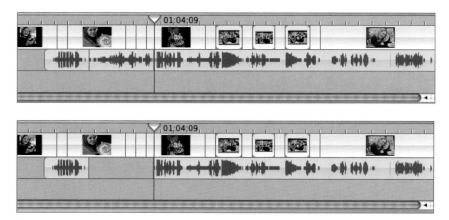

24 Slide the first part down to fill the gap that was created.

25 Slide the entire (new) "birthday" clip pair down to start where they need to—right under the birthday cake shot.

Technically speaking, the birthday cake shot begins at the start of the fade-in at its head, so position the playhead between the fade-out and fade-in, and then slide the pair of audio clips to begin here. They extend past the end of the video track because they're too long. The solution is to lengthen the picture track.

26 Select the last photo in the sequence, Jessica getting a birthday hug from her friend Rachel. You can't use the Trim tool to make this shot longer, because this isn't video; it's a still photo that has the Ken Burns Effect applied to it. The way to adjust it is through the Photos pane.

27 Click the Photos button.

28 Select the shot (again) to load it into the Ken Burns Effect workspace.

29 Adjust the duration of the shot from 8:03 to 10:00. You could guess, but it's faster to use the playhead in the timeline to get an approximation of how much material needs to be added. The picture track ends at 1:23:16, and the audio track ends at approximately 1:25:10. About two seconds will get the shots in the ballpark.

30 Click Update. The old shot will be replaced by this new, longer shot.

> **NOTE ▶** Whenever you update a shot that has an effect or transition on it (in this case, a cross-dissolve transition), iMovie will ask if you want it to automatically re-create the effect after it has replaced the shot—a good idea in most cases.

31 Drop a one-second fade-out transition on the end of the last shot.

Preview this part of the timeline. This last segment now works better, but you still must address the too-long stretch in the middle.

The easiest method is to remove shots to shorten the picture track. Using your judgment, you can visually recognize the size of the hole and estimate how many images you need to remove to approach that length of time.

32 Switch to Clip view for a moment.

33 Delete the shot of the girls from behind the paint display tiles (DSCN0106) and the one after it, too (DSCN0111).

34 Switch back to Timeline view.

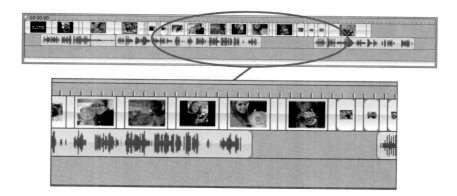

The birthday audio clip didn't slide when you removed pictures because it is not attached to anything. You don't need to adjust it yet, because you're about to do a little more moving. Since you can see the end of the "cows" audio and the beginning of the birthday video clip, you can see there's a little more of the picture track to be shortened before these line up. By measuring again with the playhead, you can see that about three more seconds need to be removed.

Rather than take little bits off lots of shots, or deleting any more shots, Christopher decides to shorten the long push in on Jessica and Rachel at the early part of the video.

35 From the Photo button, click the third shot after the opening title.

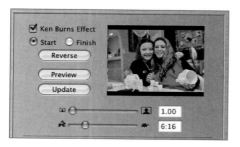

36 Change the length from 6:16 to 3:16 and click Update.

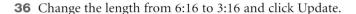

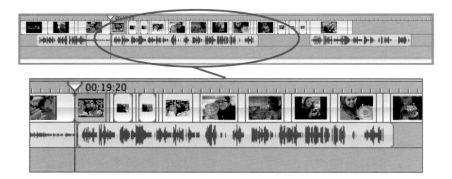

From glancing at the timeline, you can see that the end of the "cows" audio clip nearly aligns with the beginning of the cake video. Perhaps the fastest way to conclude this work is to slide the birthday audio back to fill the gap. (Or, if you prefer, line it up precisely by placing the audio in the second audio track—that way it can overlap slightly without requiring further work.)

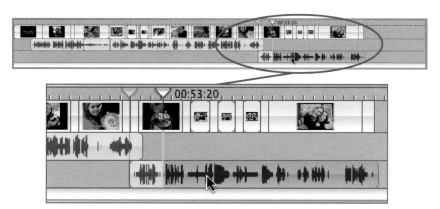

What you've accomplished is quite complex and is precisely the kind of work professional sound editors do. A QuickTime movie of Christopher's final version of this video is in the Lesson09 folder (Finished_BirthdayCD.mov).

Adding Narration While You're Working in iMovie

Recording audio with your camcorder is not the only way to get an audio-only track for iMovie. If you're willing to use the microphone built into your Mac, you have a quick and easy way to add narration directly into iMovie while you're editing.

1   Create a new iMovie project.

2   Name the project *Ceramic Process*. You're going to revisit Charlie's still photos to help him with his dynamic slide show.

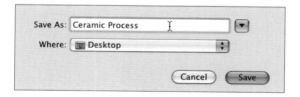

3   Open up the text document called **CeramicProcess_script.txt** located in your Lesson09 folder. Charlie originally used this material for the captions he printed out for his poster in Lesson 5. The narration tool in iMovie provides another option.

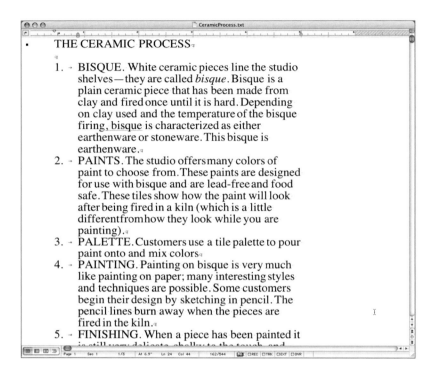

4 Click the Audio button in iMovie. The last time you used this part of the screen, you were importing music from your iTunes Library. Beneath the lists of songs is an innocuous set of items on your screen. Notice the word *Microphone*.

As you speak, or make any noise really, the microphone on your Mac is picking up the sound. The series of small rectangles stretching from the word *Microphone* to the red dot represents the volume of the sound the microphone is picking up.

5   Say something and watch the green lights expand to the right and then disappear. This means your microphone is on and working and ready to record anything you say. In audio circles, this loudness scale is called a *VU meter.*

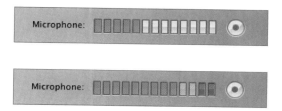

If a sound is too loud, the bar of lights will reach the yellow and then red zone. You want the sound to be loud enough, but not too loud. For most speech it's safest to stay in the middle of the green zone, with an occasional peak in the yellow or even red, as long as it's kept to a minimum.

You're ready to record.

6   Rehearse reading the first step in Charlie's report on the ceramic process. When you feel like you've got the words right, record it.

7   Click the red button to the right of the loudness meter and start reading the caption for the first photo in Charlie's album. When you reach the end of the first caption, click the red button again to stop recording.

It should take about 16 seconds to read the first bit. iMovie places the sound you've recorded directly into the timeline as a clip. Particularly for narration of this kind, where each caption is specifically for one photo, stop recording after each one to give yourself a moment to prepare and to make each caption its own discrete clip.

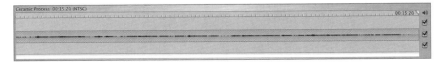

8   Read and record the next two captions, and make two more audio clips. iMovie will place these after the first one in the timeline. If you make a mistake, stop the recording, delete the clip, and try again.

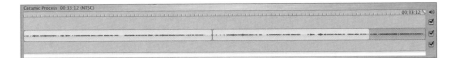

9   Click the Photos button, leaving this narration tool for a moment.

10   Open the Ceramic Process album from iPhoto to view Charlie's still photos.

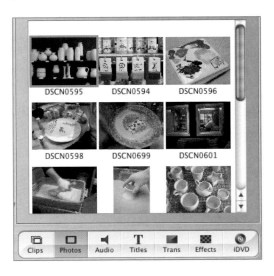

11 Click the first audio clip in the timeline: the caption for the first photo.

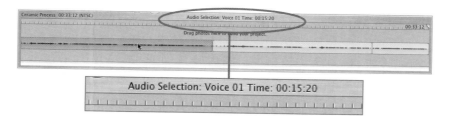

When you click a shot, the duration of the selection appears in the format of timecode in the top center part of the timeline. This clip's length is 15:20 (15 seconds and 20 frames). You're going to use this value to establish the duration of the Ken Burns Effect.

12 Click the first photo in the album—the one of white bisque. The caption should accompany this image.

13 Set the duration of the shot to 15:20. The colon between the units is important. It's not a decimal.

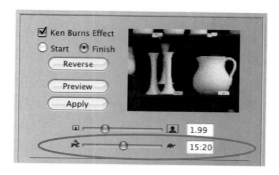

14 Set up the start and finish points for your Ken Burns Effect.

15 Click Apply. The shot will be added to the timeline, above the first audio clip.

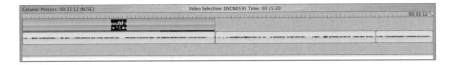

When the rendering of the effect is done, you can play the sequence.

16 Continue this process for the second and third shots.

This is a streamlined method to add narration to photos in iMovie. Rather than trying to make the sound fit the picture, you'll often find it easier to make the pictures fit the sound. Of course, all the tools you've used in the first part of this lesson apply here as well—if you needed to trim sound or picture, to rearrange clips, to cut out mistakes and adjust the results, and so on. It's not always possible to add sound while you're working, but many kinds of projects (like Charlie's) can benefit from the narration tools built into iMovie.

What You've Learned

- Sound is not ancillary to picture. In many cases, sound is more important than picture in giving the audience a feeling of completion and quality.

- You use the advanced feature Extract Audio to separate video material into its component picture and sound elements.

- You can unlock picture and sound elements before moving them around by using Unlock Audio Clip.

- Drag sound clips to any track. If you want to hear different sounds simultaneously, they need to be in different tracks.

- Use the microphone in iMovie's Audio pane to record narration right into the timeline.

10

Lesson Files	No files for this lesson
Tools	iMovie (optional), camcorder (optional)
Time	Approximately 45 minutes
Goals	Learn what kinds of events you can shoot for the best effect
	Get the best coverage in any shooting scenario
	Prepare for the most efficient and productive editing session following your shoot

Shooting with Hollywood-Style Techniques for Better Videos

Once you see how shooting and editing are related, you can see why you'll want to add different kinds of shots to round out your videos. There are also some shooting tricks you might try that facilitate your creating particularly cool results in iMovie. Not special effects, mind you, just simple concepts for gathering the right footage in order to give your videos a rather sophisticated style.

This lesson is really only half a lesson and must be approached with Lesson 11 in tandem: Shooting techniques can't stand alone and are realized only when it comes to editing with the shots they produce. In fact, even though there are no lesson files for this chapter, the illustrations that you'll see in this chapter come from the lesson files for Lesson 11.

Christopher gave you a quick taste of how shooting and editing work together in Lesson 8. At that time, you were introduced to the concept of *coverage*—that is, getting the material required to edit a scene. Now you will delve into more detail about coverage and how to get the best kind.

You don't need to prepare for a video shoot in advance, and you don't need to bring a lot of equipment to an event. But you do need to keep certain ideas in mind—primarily you have to know what pieces of video you need for editing, and you have to remember to get them during the event itself.

Now you will see how Christopher approaches shooting the birthday party in order to get the shots he thinks he might use. Getting the right shots now will make the time he spends editing much faster and more enjoyable.

How to Approach Shooting a Video

Shooting with a camcorder is in many ways the same as shooting with a still camera. All the rules of exposure and lighting apply (keep light behind you, not behind your subject), as do the rules of composition (don't always center your subject; remember the rule of thirds). It's important to hold the camcorder steady (two hands, always) and frame any shot before pressing the Record button.

But a camcorder has the added feature of motion. It takes 30 pictures every second, and consequently it can do lots of things that a still camera cannot. You can move the camera. You can zoom the lens. The camera records all of this. So in addition to basic photography skills, you need to learn some rules about moving pictures and good video.

Guidelines on Moving and Not Moving Your Camcorder

Before you get to move your camcorder, you have to come to grips with why you shouldn't. It's almost impossible to get good video when you're moving, and the material you do get is hard to watch and harder to edit.

Your camcorder is small. It's light. It fits in your hand. It seems natural to walk around with the thing recording, shooting up and down, left and right, following people around and so on. *Stop doing this immediately*.

In Hollywood, the camera certainly moves a lot, but it's not a trivial matter. Professional filmmakers get to move their cameras because of four important factors: (1) they use special equipment—like dollies and Steadicams—designed to move slowly and smoothly; (2) they have many people working together every time they set out to move the camera; (3) they get to rehearse the moves until they get them right; and (4) they are working in a controlled environment, so even if someone makes a mistake after rehearsing, they can do it again.

This isn't you. You're trying to make a good-looking, enjoyable video, and you've got just yourself and your camcorder. Once you've broken the habit of wandering around while recording and have seen the impressive results of this simple change, it's possible to add a little bit of movement to your projects to good effect.

▶ The Lingo of Motion

Before you start moving your camcorder around, familiarize yourself with the relevant vocabulary.

Pan: A move from side to side, along an imaginary horizon.

Tilt: Like a pan but up and down, like scanning a tall building.

Dolly shot: A shot from a camera that has been placed on a moving cart of some kind, to increase the stability of the camera and the smoothness of the move. A dolly is a cart designed specifically for doing this move, but you can create a cheap version by sitting on a swivel chair or in a shopping cart and having someone push it.

Tracking: Moving the camera to keep a moving subject "steady" in the middle of the frame. If you pan on a car as it drives by, it's a tracking shot.

Steadicam: A brand name of equipment that straps a camera to a camera operator in such a way that he or she can walk around while the device holds the camera steady. It uses gyroscopes and other mechanical means to keep the image from bouncing too much. These are prohibitively expensive for consumers, but mini versions (costing in the hundreds of dollars) are pretty good for amateurs.

Your Pans and Tilts

The best way to move the camera, of course, is to use some equipment of your own: a tripod. A regular tripod is designed to hold a camera steady or still, but in the video and film world, tripods often include a *fluid head*, a rather pricey feature that provides smooth and controlled movement.

A fluid-head tripod will allow you to make beautiful, smooth pans and tilts. But even then, the camera motion must be very slow and deliberate. There is a natural tendency to pan for a long time—along a coastline, perhaps—but if you look closely at pans in movies, they are actually quite short: just little moves from here to over there a tiny bit. Not 180 degrees, but rather more like 10 degrees. If you don't have a tripod, it's almost impossible to make a pan or tilt look smooth and professional. They are fun to do, but when it comes time to edit, you'll often end up skipping past them and opting for steady shots because moving shots look so bad.

Most of the time, you won't be using a tripod anyway (let alone one with a fluid head), and you must improvise. Creating a moving shot without extra equipment falls in the danger zone, and the responsibility is on you to restrain your use of pans and tilts and to be controlled when you do try them.

If you don't have a tripod and you feel compelled to pan or tilt, hold your body very stiff, hold the camera close with your elbows tight to your body, and then move the camera just a nudge between two relatively close points. If the move is short enough, sometimes the pan will be slick and usable.

Tracking

Pans and tilts are troublesome partly because you are just sort of looking around with the camera, leaving the audience searching everywhere in the frame for something to focus on. Tracking works a little better, however, because you follow an object and (generally speaking) keep it in the middle of the frame. The audience knows what it is watching in a tracking shot, and consequently the technique can be very interesting and effective. It takes some skill to follow a moving target, so practice as much as possible before you actually record the shot.

Think of moving the camera as a special effect—fun to do, cool looking, but only something done once in awhile, for good use at just the right moment.

Using and Ignoring Your Zoom

Everything just stated about moving goes for zooming as well. When shooting, don't zoom. It's really, really tempting, and it feels slick while you're doing it, but the resulting video is less than ideal.

Of course, the zoom control is critical to your videos. It's front and center—under your index finger—and second only to the Record button itself in importance. If you don't get to zoom, why is it there?

Instead of regarding this as a zoom, think of it as a big ol' bag of interchangeable lenses. What's great about the zoom lens on your camcorder is that it's equal to a bunch of lenses in one. Zoomed out, you see the big picture with a wide-angle lens. Zoom in a little or all the way, and you've got a telephoto lens, up close and personal.

Use the zoom to help you frame your shot, using your rules of composition and thinking about the coverage you want for editing. Once you've set the zoom, you can then record—without touching it. After you stop recording, you can adjust the zoom and record again.

TIP ▶ Once you're comfortable with the way shooting and editing are interrelated, you may find yourself leaving the camcorder on record while you zoom—from wide shot to close-up, for instance. The difference is that you're doing so only to get from one shot to another quickly, and you know you will be cutting out the zoom part when you're editing.

A camcorder won't let you zoom carefully or slowly enough to produce good zoom shots. But you can create the same effect by shooting two or three unmoving, unzooming shots of an object with your camera set to wide, then closer, then as close as you can. Cut these shots together, and you get a professional looking "push in."

Christopher began recording his video from the far corner of the studio. He wanted to get a nice, basic shot of the event from this initial position, but while he was there, he chose to cover himself by getting a couple of additional shots. Here's what he did:

1   With the camera zoomed out as wide as possible, he recorded the room for about 15 seconds. He held the camera above his head and used both hands to steady the shot.

Wide shot (also written as "WS" or "Wide")

This is a *wide shot,* which is defined as any shot in which the subject is fully inside the frame—a person seen from head to toe, for instance. The wider a shot and the more details present in the frame, the longer the piece of video needs to be so that the audience can get oriented and see what's going on. Because the party group is so tiny in the frame, this shot is actually an extreme wide shot (EWS).

2   After Christopher stopped recording the wide shot, he zoomed in a little bit—about midway between the widest and the closest settings. Once he framed this shot, he recorded again for about 10 seconds.

Medium shot ("MS" or "Med")

This is a medium shot, in which you can see a person from head to waist. Medium shots should make up the bulk of your video material. They look good on TV and achieve a nice balance between being close enough to show what's going on and far enough to provide some perspective.

3 Finally, Christopher zooms in all the way to get a close-up shot.

Close-up shot ("CU" or "Close")

Close-up shots are nice and often look more attractive than other shots because the subject is so clear. A close-up comprises just a person's head, and traditionally you crop off the top of the head to get a little closer. It's the eyes where the expression is communicated, and the top of the head is considered superfluous.

An extreme close-up (ECU) is common too—just the eyes or just the eyes and nose.

TIP ▶ When working with a camcorder, it's easy to shoot everything too close. The LCD is often so small that it makes your subject look boring unless you get *really* close. Fight this urge, and trust that when you see the video on your TV set, the close-ups will freak you out with their intensity. The medium shot is the main kind of image you are looking for. Close-ups are powerful and a little scary, and they should be used more sparingly than it may seem.

These naming conventions aren't rules so much as guidelines designed to help you distinguish the shots you are recording and to help you keep your shots distinct.

Why the need? Because when you edit, you cannot juxtapose two shots that are too similar. It ends up looking jarring, like a mistake. So although it's easy to cut from a wide shot to a close-up, cutting from a medium shot of a person to something only a tad different, say to just their head and shoulders, likely wouldn't work. By recognizing the difference between shots and making sure they are appropriately distinct, you get material you know can be edited.

When you shoot scenes, you don't always need all three shots of each moment, but you should record at least two. That way, even if you get no other coverage, you have some way to edit the material into a video with impact.

> **NOTE** ▶ You can shoot a close-up with your camcorder even when the zoom setting is wide angle (just stand really close to your subject) or tele-photo (stand farther away). So, there isn't a direct relationship between the zoom—in photo jargon, the *focal length*—and the size of your subject. In the end, when you work in iMovie, you won't care about wide angle or telephoto, but you will care about the distinct look of close-ups and medium shots.

Determining What to Shoot

The central element of the subjects you shoot needs to be relatively repetitive. And it should be something that is ongoing—like girls painting and talking. Or people eating dinner, kids building with blocks in the living room, or ath-letes playing soccer. While it seems like these activities consist of very random actions, all involve a certain repetitive motion (painting, eating, running), and this is what allows you to get Hollywood-style coverage of the event without having to interrupt the action and ask everyone to do it again.

Unlike still photography, your videos should have at their core a *scene*. For professional filmmakers, a scene is a scripted event that takes place between a set of characters in a fixed location. For you, the moments you shoot with video probably are not planned events. You're just minding your own business and wham, something cool (cute, amazing, unbelievable, funny,) starts to happen. You think, "Man, I wish I had a video of that," and then you run off, get your camera, and run back. The event that started this is the core of your scene.

At the birthday party, there are in fact lots of little scenes. There's the scene you worked on in Lesson 8 in which the girls are at the shelf of bisque selecting what they want to paint. It's small, it's fast, but it's a scene. In the current lesson (and Lesson 11), the girls are sitting and painting, and this too is a scene.

Christopher wanted some video of the girls painting, so, in order to be as non-invasive as possible, he began shooting video from a distance across the room. This is a good strategy. In many videos, you will want to start discreetly from far away—zoomed in, if necessary—and then work your way closer, remembering not to shoot as you move but rather to move, frame, and then shoot.

Your first task is keeping the core (repetitive) activity you are shooting in mind and getting the coverage that you need to edit.

Getting Coverage in Your Scene

We touched on the relationships between shots in Lesson 8. There you learned that each shot needs to have at least one other corresponding shot with which it has a natural dynamic. This section is going to outline the most important (and easiest to get) shots that create this dynamic.

Christopher is not doing a documentary on ceramics or even on his daughter; he's just making a sketch of a moment in her life. The still photos were far better for getting bits and pieces of the whole event (arriving, painting, chatting, and eating cake). The video is intended to preserve a moment and make it interesting. The moment he chooses is the painting.

Earlier in this lesson, you saw Christopher start the shoot by going to the edge of the room and shooting both a wide and a close-up from there. This is the first guideline for shooting: Get multiple shots from each position.

Multiple Shots from Each Position

You don't want to move around too much with your camera. You want to get the coverage you need from just a couple of fixed locations. Maybe two. Or three. If you're good, maybe four. But not 10. A common mistake is to shoot a little bit from here, wander around, shoot some more from over there, stop for a while, and then shoot from some new location. All of this will be more challenging to put together into a cohesive video.

From whatever position you make your first shot, you want to get two shots. When Christopher made his first wide shot of the girls painting, he recorded for about 10 seconds and then stopped. Then he did the important thing: He zoomed in for a closer shot and recorded again, for 10 more seconds. If he was not in a hurry, he might have shot three shots from this location (a wide, a medium, and a close-up), but at least two are critical. Make two shots, then move to the next location.

TIP ▶ A wide shot will often answer the question "Where are we?" A medium shot will answer the question "Who is here?" A close-up will answer the question "What is going on?"

Shots and Reverse Shots

Once Christopher got to his first position and recorded a couple of different shots from there, the question arises: Where to go next? The answer is easy. Once you've shot everything you can see from the first vantage point, move to the other side of your subject and shoot back toward where you were standing. In very general terms, you're moving about 180 degrees from where you started. The name for this is the *reverse shot*.

> **NOTE** ▶ Technically speaking, you're not going to move exactly 180 degrees opposite your original position. It's going to be closer to 120 degrees, but it's a detail that you can refine once you're in the habit of getting a reverse shot.

When you are done shooting from the reverse position, you'll have two sets of shots (called, of course, shots and reverse shots); and those have a very specific dynamic between them. As long as the action is similar from both positions, these shot/reverse combinations can be cut together to give a remarkable experience to the viewers—as if they were in two places at the same time.

The shot/reverse dyad works wonderfully if a pair of people are talking or directly interacting. Focus on one of the two people for the first shot and on the second person for the reverse shot. Christopher's job was challenging because instead of two girls talking and painting there were five. Still, by concentrating on two of them at a time he was able to get the coverage he needed.

Interaction between two people is almost always a compelling core to your videos. Everything else is just setting and ambience. The back-and-forth of human interplay is in many ways the precise reason you are using video and not still photography. Consequently, the shot/reverse shot is often the main element of your projects.

You don't have to load up your camcorder and follow along with Christopher for this lesson—primarily because what he's doing won't precisely match what you're going to do in any given shooting situation. Hopefully, seeing his process will still be of value to you when you shoot your own projects.

If you want to try these basic shooting guidelines, and you are encouraged to do so, set up a very basic scene. Two people sitting in chairs facing each other and playing a game—tic-tac-toe perhaps, or chess, or cards. Let the two "actors" play a real game, ignore you, and you shouldn't bother them. Shooting and getting this coverage will be straightforward and, while you won't use it for editing in Lesson 11, once you've finished that exercise, you could edit the material you just shot.

1   Find your subject, frame it as a medium shot, and start recording. This first shot should go on for a minimum of 10 seconds and probably more like 15. There are no rules; just hold still and let the person do whatever it is she is doing.

2   Before leaving the first position, don't forget to get a second shot (either zoomed closer or farther). Getting two shots is not required, but it will give you a little flexibility later when it's time to edit. You'll be glad you have them.

3   As soon as you stop recording, move to a position opposite where you were with the first shot. The easiest way to do this is to imagine a line between the subject and the person your subject is interacting with. With luck (and for easier shooting), these two people should be facing each other, sitting on opposite sides of a table or something. Walk from position 1 to position 2 and, framing the subject in a medium shot similar to before, shoot for another 10 to 15 seconds.

4   As before, it's usually a good idea to get a second shot (probably a close-up) from this same position.

When you've finished shooting from these two positions, you have the core of your video coverage. With a shot and a reverse shot, you can build a compelling moment easily in iMovie.

> **TIP** ▸ Another specific shot used often in Hollywood is the over-the-shoulder (OS) shot. Instead of having a single shot of a person alone in the frame, keep the edge of the other person's back in the frame. This shows the physical relationship between them—how close they are to each other—and reminds the audience that two people are there, not just one. In conversations on film, particularly for medium shots, they are the standard.

Get the Cutaway Shot

Shots and reverse shots may make up the core of your video, but it's almost impossible to watch these two shots all day. What you need is something else to look at, a break. Behold the *cutaway shot*. It is a close-up of something other than the people in your video. It doesn't include anyone's mouth moving. Its sole purpose is to show you details and texture of what is going on.

Any number of subjects can constitute a good cutaway shot. You'll probably find a half-dozen or more. You almost can't have too many, they're so useful. In some ways a good cutaway is almost a still photo: You frame some odd detail as a kind of still life. It doesn't have to be an image from the action (like hands painting) but instead could be anything that provides details within the environment (other people in the studio, odd bisque items on the shelves, the slide show running on the big display at the bar, and so on).

Don't shoot your cutaway shots until you're satisfied with your shot/reverse coverage. You can cheat the cutaways a little bit; they don't have to fit precisely with the shot/reverse and can often be shot very late in the event. You don't know how (or even if) you will use these shots while editing, but when you need one, you won't believe how important it is to have it. You'll end up picking one or two—whatever fits best with the video you're making. But those decisions will come later. For now your job is to get all the coverage you might need.

Here are some of Christopher's cutaway shots that he might use with the shot/reverse combinations you saw previously.

Unlike the more standard shot/reverse combinations, cutaways beg for creativity. From any position (wide from across the room, from the side getting the shot/reverse), you've always got the opportunity to point the camera in a slightly different direction, zoom in, and get a cutaway shot. Remember that fewer shooting positions is generally better. Still, in some of the shots Christopher took, he set the camera down on the table or shot from high above his head, pointing the lens down at the table.

Make Sure You Have an Establishing Shot

Finally, you'll always need at least one *establishing shot*, which shows where this event is taking place—a wide shot that depicts not only your main characters but also where they are situated. Sometimes this is the first shot you get; remember how Christopher started wide and far away before getting close for the shot/reverse? But don't be limited by a wide shot or a shot that includes the girls. The outside of the studio is perhaps a better establishing shot.

Sometimes it's natural to get the establishing shot at the end, after the cut-aways. Since the participation of the birthday girls isn't required, it's good to focus on them first and get the extra material afterward. It doesn't matter when you take the shot; just remember that establishing shots, particularly if they are wide, often need to play onscreen for a little longer than normal. Hold still (don't pan—it isn't necessary). If the venue or vista is too large for a single shot, stay in your position and point in a few different directions, changing from wide to closer as necessary. All these bits can be combined into a short establishing shot sequence.

> **TIP** Establishing shots can be exceptionally creative too. Don't just wander far away and shoot a big wide shot. Think about shooting from up high, over your head. Shoot through a window—reflections and all. Look for signage around that might help place you ("Welcome to Petroglyph Ceramic Lounge" or "Hot, Hot, Hot. Careful around kilns"). The signs are good for establishing your location, but they don't need to be full frame, dead center—just an edge of a sign or a snippet of a logo is often enough.

Looking for Story Structure

The final aspect of coverage is that of story structure—that is, finding shots that in some way represent what might be a "beginning" of your video as well as an "ending." Your video isn't just a random sequence of shots, but a short story. While you can build a sequence that is visually dynamic using shot/reverse combinations with the occasional cutaway, your videos will be better if they have a natural beginning, some climax or punch line, and then a natural ending. Only the best videos nail these story elements—you can't script them, and they don't always happen when you shoot. At best you can be looking for them so that you can record them when the moment arrives. Shooting video is a little like trick-or-treating on Halloween: you get what you can, you go home, dump the bits on the kitchen table, and see how you did. No matter how hard you try, sometimes you just don't get all the coverage you hoped to get. You can try to edit anyway, but it will be that much harder to make a great video.

A few tricks can facilitate good beginnings and endings. In the first place, since you now know not to move the camera, you can achieve the excellent effect of letting your characters move into and out of the frame. If you know where something is going to happen—say, the girls just arrived at the studio and are about to start looking for ceramics at the shelf of bisque—then you could point your camera there, start shooting, and hold still. In no time, the girls will wander into the frame. Presto: a beginning shot. Similarly, if you know they've found their pieces and are about to go sit down, frame them and hold still. They'll exit the frame and you'll be left looking at a shelf of ceramics—a nice ending.

Many natural events make good endings. People walking off into the sunset is a classic (even clichéd) finale. Somebody pulling up in a car, opening a door to enter a house, or walking into a room are all natural introductions. Shooting these moments isn't required for a video, of course. If you don't get this kind of coverage, you'll force the editor (again, you) to improvise. A simple fade in or fade out is the fallback position.

What You've Learned

- You need sufficient coverage to edit a video. With just a few simple bits, you will have enough to make interesting videos when it's time to edit.

- Shoot from a finite set of positions to get your video—at least two, and probably three or four. More than that will likely produce too much coverage, the majority of it not useful.

- Always shoot a wide shot and a medium shot from a given position. If you have time, shoot a close-up too. The medium shot is your primary shot. Make sure you have enough material from each shot.

- Wide shots need to be longer than close-ups. Think of recording your wide shots and establishing shots for around 15 seconds each. Medium shots and close-ups can be closer to 10 seconds.

- Look for shot dyads—a shot/reverse shot, a shot/cutaway shot, a shot/establishing shot. These make editing a snap and give your projects a sophisticated look.

11

Lesson Files   Lessons > Lesson11 > Start_Project11

Tools   iMovie

Time   Approximately 90 minutes

Goals   Learn how to handle the coverage you shot when editing

Use basic editing skills to create dynamic scenes

Recognize how to use interactions between characters to guide your editing

Create a high-quality archive copy of your finished video

Lesson 11
Editing and Finishing a Professional-Looking Movie

In Lesson 10, Christopher shot coverage of the birthday party at the ceramics studio. The party's over now. The cake is eaten, the brushes are washed, and the girls have gone home. Now it's quiet time, and Christopher has an hour or two to see if he can make an interesting video from the material he shot.

The techniques you've learned over the last 10 lessons all come together when a video is being developed: incorporating music from iTunes (Lesson 1), adding moving still photos with titles and transition effects (Lesson 6), and taking advantage of the fundamental editing tools (Lesson 7). There is no way around it—making a video incorporates all the tools, tricks, and capabilities of iLife. With basic coverage (from Lesson 10) and familiarity with the editing tools in iMovie (which starts right here), you can whip out a video in no time.

Getting to your Mac with your video material and starting to work in iMovie can be a little emotionally challenging. If your photographic skills are competent, most of the material you shot is good. Even so, most of the material will not end up in your project.

Keep one thing in mind (you might even want to print this out and hang it above your Mac): *Editing is not about throwing out bad material. Editing is about building something interesting and watchable.* Sometimes you toss bad bits of video, but mostly you have to get rid of many good parts to make the remaining parts even better.

If it makes you feel better, you're not really throwing anything away. It's all on the videotape you shot. That original tape is an archive. When you finish this lesson, you'll also learn how to archive your final project in high-quality digital videotape for any future uses that may arise.

Reviewing Material from the Camcorder

The material Christopher shot is in iMovie for you already. If this were your own material, and you were going to make a log sheet for your videotape (described in Lesson 8), a good time to do it would be while you imported material into iMovie.

Once you've importing the video, you can turn your attention to the kinds of coverage that you'll be editing. In this case, we'll look at Christopher's footage, which focuses on four of the girls at the party—our "characters." Since you'll be watching their individual coverage as well as their interactions, it's practical to refer to each of them by name.

Here are our characters:

Jessica   Chloe   Rachel   Alison

1   Open the **Start_Project11** project from the Start_Project 11 iMovie folder
    (in the Lesson11 folder). By now you're familiar with iMovie and will
    notice there is one clip in the Clip pane.

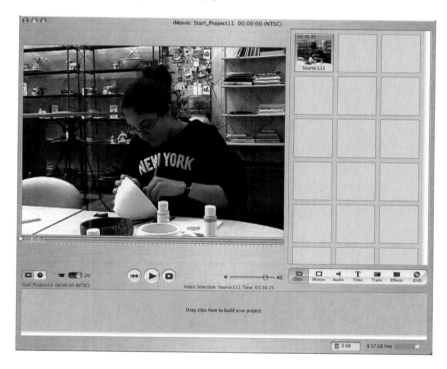

Why only one clip? Didn't Christopher get a lot of shots? Yes—but as you
learned in Lesson 8, iMovie gives you the option to break up material into
discrete clips in the Clip pane based on the camera's starting and stopping
points. In prior lessons, you saw the clips already broken into shots in the
pane. But you also have the option of not breaking up material in that way;
it isn't always helpful (as with the time-lapse video in Lesson 7)—and it may
be misleading.

As your skills increase, you won't need to rely on stopping and starting the camera to distinguish between shots. For instance, if you zoom from a wide shot to a close-up and then quickly move the camera to get a cutaway shot, all without stopping the camera, iMovie will see these continuously-recorded-but-discrete shots as a single clip. If it only gave you one clip in the pane for these shots, you might inadvertently miss part of the coverage.

Consequently, before he imported this video, Christopher disabled the preference (iMovie > Preferences > General) that tells iMovie to separate clips while it places them in the Clip pane:

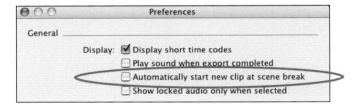

In this lesson, you'll approach the video the way it is on the videotape—and move through the "single" clip getting the pieces you need (to start with).

> **NOTE** ▶ This clip is only 3½ minutes long and is pulled from the 10 minutes or so that Christopher actually shot at the party—a necessary practicality. This makes the video easier to work with in this lesson, but it deprives you of all the coverage Christopher gathered for himself and slightly limits what you can build from this material.

2   Begin by watching the entire clip. Click the clip in the Clip pane and watch it in the Viewer. Make mental notes about what coverage is here and which shots have a relationship to other shots.

One of the most important ways to get the best cut of something through editing is by being exceptionally familiar with the material you're using. Moments as short as a second are sometimes remarkably valuable when it comes time to solve a problem during editing. The only way you'll be able to use these is if you notice them, so it's a good idea to watch the raw material at least twice before you make any cuts.

The sound of the girls talking (the production sound) is really hard to hear, and consequently it's practically useless, as you might expect. When you watch the video, it's good to notice when you see people speaking, but don't be concerned with what they're saying. In a video like this, instead of dialogue you'll end up using background music (making a kind of music video) or a narration track (as you did in Lesson 9), which parallels but does not synchronize with the video. Either way, the actual words spoken are relatively unimportant.

Time to make your first cut: but where to start? Since you can add shots anywhere to the sequence at any time, there's no need at this point to focus on what you think might be the "first" shot. Instead just start working with shots as they show up on the tape, in the order things were shot. You can decide on the order in which to place them as you build your sequence.

3   The first shot on the tape is of Alison—it starts as a medium shot and then zooms quickly to a close-up. Cut three or four seconds of each of these and put them in the workspace. Your goal is to find moments where the camera is steady and there is no zooming.

If you can't remember how to chop up these bits using Command-T and then dragging them to the timeline, review those skills in Lesson 7 or Lesson 8.

4   Continue working through the material of each girl, adding a medium shot and then a close-up, until you have a series of shots of each of the four girls painting. Your workspace will look something like this:

You've created a little mess in the Clip pane—mostly trimmed bits you don't need, and one large piece that is still untouched. That's OK; it's a different kind of workspace. You may move shots back and forth from the Clip pane to the timeline in Clip view and sometimes back to the Clip pane. In the same way that you can rearrange shots in the timeline, you can pull shots out while you work.

It's a good time to change the names of the shots in your workspace. iMovie defaults to some pretty cryptic names. Finding material and working with shots is easier if the names are useful.

5   Click the first shot in your timeline. The shot is highlighted; click the name of the shot, and you can change it. Use the naming methods you learned in Lesson 10. This first shot is a medium shot (MS) of Alison.

6   Proceed through all the shots in the timeline and rename them as follows:

This is a good start, but remember that the order in which you shoot has little to do with the order in which you will place the shots. The current organization is a little dull.

7   Try rearranging these shots by dragging the clips to new positions in the timeline. Without adding any new material, this same bunch of video can become something like this:

After this quick adjustment, the editing is beginning to create some feelings in the audience as they pick up on dynamics between the girls. The sequence begins with a medium shot of Jessica (the birthday girl), and in the same frame we can see that Rachel, on the right edge, is speaking to Chloe, who is off camera. Jessica is keeping an eye on their discussion. In the next shot, we see Rachel painting and speaking to Chloe, whom we can't see. Next the audience needs to see Chloe, who up to this point has been participating but hasn't appeared in the frame. And thus, we then cut to the MS Chloe shot.

The characters' eyes drive the direction of the edits. (An audience tends to want to see the things the characters are looking at.) Since this is a dynamic conversation—we can't really hear what they're talking about, but we can tell they're interacting—let's go back to Jessica, this time for something closer, more personal, more intense. It might have been too much to start with that intensity, but now that we've looked around, it's OK.

Again Jessica is watching Rachel and Chloe. So we move on to Rachel painting in close-up, and then Chloe returning the looks. If there is back and forth between characters, it's often good to keep the characters the same size in the frame in shots edited together (keeping close shots cutting to close, or medium cutting to medium); this provides a good visual and emotional balance for the viewer. When you "punch in" to a close-up, you want to do it for a good reason (and not just because you *have* a close-up shot).

But what about Alison? Through the whole dialogue, Alison is hard at work painting on her own and is not participating in the conversation. The medium shot of her depicts this. In truth, the close-up of Alison is superfluous.

8 Drag the last shot, CU Alison, back to the Clip pane. You may want it later, but you don't need it now.

NOTE ▸ When you want to play the sequence, it's generally easiest to pop back to Timeline view and drag the playhead to the point from which you want to start watching. Clip view is good for rearranging shots, but ultimately you will go back and forth in your workspace view while editing.

Now the stage is set for moving on, digging further into the material on the "tape" (in the Clip pane). Don't worry yet about the length of these shots—they may be a tiny bit too short or too long, but they can be trimmed later. For now it's important to pay attention to the structure.

TIP ▸ If the shots in the Clip pane get confusing, you can label the clips or delete the bits you are confident you don't need, or you can do some of both. Be sure to keep an eye on the "big" piece—most everything here is a few seconds long, but one clip is more than two minutes long. Get familiar with looking at the durations of the clips to help orient yourself as to what is what. Bits of video you delete go in the trashcan in iMovie—as long as you don't empty the trash, it's possible to restore the deleted pieces.

9   Go back to the big hunk of video in the Clip pane that you haven't worked on yet. The next shot you come to as you play it is a close-up of some hands. It's a cutaway shot. Cut out about three seconds of this and use it in the sequence.

Once it's cut, the question is where to put it. It doesn't make sense to drop it at the end of the sequence. This is a close-up of Jessica painting; it could go between a shot of Jessica and one of another girl, or you could break one of the shots of Jessica in two and drop it between them. Based on watching what is going on in each of Jessica's shots, it makes the most sense to place it between the close-up shots.

10   Drag the cutaway shot to after the CU Jessica shot.

It makes sense here, as Jessica looks down in the close-up shot right before we move to the cutaway. If she were already looking up at Rachel at the end of the close-up, it might not work as well. It also fits nicely, because when the sequence cuts to Rachel, she's painting, too.

After the cutaway of Jessica painting is one of Rachel painting.

11   Clip out another few seconds of Rachel's cutaway shot and place it in the sequence after the medium shot of Rachel.

Placing it here not only makes logical sense (we just saw Rachel painting, and now we can see more detail of what she is doing), but also helps the pacing. It now takes a moment longer before Chloe responds to Rachel, so you begin to feel that they aren't having just a conversation, but one punctuated by painting and watching each other paint.

There's one more nice cutaway—a top-down shot (a shot taken from overhead) of Chloe working on her cow picture. It begins with Chloe looking toward Rachel and ends with her looking down. The ideal now is to find a point that connects with these moments in the sequence you've built.

12   Play the sequence and look for a good place to put the cutaway of Chloe. What you'll notice is that all the shots of Chloe begin with her looking up toward Rachel and end with her looking down at her plate. Consequently, the choice may be to place the cutaway after either the medium shot or the close-up of Chloe, and then trim the cutaway shot so that it begins after she looks down.

13   Insert Chloe's cutaway after the close-up.

14 Change to Timeline view. Using the Trim tool, shorten her cutaway shot to begin after she looks down.

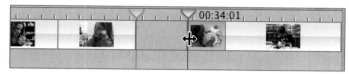

Before shortening the clip

After shortening the clip

Now the cutaway is much too short.

15 Use the Trim tool again, this time on the tail end of the cutaway shot, to add more time. Keep an eye on the shot in the Viewer window to make sure you're adding the material you want to add.

This is pretty good. It's far more interesting to watch than the raw material, particularly now that the order has been changed. Remember that all the material for this little sequence was made from one shot of each girl, with a little zoom to create two bits of coverage per position. Add to that a tiny bit of cutaway detail, and the result is a rather compelling (and maybe emotionally realistic) 38-second scene.

16 For the sake of this lesson, spend a moment cleaning up the Clip pane. Selecting shots and pressing Delete on your keyboard, delete the trimmings that you aren't using, leaving only the CU Alison shot that we specifically placed here and the balance of the source material.

Before cleanup

After cleanup

NOTE ▶ When you delete shots, they go into the trashcan at the bottom of the window—you'll notice that the number of megabytes (MB) grows as you throw out more material. iMovie will keep shots here until you empty the trashcan. Unless you are out of space on your Mac, don't empty the trashcan until you're done with your project, just in case you toss something you shouldn't.

More detailed trimming will be appropriate once you've completed a first pass of the whole scene. Then you can balance the length of the shots with each other and make the pacing feel inviting. But for now, the first part of this sequence is done, and it's time to move on to the next bit of coverage.

Editing a Dialogue Scene

From here, the coverage moves into the shot/reverse shot material of Alison speaking with Jessica. Later, Rachel joins the conversation—which makes the editing a little more complicated but not beyond your control.

In this part of the scene, you'll use the basics of shot/reverse shot to build a dialogue (even if you can't make out what people are saying). You'll do this at its simplest form—but you can use the same coverage and simple techniques to build quite complex and sophisticated sequences.

1   Begin by finding a medium shot of Alison in which she is clearly speaking to Jessica. Clip it out, keeping it as long as you can—for this one, almost nine seconds.

2   Drop it into the timeline.

Notice the difference between this shot of Alison and the one just before it in the sequence. They're both medium shots, but the second one has the edge of Jessica in the frame. It's an over-the-shoulder (OS) shot, which is important in dialogue scenes to help the audience maintain a connection to the interaction between two people. You'll notice that all the shots in the dialogue are OS shots.

3   You don't need both shots of Alison. Get rid of the first one of her painting alone in frame (called a "single" by filmmakers). Since you might want it later, drag it back to the Clip pane.

4   Find the reverse shot that matches this first shot in terms of the size of the characters in the frame. It's a medium shot of Jessica, over Alison's shoulder. What you're looking for is a moment in this shot where Jessica is speaking. Ideally she'd look up to make the connection to Alison, but unfortunately because everyone is painting while they talk, eye contact is infrequent.

When you find a moment where Jessica speaks, clip it out. It may be short, but as long as it's more than a couple of seconds, it's OK. You also may need to be careful to clip out a shot that doesn't include a zoom.

TIP ▶ Use the arrow keys to move frame by frame forward or backward through shots in order to locate the exact frame to cut on—where there's no zooming or moving.

5   The place you want to insert Jessica's shot is not after Alison's shot but within it, right after Alison finishes speaking. (Watch for her to finish moving her lips, since you can't really hear her well.) Change to Timeline view, and then stop the playhead right after she speaks.

6   Split this clip at the playhead (Command-T) to create two clips.

7   Drop the shot of Jessica between these two clips. To insert shots into the timeline, you don't necessarily have to be in Clip view. Dragging clips from the Clip pane into the timeline works fine.

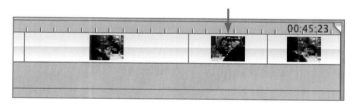

Now this scene is starting to have the flow of a dialogue: Alison speaks, Jessica listens and then speaks, and then we see Alison again.

8   Roll further into the raw source material to find another medium shot of Jessica speaking, and clip some of it out. Notice that in over-the-shoulder shots you can often tell that the person with her back to the camera is speaking, even if you can't see her lips moving. This can be useful and effective for the dialogue.

9   Place this shot at the end of the sequence, after the medium shot of Alison.

NOTE ▶ Notice how in both the shot and the reverse shot Jessica is on the left side of the frame and Allison is on the right. This is good form. The effect is created because when Christopher shot the reverse, he was about 120 degrees from his first position, on the same side of an imaginary line he visualized between the girls.

10 Instead of continuing ahead in the raw source material, you may recall that all your medium and close shots of Alison were trimmed out earlier and still reside in a hunk of film you've set aside. Go back to the close-ups of Alison in the Clip pane and find a few seconds of her speaking, with her head up (as we can see she is doing in the OS shot). Here's one:

11 Cut out a few seconds from this angle and place it after the last shot.

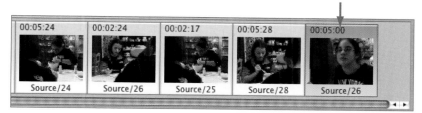

In this case, the CU Alison shot ends when she looks away from Jessica and toward Rachel to bring her into the conversation. Using her line of sight as the cue, you are now free to explore the shot/reverse between Alison and Rachel.

12 Find a short shot of Rachel speaking to Alison—a medium over-the-shoulder shot.

13 Cut out a few seconds and add the piece to the end of the sequence.

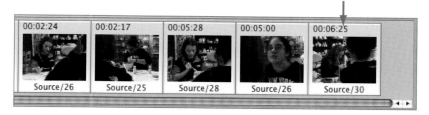

NOTE ▶ You can't trust the names iMovie automatically adds to clips as you chop up material in the Clip pane. It uses numbers that are available, and some numbers become available again and again as you use the pieces in your sequence. In the end, you may have multiple shots with names like Source/26. Again, if you're relying on names to guide you, rename shots in the Clip pane or timeline to help keep oriented.

Finally, end this dialogue with a shot of Jessica to give it some closure. You could continue indefinitely, cutting back and forth, medium to close, person to person. But your job as editor is to make the hard judgments and know when to stop.

14 Find a CU Jessica shot from the trims.

15 Cut out a few seconds and add the shot to the end of the sequence.

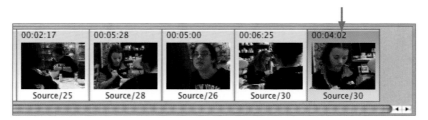

As you roll through the end of your raw material—the final moments of video Christopher shot—you'll see a few more cutaways and finally a wider shot, an establishing shot, of the group painting.

The video doesn't need the cutaway shots (although you could experiment by dropping short bits into the scene). But it does need the wider shot. There is precious little material shot from a distance to give the audience any sense of where we are or the overall relationship between the girls sitting and painting.

16 Cut five seconds from the wide shot and add it to the sequence as the very first shot—ahead of the initial work you did in this lesson.

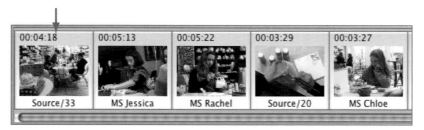

That really helps set up the coming scene. While there are other places it could go (and it can be a little clichéd to open *and end* with these wide shots), you can't go wrong structurally using the wide shot as a pair of bookends.

17 Add another segment of the wide shot to the end of the sequence.

18 Add a one-second fade-in to the opening shot and a one-second fade-out to the final shot.

TIP Special effects are fun when you're playing around or when you want to impress friends with the power of your software, but in real videos they are not only unnecessary in most cases, but actually distracting. Skip special effects in your videos and use transition effects sparingly.

19 The sequence is done, unless after you watch it a few times you see places you could trim in or out by a few frames. Use the Trim tool at the transition points to tweak edits. In particular, watch out for blips in sound where you may have cut right in the middle of a word or sound. Add (or delete) frames to soften any jarring edges.

Add Background Music

While this kind of video works pretty well with the simple ambient sound that goes with the images, sometimes it's better to drop in a more professional soundtrack.

1   Click the Audio button and access your iTunes playlists.

2   Position the playhead in your timeline at a point where you want the music to start. In this case, starting at the beginning is logical, but on some videos—those with titles, for instance—you might want to start the music midway into the title display, or after the title appears but before the video images start. Regardless of where you drop the music, you can easily slide it around afterward if you don't like the location.

3   Select a track to add to the video.

4   Click Place at Playhead. Alternately, you can just drag the name of your song to your timeline.

iMovie will import the clip, and a purple bar will appear on one of your audio tracks.

5   If the song is longer than the video track, cut it off after about one second following the end of the picture, using Command-T, and delete the tail.

> **NOTE ►** If you're using GarageBand to generate a background track (Lesson 12), use the duration of the project in iMovie to guide your music creation. In this case, the video project is 1 minute, 15 seconds, 24 frames long. Round it to 1 minute, 16 seconds, and use that as your guide in GarageBand.

The most important aspect of background music is the *mix*—that is, the balance between the loudness of the music and the loudness of the audio track of the video.

6   Click the "Edit volume" check box at the bottom of the iMovie window.

This lets you change the volume of the entire track by using the slider (or typing in a percentage) or change the volume at precise locations in the song by manipulating points on a line. For now, just change the volume of the entire track to 30 percent, which is appropriate for a background track.

> **TIP ►** To change the volume at specific points within the track, click the line superimposed over the audio track. Big yellow dots will appear on the line. You can then raise or lower the volume at one of these dots without changing the entire track's volume. By choosing these dot locations carefully, you can achieve an impressive sound mix. More on your sound mix in Lesson 12.

Saving Your Video

Once a video is finished, it can be distributed for the enjoyment of others and the deep satisfaction of the creator. iMovie provides a number of avenues of distribution, but before turning your attention to sharing, you should explore the most important output option available—creating an archive.

Unlike music, video is remarkably large relative to typical hard disk storage capacity. At five minutes of video per gigabyte, finished video in even a small collection can overwhelm a typical Mac. Consequently, archiving video is imperative. While it's great to be able to burn DVDs and CD-ROMs, put videos on the Internet, and even email them, all of these methods are for distribution—they take the high quality of your digital video and squeeze it down to fit into a given format. The quality of a true archive needs to be as high as you can manage; the perfect archive for your videos is back in the digital videotape format from which they came.

Ideally you'll have a special videocassette allocated for only finished videos, so they don't get taped over or lost among the hours of video you shoot. Lesson 8 mentions some specifics for organizing and labeling tapes, but for now let's just say you have a master cassette onto which you plan to record your video before you remove it from your Mac.

The process of getting video from iMovie to your camcorder is straightforward.

1   Connect your camcorder to your Mac using your FireWire cable.

2   Make sure your tape is in your camera and is cued up to the spot where you want to add video. Of course, your camcorder must be turned on and set to playback (VCR) mode.

3   From within iMovie, go to File > Share. This will open the Sharing window, which displays a number of options.

4   Click the Videocamera button.

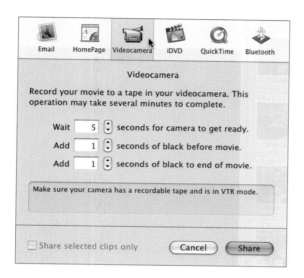

5   Click Share, as the default settings are appropriate for most situations.

iMovie takes control of your camera from this point. As long as you are cued up to the right spot on the tape, iMovie will put your camera into Record mode and then start playing the video. You may want to have your LCD swiveled out so you can see the video while it's being recorded. When iMovie is done, it stops the recording process.

6   Check the videotape. Rewind it and watch the video to make sure the recording was successful and that there were no technical snafus along the way.

7   When you're done checking the tape, re-cue it to a spot in the black material that follows the recording. By always starting to record over these black pieces of "leader," you guarantee that timecode will count continuously. This also gives you a moment to make sure you're not going to record over something you didn't mean to.

TIP ▶ The one second of black and the beginning and end of the movie are sometimes more functional for spacing out videos if you change them to five seconds. It gives you some room to breathe.

Now that a copy of your video is in DV format and is safely back on tape, you can output other formats of your video for distribution. Eventually you can delete the project and media from your computer, knowing that if you need to you can bring the project back into your Mac for new output options or a little re-editing.

Uploading Your Video to the Web

Once you're done archiving, it's a fine moment to share your video with the world (or, maybe just your friends). In the same way you created the archive, you can place the movie on your .Mac account.

1   Choose File > Share. Select HomePage. You can rename the movie or leave it as is.

2   Click Share and the movie is compressed and copied to your iDisk. It takes a few moments to perform these functions.

3   Once the file is uploaded, you're coached through the process of selecting a theme for the Web page and then publishing the movie.

4   Choose a theme. Christopher picked a movie projector theme and then went on to customize the page.

5   Finally, after you select Publish, the page is loaded into the .Mac Web site, and you are given the Web address for viewing the movie.

What You've Learned

- Roll through your material in the order you shot it, in search of bits to use.

- Use Command-T to chop up your raw material into usable bits.

- Click shots in the Clip pane or the timeline to change labels to readily identifiable names.

- Alternate views of your workspace from Clip view to Timeline view while working: moving shots around, dragging shots out, playing, and trimming.

- Build structure first. Use cutaways after you've set up the structure.

- Don't use every shot. In a first pass through your material, it might be OK to start by including everything you shot in your sequence, but you'll want to quickly become discerning and remove unnecessary angles as well as material that runs long.

- In general, the sound recorded with the video is difficult to hear. Don't try to use it or follow the conversations too closely. It's good ambient sound, but it's less useful as the driving force of the video.

- There's no need for special effects. The strength of the video is in the action and dynamics onscreen. There's no need for transition effects either, except in the opening and closing moments.

- Add background music from iTunes to match the duration of the video.

- Use "Edit volume" to adjust the mix of the music track to the sound recorded with the pictures.

- Use Share to create a high-quality digital archive of your video back to your camcorder. If you have a .Mac account, you can also quickly share your video to the Web.

12

Lesson Files

Lessons > Lesson12 > Finished_Timelapse_Project7 alias

Lessons > Lesson12 > Finished_Timelapse.music.mov

Tools

GarageBand

Time

Approximately 90 minutes

Goals

Learn how to build an original music track from prebuilt instrument loops

Adjust the length of loops

Adjust the relative volume of tracks for a balanced mix

Export custom music to iTunes and place it in your videos

Lesson 12

Creating Unique Music for Your Projects

Creating new music is a great deal more challenging (and can be more rewarding) than loading your CDs into iTunes and listening to them on your iPod. The release of iLife '04 includes a new application that addresses the fun and complexities of music creation—GarageBand. GarageBand is an obvious coup for musicians, wannabe musicians, and those with hidden musical talents and dormant dreams. The world of copyrights and permissions may lead even less-musical types to explore creating their own acoustic content rather than ripping other people's tunes. In the case of, say, music that's played with movies and slide shows in the public arena, even a musically challenged business owner can quickly make some original music with no fear of recrimination.

Some people may need to avoid GarageBand for a while. It isn't as simple or intuitive as the other iLife products. Whereas all the rest (iTunes, iPhoto, iMovie, iDVD) take in existing digital content, manage it, organize it, and prepare it for output, GarageBand synthesizes content from a virtually blank slate. If you don't have the time or inclination to make your own music, there's nothing wrong with settling into your great CD collection with iTunes and skipping the rock star bit altogether.

But you should at least try it. This lesson is designed to provide a short and safe look around. Who knows—you may even discover a deep, lurking talent for making your own music. It's powerful, exciting, and (dare I say it?) narcotic. You may not be able to stop once you lay down your first tracks. Even without a guitar or keyboard, you will be on your way to making original music with GarageBand after this lesson.

Creating New Music

Jennifer likes taking pictures and enjoys the process of making videos (as long as it's quick). But she really doesn't have any musical aspirations or, frankly, skills. Still, as a business owner she has an obligation not to accompany videos and slide shows in her retail studio with the copyrighted music she listens to on her iPod. Charlie shouldn't either—playing his music in presentations he makes at school is technically improper, but since he's a kid and the use is non-commercial (and probably one-time), he can get away with it. Charlie's interest in GarageBand is far more extensive than making background music—he's a great guitar player, and uses GarageBand to help him practice and record his professional-sounding tracks without needing to coordinate with a group when he feels like jamming. Christopher is allowed to use copyrighted music from CDs in his personal home projects, but he's attracted to GarageBand because he wants music in his videos that sounds hip but without lyrics—since they might compete for the attention of the audience. Jennifer *needs* music, however, and she has a limited budget.

It's always an option to buy the rights to some music, or find some royalty-free tunes. (There are many sources online.) Apple provides a large online assortment of short musical riffs if you have a .Mac account. Called Freeplay music, it's on your iDisk in the software folder for .Mac members.

But even with that viable option, the Freeplay songs—like virtually all prepared music—have preset lengths (10 seconds, 30 seconds, 1 minute) that may not meet your project's specific needs. And ultimately, they are publicly available tunes (although you cannot use them commercially), and you may want something a little more customized. For a small business, the cornerstone of a successful operation is often being unique. For Jennifer, her brand and business is all about creativity. Confronting her fears, Jennifer launches into GarageBand to make some very simple, quick background music for her in-studio presentations.

1   Open GarageBand.

The project begins by establishing some basic parameters for the song you'll create. The New Project window opens.

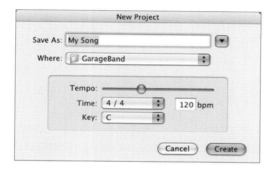

2   Give your song a name, but leave the rest of the defaults set as they are and click Create. This will open the main window for music creation. The project is saved in the GarageBand folder, which resides in the Music folder in your Home.

3   Move your pointer to the Grand Piano keyboard and click some ivories on the instrument sitting in the middle of your window. You should hear the pinging of a grand piano. (You're making music!)

If you had an electronic keyboard with the appropriate USB connector, you could connect it and play that Grand Piano interface using your full-size keyboard. But Jennifer doesn't have a keyboard sitting around, so she's going to get rid of this onscreen diversion altogether.

NOTE ▸ If you *did* plug in a USB keyboard, you'd need to connect it to your Mac prior to launching GarageBand in order for it to be enabled.

4   Click the red button in the top-left corner of the floating onscreen Grand Piano interface. The keyboard will disappear, although the green Grand Piano track it was related to remains onscreen. It is okay to leave this track here, but you won't be using it. (More about "tracks" in a moment.)

Now that the window for music creation is mostly empty and ready to go, how to start? Since Jennifer has no intention of playing any instrument or singing into a microphone, she needs to find some music.

5   Click the Browse button (with the eye icon) on the bottom left of the window.

This opens the Loop Browser: the place where you'll search for, listen to, and ultimately select the appropriate instrumental loop to add to your song.

A *loop* is a small segment of music that can be played over and over, popping from the end back to the beginning to sound like a smooth, continuous musical track. A loop is short, lasting perhaps only one to four seconds, and can repeat indefinitely. A typical real-world loop might be the drumbeat in a rock song—it may be basically the same rhythm, keeping time for the length of the song. One-person bands often use machines to generate repeating loops of sound to play along with. The Loop Browser provides access to hundreds of loops that come built into GarageBand.

The menu side of the Loop Browser

Although there is certainly no single way to build a musical track for your videos and slide shows, and no wrong way, Jennifer is going to follow an easy way.

6   Select Drums from the Loop Browser. This will reduce the number of options to only the drum loops. The remaining categories are grayed out.

Just to the left of the Volume slider, you can see that there are 280 loops that can be classified as drums. Jennifer needs one. On the far right side of the Loop Browser are all 280 search results that meet the conditions specified on the left.

	Name		Tempo	Key	Beats	Fav
🎵	80s Pop Beat 08		110	–	16	☐
🎵	80s Pop Beat 09		110	–	16	☐
🔊	80s Pop Beat 10		110	–	16	■
🎵	Ambient Beat 01		100	–	16	☐
〰	Blip Synth 01		90	–	2	☐
🎵	Classic Rock Beat 01		140	–	16	☐
🎵	Classic Rock Beat 02		140	–	16	☐
🎵	Classic Rock Beat 03		140	–	8	☐

The six columns have some interesting information. The leftmost column shows an icon, either a green music note or a blue waveform. The green note indicates the loop is MIDI—that is, a computer-generated sound. A MIDI loop is not a recording so much as a mathematical instruction for playing music. It has properties that make it attractive to the beginner. Most important to know is that when you merge MIDI loops, the computer can work for you to make them sound good together.

The blue waveform represents an audio file, not unlike the files in iTunes. This is an actual recording of sound. The Mac cannot augment this sound to make it fit with other sounds the way it can with the MIDI loops. Audio files are less malleable as raw material for beginners and are a little harder to make sound good. For that reason, don't use them for this lesson. Focus on the items with green notes, the MIDI loops.

Besides the name of the loop and the icon, you can ignore the rest of the columns. But if you're curious, what you've got is the loop's *tempo* (a measurement of how fast a song will be played), its *key* (not relevant to drums, but a reference to a song's position on the musical scale), and its *beats* (the number of beats per measure, the unit of a song). Favs (favorites) is a convenience for you to mark loops you like so you can find them quickly later on.

When you use loops in GarageBand, the software automatically adjusts their listed values to fit together. So you don't need to limit yourself to selecting loops that have matching tempo, key, or beats.

7   Single-click an item and it will start to play. Explore different loops in this way. Feel free to make notes about the ones you like, or click the Fav check box to easily search for the loop later. Click a playing loop and it stops.

8   Scroll down through the list of drum loops to Straight Up Beat 02.

9   Click and drag Straight Up Beat 02 to the space under the Grand Piano track. If you drop it in the Tracks column, GarageBand creates a new track for the loop and places the music at the beginning of the timeline area to the right of the Tracks and Mixer columns. This region is the musical workspace.

You have now created a new track for the drum loop and added the loop to the numbered timeline on the right, starting at the 1.

The little dark bars and dots in the green loop represent the notes. The vertical red line at the head of this loop is GarageBand's playhead. From the numbers in the timeline ruler, you can see that this loop is two measures long.

NOTE ▶ Unlike movies and the timeline in iMovie, music is built in measures, which are counted along the ruler. A measure is a musical unit but not a fixed span of time, so it varies depending on the song. Notice the number 1 at the beginning of the timeline, rather than a 0 as you'd find if this were a time scale. The 1 denotes the beginning of the first measure. A loop that extends from the 1 to the 2 is one measure long. Similarly, a loop that extends to the 7 results in a piece of music six measures long.

10 Click the Play button in the shuttle controls at the bottom of the window, and the music will play, continuing forward right past the end of the loop and into silence.

Did you hear it? It was short.

11 Move the pointer to the edge of the green loop in the timeline. The great thing about loops is that you can repeat (or loop) them.

When the pointer approaches the edge of the loop, it changes into one of two tools. If you point at the middle-to-lower edge of the loop, you'll see a Trim tool, which extends or shortens the loop segment itself. When the pointer moves up to the top edge of the loop, it turns into the Loop tool, which lets you grab and drag the loop forward in time, rolling out more and more loops (or parts of loops) as you go.

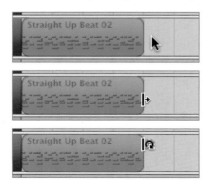

12 Use the Loop tool to click and drag the loop to extend to the end of the sixth measure (and thus to the 7 on the scale).

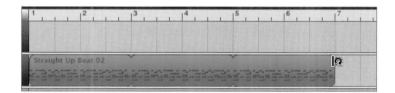

13 Now go back to the Loop Browser and click Reset (in the top-left corner of the browser). This brings you back to the top level of the Browser so you can dig in and find your next piece of music.

14 Click Bass. A reliable method of building a bit of music is to start with the drums, add bass, and then end with something more melodic like a guitar or piano.

Instead of scrolling down the column of the 166 bass loops that were found, you can further refine your options by selecting one of the attributes on the right side of the Loop Browser.

15 Click Cheerful; the number of options is reduced to 52.

16 From the resulting bass selections, look around until you find Funky Pop Bass 01. (It should be on top.) Click and drag it up to the empty track region beneath the Drum Kit track.

	Name	Tempo	Key	Beats
♪	Funky Muted Bass 01	100	C	8
♪	Funky Muted Bass 02	100	C	8
♪	Funky P♪ Funky Pop Bass 01	96	C	16
♪	Funky Pop Bass 02	96	C	16
♪	Funky Pop Bass 03	96	C	8
♪	Funky Pop Bass 04	96	C	8
♪	Funky Pop Bass 05	96	C	8
♪	Funky Pop Bass 06	96	C	16

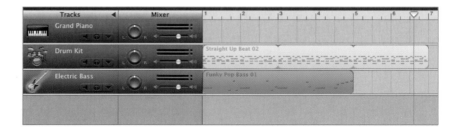

17 Drag the playhead back to the beginning of the timeline (the left side of the tracks) by clicking in the ruler portion of the timeline and then dragging left. (Alternately, you can click the Cue to Start button in the shuttle controls—the backwards arrow against a vertical line—to pop to the beginning of your song.)

18 When the timeline is positioned at the start of the tracks, click the Play button (or press the spacebar on your keyboard).

NOTE ▶ The entire loop in the Electric Bass track is four measures long—meaning it repeats itself half as much as Straight Up Beat 02. This tends to make it less repetitive sounding. You can see how long the original loops are by the small indentations in the edge of the loop as it repeats in a track. In general (but certainly not always), it sounds better when you add loops in these full units—notch to notch.

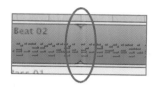

Sounds good—pretty cool, pretty easy. Let's get one more track, one more instrument.

19 Go back to the Loop Browser, reset the options, and then find Piano > Classic Rock Piano 02. Drag it to the track space under the Electric Bass track.

GarageBand does its best to make these disparate instruments sound good together. If the tracks are in different keys (Classic Rock Piano 02 is in the key of D; Bass is in C), GarageBand transposes one to match. If the tempos are different, GarageBand slows them down (or speeds them up) to synchronize them with the tempo you chose when you opened the project. (The default is 120 beats per minute.) But even after this clever work, many tracks will sound really lousy together. If you're not really musical, your best option is to experiment a lot and work hard to keep it simple.

TIP ▶ In the world of background music, very simple arrangements work well. It's not a cop-out. One or two tracks—sometimes just a drum, other times just a clean piano with a shaker—often are all you need to enrich your videos, particularly those with dialogue. You don't want the music to compete. You only want it to enhance the texture and mood.

The three tracks in your workspace may be all you need for the background of a video. If you dragged the loops so that they all extend to the same length, you might consider yourself done. But Jennifer is not satisfied with the Classic Rock Piano 02 loop. The piano is nice, but it's too busy for her taste.

20   Select the Classic Rock Piano 02 loop and press Delete on your keyboard. The piano track remains, but the loop of music is gone.

21   Grab the Funky Pop Bass 01 loop from its position in the Electric Bass track and drag it down to the Piano track. Now play it.

Notice that? The notes that the bass was playing are now being played by a piano. This is because the loop is a MIDI loop. It means that you can instruct the Mac to play it as if it were any instrument, depending on the track you place it in.

NOTE ▶ If you want to hear something truly odd, drag the drum loop down into the bass track. That percussive music is quite unusual when "played" by an electric bass. Drag it back to its starting point when you're done—too avant-garde for the ceramic studio.

22 Instead of dragging the Funky Pop Bass 01 loop back to its rightful spot, Option-click and drag it back. This will copy the loop, leaving one in the Piano track and placing a duplicate in the Electric Bass track. Now you have the same music, the same notes being played simultaneously by different instruments.

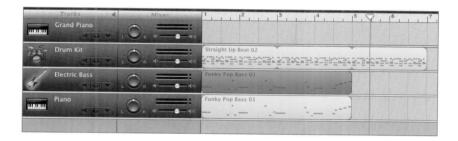

Doubling up makes the notes a little richer and is a great effect to apply when you're looking to add some musical sophistication with little risk of it sounding bad.

23 Drag the loop in the piano track to delay it by two beats (in this case, half a measure). This offsets it from the Bass track playing the same tune—another interesting musical touch that works for short periods without becoming grating.

24 Use the Trim tool at the tail of the piano loop to shorten the music to end when the bass ends.

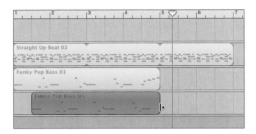

TIP A razor blade is really the only tool you need to edit—whether it's video or audio or music. GarageBand provides a chopping tool identical to the one in iMovie. Command-T breaks a selected track at the playhead (called *Split* in the GarageBand Edit menu). Using Command-T with the Move and Copy functions you've already used will let you build far more interesting combinations of loops (or parts of loops).

GarageBand is all about loops, and you've been working with a series of musical loops. Now it's time to loop your tracks.

25 Down in the shuttle controls is a button that repeats your music over and over—the Loop button. It's a pair of curved arrows. Click it.

When Loop is selected, a yellow bar pops into the ruler area of the timeline. This yellow region determines what section of your creation will be looped.

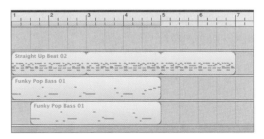

By clicking the end of the yellow bar, you can drag the loop duration in or out to be shorter or longer, whatever you prefer for evaluating the music you've created.

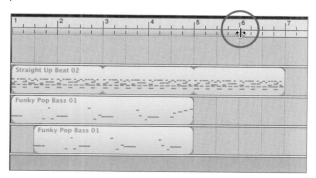

26 If your loop region is not aligned with the 5 in the ruler, drag the end of the yellow bar so that it is.

27 Click the Play button. No matter where your playhead is parked, it will always pop to the beginning of the yellow bar to start playing. When it reaches the end of the bar, it will pop back to the beginning and continue, no matter how far your music extends. Now you're looping.

Mixing Your Music

You put three tracks together in GarageBand, and it placed them where you wanted with the instruments you selected. But you may want to make more fundamental adjustments to the music before you decide you're done. The art of determining the relative volume of each track, as well as whether you hear music from the left speaker or the right, is critical to the musical experience. Setting up these parameters is called *mixing*.

Between the Tracks column and the workspace you've been using is the Mixer.

The Mixer provides some volume and pan controls for each track (known as a "slice") of your creation. These settings are not variable within the track but remain fixed for the entire track. The pair of bars above the volume control are *peak meters,* which alert you to sound that is loud enough to result in distortion when played in most audio equipment. It's OK if the red lights on the right edge flash a little during a loud piece of music, but for the most part the lines need to be in the middle of the bar and mostly in the green. A small vertical bar appears in each meter to indicate the peak level reached as the music volume pulses.

Move the Volume slider around to get the sound volume of one track to balance with the others. Use the Pan knob to move the sound from one speaker to the other—or balance it between the two. Sometimes when you have lots of instruments, you want them to appear to occupy different locations in space, and you can do this by selecting how much you hear with each ear. For the music we're working with, there is little need to mess with the balance.

If you want the volume of a track to vary during the playing of the track itself—known in the business as using a *dynamic fader*—you must leave the Mixer and look in the Tracks column. You'll see three buttons there; the one on the right is a small triangle, which reveals your work for adjusting volume variably.

Clicking the triangle will reveal a new track below the one you're working on.

By checking the Track Volume check box, you will have the ability to move a line to increase or decrease the volume. You'll also be able to click the line to add points at which you can change the volume—very much in the way you can dynamically adjust the volume in iMovie.

This process is a little more complicated than what, say, Jennifer is interested in pursuing. Uncheck the Track Volume box and close this dynamic volume control. Far more useful at this point are the other two buttons in the Tracks column.

Listening Only to the Tracks You Want

Two buttons give you two great track-auditioning capabilities in GarageBand. The first, the Mute button, is represented by a little speaker. Click it and it turns blue, indicating the track is silent.

Muting a given track lets you get rid of it (temporarily) as you develop the mix of your song.

The opposite of muting a track is soloing it. The Solo button is indicated by a headphones icon. Clicking it lets you hear *only* the track selected.

The Mute and Solo buttons can be used at any time during the editing and mixing of your music.

Adjusting Your Time Scale and Working with Real Time

All of this musical notation—keys and measures and tempos—are great for the musically inclined, but Jennifer has had no musical training. All she wants is a loop that will run as long as her video. She knows her time-lapse video (from Lesson 7) is one minute long. How does that translate into measures?

Luckily, no math is required. At the bottom of the workspace is a digital counter.

The music note to the left of the numbers indicates that the counter is displaying musical measurement. For more practical applications of your music, change the counter to display time measurement by clicking the note.

The note becomes a clock, and the display changes to show hours, minutes, seconds, and thousandths of a second—perhaps more accuracy than you need. Now, by positioning the playhead in your music, you can see how long your music is running—or where you are within a piece of music.

> **NOTE** ▶ When you loop a bit of your music, the counter restarts at zero, the beginning of the loop, no matter how many times the loop repeats.

The ruler across the top of the workspace is always expressed in measures. And measures do not consistently relate to elapsed time in different pieces of music. But as you build your music, and the length of your song increases, you may need to see more duration of your tracks at a glance.

The Zoom control for the workspace is (somewhat cryptically) nestled at the bottom of the Tracks column.

Click and drag the knob to increase (or decrease) the time span represented on the right side of the workspace. Whenever there is more to see than what is shown in the window, the familiar Mac scroll bar is available along the bottom of the workspace.

The measurement of time is the ideal way to find events in your video and make them correspond to moments in your music.

1   Open Lesson12 > Finished_Timelapse_Project07 alias > **Timelapse Video**.

This is the finished version of Jennifer's illustration of the Italian brush-stroke technique. With the titles and fade-out, the video is precisely 1 minute, (0 seconds) and 7 frames long. The music for this should probably be relatively subdued. The only musical cue—that is, the only instance in the picture where she might want to have a corresponding change in the music—is when the video goes from the medium shot to the closer shot.

2   Move the timeline to the point where the video cuts close.

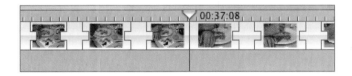

The counter at the playhead indicates this is 37 seconds, 8 frames from the start. This will be our cue point.

3   Go back to GarageBand. With the counter set to display time measurement, you now have three factors to keep in mind as you develop your music: The song starts at 0; something happens at 37:08; and the song ends by 1:00:07.

As you continue to work on your tracks, these cue points will be central to the creation of the structure you build in your song.

Combining Loops from One Family to Add Variation to Your Songs

Keeping the music simple is often the key to building a successful track of background music. But you can use a number of simple strategies to make your music slightly less repetitive.

1   Start from the song we've been building. Click the Loop button in the shuttle controls to turn off that feature, as it won't be necessary for the time being.

2   Delete the Drum Kit track—the whole track, not just the loop of music placed there. With the track selected, choose Track > Delete Track. You're going to continue reshaping your song until it feels appropriate for the time-lapse video.

It's also good to know that in the process of sculpting a song, you may create many tracks, add more to them, and either mute or totally delete parts as you go. In this case, ignore the Bass and Piano tracks and explore some different sounds.

3   Mute the Electric Bass and Piano tracks.

4   Click Reset in the Loop Browser. Find the guitar loop called Southern Rock Guitar 01.

5   Listen to all the tracks in the Southern Rock Guitar family (01 through 05). Notice the similarities and differences. Some of the loops lend themselves to long stretches of video, and some sound more like emotional transitions.

6   Click and drag Southern Rock Guitar 02 to the track under the Piano track.

This has a nice sound to it. The loop comprises four measures, which—according to the counter—is eight seconds long. This is pretty long by loop standards. It means the sounds in it repeat only every eight seconds, which is good for a loop that will play over and over a few times without getting too repetitive.

7   Drag the guitar loop out for 12 measures (to the number 13). After listening to it, that's about as much as Jennifer can take before she wants to hear something else. Change your scale using the Zoom slider on the left to see more of the ruler. (Thirty measures is about one minute—the length of the time-lapse video this song will be for, so make sure you can see at least that far.)

8   Click and drag Southern Rock Guitar 01 to the same Acoustic Guitar track, following the first loop. It is also a pretty long loop, and it sounds similar enough to Southern Rock Guitar 02 that they form a nice duo—an almost imperceptible variation, but enough difference to eliminate some of that repetitive feeling.

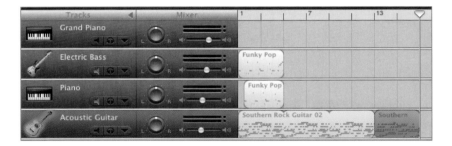

9   Drag the Southern Rock Guitar 02 loop out by one more full loop— another four measures—and play some (or all) of the resulting music.

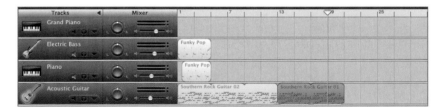

As you're playing, watch the time counter. Somewhere in the middle of the added area, the counter says you're at 37 seconds. According to your notes, that's where the video cuts from the wider shot to the closer shot, and you want a transition in the music here. The transition could be a different instrument, maybe a new track, or just a musical interlude of some kind.

10   Park the playhead on the measure closest to 37 seconds. GarageBand snaps the playhead to the measure boundaries; the closest is at 36 seconds.

There is a nice musical transition in the Southern Rock Guitar family, loop 05.

11 Click and drag Southern Rock Guitar 05 to the Acoustic Guitar track, and drop it over the end of loop 01, aligned with the playhead.

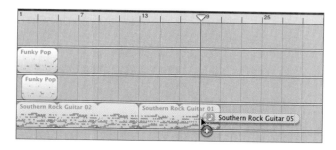

Play the track. The transition works, but loop 05 is short; it feels like you need more of it to be satisfying.

12 Drag loop 05 out by another full repetition, to the measure 23 line.

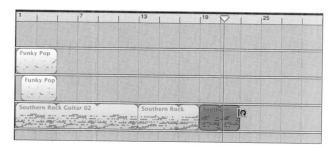

13 Click and drag loop 01 onto the track to follow loop 05. This should bring the sound back to a familiar verse. After playing one loop, the song's overall duration is only 52 seconds; the song needs to be longer to fit with the video.

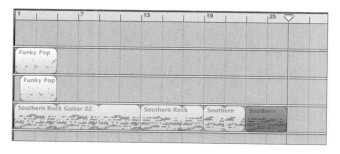

14 Drag loop 01 out until the song is 1 minute long—30 measures. You could end it here, but it would sound better to make it slightly longer and fade the music out after the video ends. Editing the song is best done here, from within GarageBand. The actual musical fade-out could be done (earlier in this lesson, you learned about the Track Volume check box), but it is sometimes better to do that fine-tuning with the video while in iMovie after the song is imported. Either way, drag loop 01 out a couple of beats further, a couple of seconds more than one minute.

This is a nice, simple track of acoustic guitar that even without drums and bass seems to feel light and dynamic enough for the video. To give the guitar just a touch of texture, a small amount of percussion would probably help. A drum is too much, but let's try a shaker.

15 Reset the Loop Browser. Select Shaker and find Shaker 16. Nothing fancy, just a little salt for the stew.

16 Click and drag the Shaker loop to the track underneath the Acoustic Guitar track.

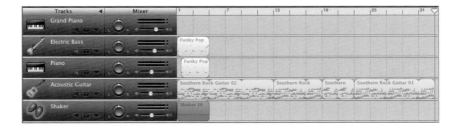

This starts the shaker immediately at the beginning of the song. Sometimes it helps to break up the repetition of a long track by staggering the introduction of other instruments.

17 Slide the Shaker loop to begin after the Guitar loop completes its first cycle. Look for the notch in the Guitar loop if you want to see the unit of the actual music loop before repeating.

18 Drag out the Shaker 16 loop all the way to the end of the Guitar loops.

Play the tracks. The shaker is a little loud; it needs to fall into the background more.

19 Reduce the volume of the Shaker track using the slider in the Mixer until the sound is audible but not noisy.

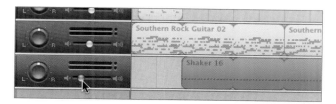

TIP ► Songs tend to have familiar structures—sometimes as simple as verses and chorus. Verses have one kind of sound, and the chorus has a different but compatible sound. If you call the verses *A* and the chorus *B*, a song's structure is often something like A-B-A-B or A-A-B-A.

Getting Your Music into iTunes

Getting music from GarageBand into iTunes is a necessary first step to being able to use the music in your other iLife applications (iPhoto, iMovie, iDVD), and it's incredibly easy.

When you're done making a piece of music (or even before then—you can make interim versions to your heart's content), you can export the music directly into iTunes.

Before exporting for the first time, you may want to verify the settings for precisely where GarageBand will place this music in iTunes and how it will label it. (Remember, you can change the labels in iTunes if you're so inclined, but it might be better to make sure it's set up properly here first.)

1 Choose GarageBand > Preferences.

2 Click the Export tab. Here you can confirm (or set up) how the music will go into iTunes.

If these settings are good, close the window (with the red button). Now you are ready to export, and you know where the music will end up when you do.

3   Choose File > Export to iTunes.

This will mix your entire sequence of music (not just the part indicated by the yellow loop bar) down to a single track. This is referred to as a *mixdown*.

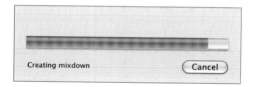

NOTE ▸ A mixdown is the musical equivalent of the rendering of special effects that's done in iMovie. The program takes a bunch of discrete elements and—through some computer processing—combines them into a single element. If you make a change to some part of the original parts, the computer has to do it again to keep the combination current. Faster computers—with more MHz in the CPU—do these kinds of tasks fast.

The process takes a few moments, but when it's done, the song is placed in a special playlist in iTunes.

After exporting, your Mac will automatically open iTunes (presumably so you can play it there). If you want to see the song you've created, browse in iTunes and go to the designated playlist. Your music is waiting for you there. And of course, it is now also accessible from the other iLife applications for use in your slideshows, DVDs, or movies.

NOTE ▶ You can export to iTunes at any time while you are working, to create interim versions of tracks. But remember that if you change the music in GarageBand, it's not automatically reflected in the song in iTunes. You need to export again to get the current version.

Finally, reopen iMovie if it's not still open.

4   Open Lesson12 > Finished_Timelapse_Project07 alias > **Timelapse Video**. Park the playhead at the beginning, for good measure. This is where you want the song to begin, during the opening titles.

5   Click the Audio button to access the iTunes playlists.

6   Open the playlist to which you exported your music. For Jennifer, it was the Petro Playlist.

7   Select the song.

8   Click the Place at Playhead button. The song is immediately imported and dropped into an empty audio track aligned with the playhead (which should be at the start of the video).

Play it and see how the song syncs with the picture. The only thing left to do is fade out the music after the video ends.

9   Check the Edit Volume check box. This adds a volume control line to the audio tracks.

NOTE ▶ This method is comparable to performing the same kind of work in GarageBand using the Track Volume check box.

10   Click the line in the music track at a place where you want the song to fade out. A yellow dot will appear here, and a smaller, purple dot will also appear to its left. These two points control the beginning and end of the fade-out, with a curve of steadily decreasing volume spanning between them.

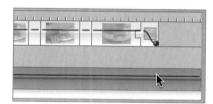

11   Drag the yellow dot to the position at which the fade-out should be completed, and pull it down to a volume of zero—the lowest you can drag it.

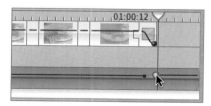

12 Drag the purple dot back to the position you want the fade-out to begin—probably in the middle of the video fade-out, but the precise location is pretty subjective.

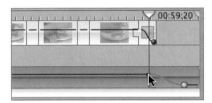

When you like the relationship of the video fade-out and the music fade-out, you're done.

13 Click the Edit Volume check box again, which preserves your settings and keeps you from changing them accidentally.

Play the entire video now, with the song mixed in. The two should fit together pretty well, and the fade-out at the end should get softer as the picture disappears, but should end a moment after the video is gone. That's a nice conclusion and typical in professional videos. Good job.

What You've Learned

- Click the Browse button with the eye icon to use the Loop Browser.

- To find the instrument you want using the Loop Browser, select instruments on the left, add more criteria on the right, and view the results in the scroll window on the far right.

- Drag a loop to the Tracks column to add the music in its instrument track.

- Click the trailing edge of a loop to edit it or repeatedly loop it out; click the trailing lower edge for the Edit tool and the trailing upper edge for the Loop tool.

- Use the Volume slider in the Mixer to adjust the relative volumes of tracks for a balanced mix.

- Solo or mute tracks using the buttons in the Tracks column.

- Toggle the counter from musical notation to elapsed time by clicking the note icon in the counter window.

- Use Preferences > Export to set up the location in iTunes where exported music is placed.

13

Lesson Files	Lessons > Lesson13 > Start_BizOwnerVideo13
Tools	iMovie, iPhoto, .Mac account
Time	Approximately 40 minutes
Goals	Grab still images from videotape
	Move folders of images into iPhoto
	Show off your iPhoto slide shows on the Internet with Apple's .Mac service

Putting Your Slide Show on the Internet

DVDs are great for small distribution, and digital video cassettes make good archives and are often fine for watching videos at home. But sometimes it's important to get your material out to a wider audience— on the Internet. At the end of Lesson 11, you saw how quickly you can upload a finished movie directly from iMovie to a Web page at Apple's .Mac Internet service. Now you're going to see the corresponding simplicity of uploading a slide show to the Web.

Throughout the lessons in this book, you've been learning to improvise. Not everyone has a digital camera and a camcorder, and even if you did, you don't always use them both in every situation. In Lesson 6, you learned to make a movie with photographs from a camera. Now you're going to learn to make a slide show with video from a camcorder.

The studio owner, Jennifer, doesn't use her still camera very often; she is more comfortable with her video camcorder. She sees iMovie as a tool that helps her find just the right frames of video, grab them, and turn them into photographs that she can then manage easily in iPhoto.

iPhoto makes it easy to organize the stills into albums and upload them to the Web for presentation. While the image quality of video frames is far inferior to that of dedicated still cameras, the Web demands that images be compressed, and therefore degraded from the high resolution you get in prints. The lower resolution of a camcorder makes it a perfectly suitable *camera* for shooting photographs for the Web. Jennifer keeps a gallery of shots from around her studio online and updates it often. It's easy because she pulls the still shots from the videotapes she shoots and uploads them to her company Web site with iPhoto.

All of this is contingent, of course, upon having an account with .Mac, Apple's suite of Internet services, including Web hosting. As a sophisticated Macintosh user for many years, Jennifer initially imagined a user-friendly Internet account like .Mac to be unnecessary. Her company maintains a Web site on a local hosting service, and she has been very happy with it. Still, the .Mac account is more than an ordinary Web host; it's one that's highly tuned to work with the iLife applications. In the same way that music effortlessly moves from iTunes to iMovie and iPhoto, .Mac interacts with iLife to make Web pages, slide shows, and movies easy to build, update, and share. After years of conspicuous avoidance, Jennifer got a .Mac account to streamline all her iLife work—and she even found a way to integrate it with her existing Web site for maximum effect. (For more information on .Mac accounts, see the Getting Started chapter.)

This lesson has two distinct parts, both of them simple and both important. The first happens in iMovie—the process of grabbing a bunch of still images. The second happens in iPhoto—building a slide show and putting it on the Internet through a .Mac account.

Getting Still Photos from Your Video

At some point, you'll face the choice of grabbing either your still camera or your video camcorder. You can't always shoot with both. You saw in Lesson 6 how to turn still photos into a dynamic slide show. Now you will see how to turn video into acceptable-quality still photos. It begins in iMovie.

1   Create a new folder on your Desktop called Petroglyph Stills, where you will store all the photos you'll get from your video. This isn't required, of course, but it streamlines the process of moving the images into iPhoto. (If you can't remember how to do this, choose File > New Folder.)

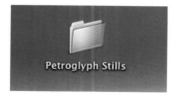

2   Open Lesson13 > Start_BizOwnerVideo13 > **BizOwnerVideo**.

Only one clip is here; the truth is you don't need to do any editing. Right now you're using iMovie for its capability to grab still images from video.

3   Click on the single clip and shuttle through it in the Viewer until you find a frame to grab. Pick any shot that appeals to you. Since a camcorder records 30 frames every second, there are many to choose from.

4   When you find a good shot, use the arrow keys on the keyboard to move forward and backward a little until you identify just the right frame.

5   Choose File > Save Frame As.

6 Name the image and select a location on your Mac for storing it. In this case, select the folder you created on the Desktop to keep your frame grabs from this (de facto) roll.

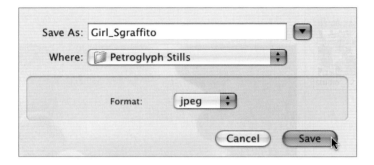

The default format for the image is JPEG. This is a good fit with iPhoto, so don't change it.

TIP ▶ If it's a challenge to navigate your computer by way of the Where pull-down menu, you can always deposit images on your Desktop and organize them in a folder later.

And that's it; the still is created and placed in the folder you selected.

7 Continue through this process until you have made a still from each unique shot on the videotape—around 19 of them—and placed them in the Petroglyph Stills folder.

That's all you need from iMovie. Close the project (no need to save anything; you didn't do any editing). Now you're going to move back to iPhoto.

Putting Digital Files into iPhoto

Just as you did in Lesson 3, you're going to bring photos into iPhoto. And as you did there, you'll add folders of photos as if they were rolls. (Before, however, you were simulating importing rolls from a digital camera.)

1 Open iPhoto.

2 Drag and drop the Petroglyph Stills folder of photos from the Desktop onto iPhoto's Source column.

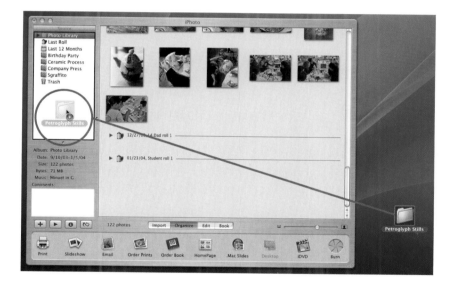

You can import a folder by dropping it in the Organize window, but you might as well take it right to Sources—this creates an album for you, with the name of the folder (Petroglyph Stills), and loads all the photos into it (as well as into the Library).

Now all the stills from the video are in iPhoto, in an album and ready for you to organize.

3 Open the Petroglyph Stills folder.

4 Rearrange the photos to your liking. As with editing video, they don't need to be in the order you shot them—and in fact, they probably shouldn't be. Drag and drop the photos into a new order.

5 When you're ready to put your slides on the Internet, click HomePage.

NOTE ▶ You might notice the .Mac Slides option—which at first glance appears to be the perfect choice. However, .Mac Slides is a completely different feature that allows slides to be "played" on your Mac (or anyone's) as a screensaver. As you update the slides, it automatically updates the screensaver. The problem is that .Mac Slides accommodates only one slide show at a time—uploading a new album replaces the old one—consequently, it's not necessarily the ideal option for a business owner, or family, who may have a series of slide shows to share.

Clicking HomePage will let you access your .Mac account and open the album in a preset template.

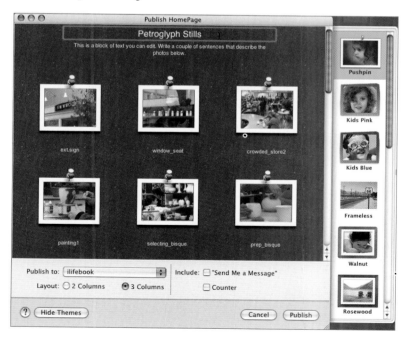

The names under the images come from the file names of the photographs. The style of the page is set according to your choice from the themes, presented along the right side of the window. Try a few different themes to see what they look like, but ultimately come back here, to the Pushpin theme.

6   Change the text on the page. You can change the title at the top of the page, the small block of text under the title, and of course the captions. Write a pithy description in the text block by first clicking the title. Click the photo names to change them into captions.

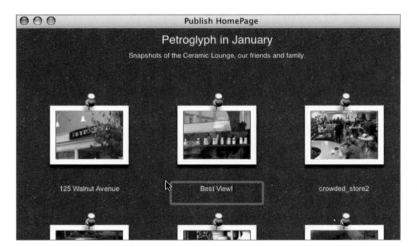

When you've got the page the way you'd like it to be seen online, you're ready to publish it.

7   Click Publish.

Immediately, iPhoto makes a connection to your .Mac account—in particular, your allocated iDisk space—and uploads the photos from your computer to the .Mac server.

In a few moments, the transfer is complete, your page is published, and a window pops up to alert you. You can visit the page directly, go back and edit the page if you'd like, or just click OK and the window goes away.

Your .Mac account will email you (or the person listed on the account as the contact) with information about your new page—including the URL—as well as some other tips. So, although you may have the urge to write down this long Web address, you'll have other opportunities to save the page as a bookmark or email the URL to friends and family or a mailing list of customers.

8   Click Visit Page Now.

Your default Web browser will go to your new Web page. It will look pretty much the same as it did while you were building it, with the addition of one particularly interesting option. There's a button near the top that turns this Web page into a slide show. It's not an automatic show as in iPhoto; instead, viewers can manually move from slide to slide at their own pace.

9   Click Start Slideshow.

The slide show opens in its own window and can be navigated with the arrows in the bottom-right corner.

10   Peruse the slides you uploaded to the Web.

Of course, this method for uploading images from iPhoto to the Web works regardless of where the photos came from—video camera, still camera, scans, and elsewhere. As long as images are in iPhoto, they can be shared by way of your .Mac account this easily.

What You've Learned

- You can use videotape as a quick source for still images that will be printed small, emailed, or posted on the Internet.

- Use the Save Frame As feature in iMovie to create still frames from video.

- Drag folders of still images to iPhoto to create the equivalent of rolls of these images.

- Use HomePage to build Web pages of your stills and to generate user-controlled slide shows.

14

Lesson Files

Lessons > Lesson6 > Sgraffito Technique.mov

Lessons > Lesson12 > Finished_Timelapse_music.mov

Lessons > Lesson14 > Timelapse Video alias

Tools   iDVD, SuperDrive

Time   Approximately 90 minutes

Goals   Learn how to make DVDs that include movies
and slide shows

Learn how to customize DVD themes and menus

Burning DVDs of Your Videos and Slide Shows

It's great to be able to flip open your iBook laptop and present a slide show live, but there are times when you want to leave the slide show with someone, such as your family, to watch at their own convenience. Similarly, once your videos are archived onto digital tape, it's likely that you will want to distribute them. A DVD is a remarkably convenient way to distribute digital content, and burning a DVD has never been easier.

Christopher can't wait to make a DVD to send to Jessica's grandparents. They live in another town and are hungry for photos and videos from her life. Charlie's parents just got a SuperDrive to burn DVDs, and he archives his video journals onto the discs and removes them from the family Mac to conserve hard disk space (and maintain a little extra privacy). The ceramics studio has a large flat-panel display that customers often watch. Studio owner Jennifer cycles through a few DVDs each day—presenting slide shows of finished pieces (to give customers ideas for their own projects), quick techniques to try (like the sgraffito step-by-step), and other creative touchstones (the time-lapse videos are always crowd-pleasers, both instructive and entertaining).

In the same way that all the iLife applications integrate so effortlessly, adding music to slide shows or adding still photos to videos, burning a DVD in iDVD is just as painless with its direct connection to your music, your photos, and your movies.

Getting to Know a DVD

DVDs are for more than playing movies. A DVD can play all kinds of media—from videos to slide shows to music—but it's also a big storage device. A DVD holds 4.7 GB of data—actually more like 4.3 GB (the discrepancy is partly because of the way computers measure the capacity). There are primarily two types of DVDs. One kind holds movies (a regular DVD), and the other holds software and files (sometimes referred to as a DVD-ROM).

iDVD has the great capability to combine these attributes. You can play movies from your disc, and you can also store files in folders that recipients access by popping the disc into a ComboDrive or SuperDrive (or any other DVD player hooked to your Mac). In the latter case, the DVD would be just like a giant CD-ROM.

NOTE ▶ At first there were only CD players in Macs. Then there were drives that would both play and record CDs. Then came DVD players. Since the DVD format is *backwards compatible*, as they say, a DVD player can also play a CD. Next was a drive that could play the DVD, but both play *and record* a CD. This is a great set of features, and Apple sells this as a ComboDrive. Finally, there is the DVD player and recorder, which also plays and records CDs. This is a SuperDrive.

The video and other media content on a DVD must be encoded in order to play on your DVD player and TV. The files are squeezed to fit on the disc (*compressed*), which decreases their quality slightly but makes them considerably smaller. The digital video files you work with in iMovie are large (1 GB per 5 minutes of video, as you may recall) but after iMovie prepares them for the DVD, the same gigabyte can hold between 15 and 30 minutes of video (depending on some of your preferences in iDVD, but don't worry about that now). Consequently, a DVD can hold up to two hours of your videos.

NOTE ▶ This compression is one reason you can't go backward, moving videos from DVDs into iMovie, without a lot of work.

TIP ▶ Because of the way iDVD squeezes video to fit on the disc, recording less material to the disc (say, an hour or less) will yield slightly better quality than putting on more. For the best quality, keep the length of your DVD material under an hour.

When you use a DVD for data storage (as a DVD-ROM), you don't want to compress files at all—you want to leave them exactly as they are. iDVD has the capability to manage all of this, which is one of the excellent features of the product.

TIP ▶ There are many, often confusing, DVD formats, which you may have come across once you got a SuperDrive. There's DVD-R, DVD-RW, DVD+RW, and more. While most are generally interchangeable and play in a ComboDrive as well as typical consumer DVD players, some won't. Never mind the subtleties between formats; the blank discs available from Apple tend to record easily in SuperDrives and play without problems on most players.

Getting an iMovie Movie Ready to Burn

Once you finish making a video in iMovie, there's not a lot you have to do to put it into iDVD, but there are a few things you might *want* to do. The most fun of all the options is to add *chapters* to your movie. (Chapters are midpoints in your video that can be directly accessed from the opening DVD menu.) This way, for longer videos, you can choose between playing from the start or popping to specific locations within the movie, which saves you from having to fast-forward every time you want to watch a specific part of the video.

None of Jennifer's videos is long enough to really merit chapters, but since adding them is easy enough, it's worth seeing how it's done.

1   Open the Lesson14 > **Timelapse Video alias**. This is linked to the project you worked on in Lessons 7 and 12.

2   Place the playhead at the edit between the wide shot and the close-up. (If you have trouble finding it, the running time at the playhead is 37 seconds and 8 frames.) It's the only change in camera position in the entire video, so it's a plausible choice for this demonstration of chapters.

3   Click the iDVD button from the array of buttons beneath the Clip pane.

This changes the pane into the iDVD Chapter Markers workspace.

4   Click the Add Chapter button when the playhead is positioned at the location in the video where you want to add a chapter.

This does two things: It places a little yellow mark in the timeline to denote the chapter mark, and it adds details about the chapter mark to a list that will grow in the iDVD Chapter Markers pane.

5   Click the chapter title, and change the name from the default "timelapse raw/15" to the information you'd want to describe this chapter on your DVD.

This information is saved as part of iMovie's data about your video. When iDVD examines an iMovie project in preparation for bringing it into your disc, it sees this chapter information and places these markers into the DVD menus it makes.

6   Save and close your project. All your file preparation is complete. You're done with iMovie for now and ready to work with iDVD.

There are two ways into iDVD. You can launch it and then pull in content, or you can start from inside iMovie (presumably where you are, having just added chapters to your movie) and access iDVD from the content side. Either way, iDVD lets you drop more than one movie onto a DVD and more than one kind of project (like a slide show) as well.

In this lesson, you'll follow Jennifer as she builds a DVD for her studio, including much of the material you and she have been building throughout this book.

iDVD gives you direct access to iTunes, iPhoto, and iMovie through its connection to the Music, Photos, and Movies folders in your Mac's Home folder. By default, music and photos reside in these folders when you use them in iLife, but movie projects often get saved all over a computer. Your iMovie projects should reside in the Movies folder. iDVD is designed to look into an iMovie project file and extract what it needs in order to make the DVD, both the edited video and the chapter information you create. This is a remarkable feature and makes your job of DVD creation much simpler.

If you create QuickTime movies of your completed iMovie projects (using the Share exporting option), save these to the Movies folder as well, particularly if you want to access them from iDVD. The movies you'll be using in this lesson came on the book's DVD and need to be positioned in your Home folder before we can work with them in iDVD.

Move the following finished project files from their position in the Lessons folder into the Movies folder in your Home folder:

- Lesson6 > **Sgraffito Technique.mov**
- Lesson12 > **Finished_Timelapse_music.mov**

NOTE ▶ If you want to access QuickTime movies from locations on your Mac *besides* the Movies folder, you can expand your options through the iDVD Preferences (under the Movies tab), although this won't work for entire iMovie projects. It's generally best to keep everything in the Movies folder.

Building a DVD of Your Movies

When you load a DVD into a DVD player, usually the video doesn't begin playing right away. Instead, what you most often see is a menu that introduces you to the content on the disc. It might say what the disc is about, what different videos it contains, and maybe give you options for accessing specific chapters within a video. The menu provides information and access, but it can also have personality.

Half the fun of iDVD is customizing these menus. While there are some practical considerations about what theme your DVD has, in general the choice is entirely personal, and any will do.

1   Open iDVD.

There are a few ways to do this. The first is through the Share option in iMovie, which includes an iDVD button. We won't use this method right now, but sometimes it's a great way to initiate the process, particularly when you want to burn a DVD of the movie you just completed in iMovie, but nothing else.

In many cases your DVDs are compilations of different videos and photos. Consequently, let's not start from a particular iMovie project but rather from iDVD itself, pulling in content you want to have on the disc. To do this, you'll need to open iDVD from the Dock (or from the Applications folder).

2   Name the project (the name will end up being the name of the DVD you're going to make), and make sure it will be saved where you want it. Jennifer is calling her disc PetroDVD.

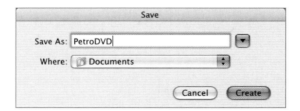

Your Mac defaults to placing projects in the Documents folder, which is fine, but you might change this to the Desktop (by using the pull-down menu) if that's the way you like to work. Jennifer is going to keep hers in the Documents folder.

3   Click Create. This launches iDVD. When it's open, you'll see one of the DVD templates onscreen in the iDVD workspace. The odds are good this theme isn't the one you're looking for. You have many to choose from.

At the bottom of the window is a series of buttons that will help you build and customize your DVD.

4   Click Customize.

The Customize button opens (and closes) a sidebar that presents your DVD themes. The sidebar (which actually lets you access a few different workspaces via four buttons at the top) will appear on the left of the main window.

You'll notice that when you click a theme, you get to explore its details in the big window to the right.

TIP A template for a wedding theme doesn't necessarily have to be used for a wedding. It might be a good look for a disc about your child's first years, for instance. Don't be fooled by theme names. When you look at a theme template, you'll see it's just some stock elements and colors. Wedding Bronze One, for instance, shows a curtain rippling and provides space for you to add a photo—there's nothing inherently "wedding" about it. If you don't like following the crowd, one nice way to customize your disc is to augment prebuilt themes and use them in original ways, all of which you'll learn in this lesson.

Scroll through the options available, looking for one that feels appropriate for Jennifer's ceramics studio.

5   Select the Pop Art theme. Although each theme is slightly different, all work in the same way, so even if you experiment with only one theme, you can learn the basics of building discs and designing menus.

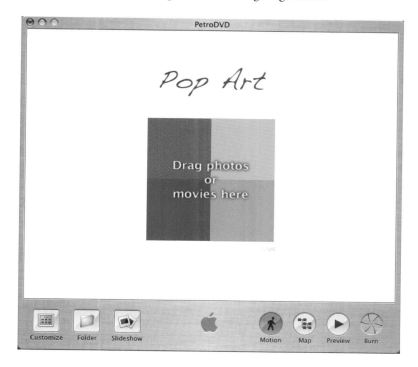

Like most theme templates, this one has a title on top—which you can change simply by clicking it and typing a different title. (The typeface and size are set, though you'll shortly learn how to modify them.) There's also a space that instructs you to "Drag photos or movies here." Not every template provides a space that accommodates both photos and movies—some hold only one or the other.

The question onscreen does beg the question: Drag photos from where? From iPhoto, from the Desktop, from somewhere else? Of course, the answer is from everywhere.

Here is a photo being dragged from the iPhoto Library open in another window.

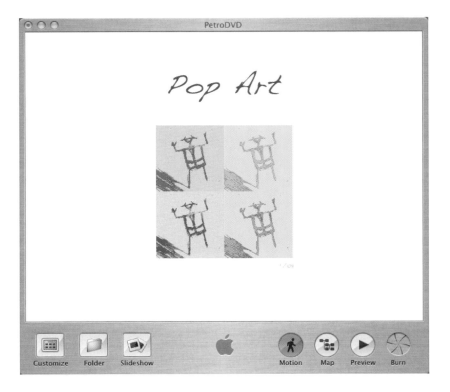

To make it easier to find photos, or movies if you're looking for them, iDVD provides inside access—much like what iPhoto and iMovie offer.

6   Locate the set of four buttons at the top of the Customize pane on the left side of the main window. You've been working in Themes. Click Media.

Under the row of buttons is a pull-down menu that connects you to the appropriate iLife application (or more specifically, to the corresponding folder in your Home folder: Music, Pictures, or Movies).

7   Choose Audio.

You will see your Library and playlists from iTunes.

8 Choose Photos.

Here is another workspace that lets you add photos by dragging them into the main window when appropriate.

9 Drag the photo of the petroglyph (DSCN0261) to the center of the template so that your menu looks like Jennifer's. (This photo is from Jennifer's L4.Biz roll 1 that you loaded in Lesson 4.)

10 Choose Movies. The two QuickTime movies (with the .mov suffix) are available here—earlier in this lesson you dragged them into the Movies folder from the DVD's Lessons folder.

These two short videos are key elements of the DVD Jennifer wants to create.

NOTE ▶ The image quality of these videos is not comparable to finished projects in iMovie. iMovie is always working at the full quality of the video from your camcorder—called DV video quality—and it's very good. These particular QuickTime videos were necessarily compressed to be small enough to fit on the enclosed DVD with all the rest of the content for this book, and consequently lost a fair amount of resolution. Keep in mind that your own projects and DVDs will have better-looking video than these examples.

11 Click **Finished_Timelapse_music.mov** and drag it to the template. Drop it on the template anywhere but on that graphic in the middle of the screen—if you put it there it will replace the photo already placed with the movie you're dragging. These theme templates often contain some kind of graphical element that can present moving video—but don't mistake these for the places you drop your videos.

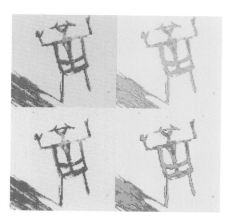

When you drop the movie onto the template in any of the white space around the graphic in the middle, a link will be created to the movie from here.

12 Drag **Sgraffito Technique.mov** to the DVD template as well.

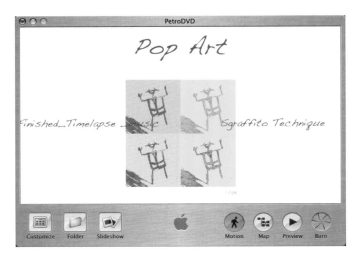

This particular template forces titles to alternating sides of the graphic in the middle. You'll find that different templates have their own idiosyncrasies as far as how they handle title placement, line breaks, and other minor issues.

Now that both movies are set up for the DVD, it's time for a little cosmetic work. Let's fix the titles.

13 Click **Finished_Timelapse_music.mov** and change the name to something more descriptive and user friendly, such as Italian Brushstroke. Change the second title as well. Since both of these movies are essentially examples of techniques, Jennifer decides to save visual space by removing the word "Technique."

One of the minor irritations of this template is that the titles overlap the graphic image a little. This makes the word "Brushstroke" hard to read. Jennifer could force a line break between the words in that title, but she opts to finish the DVD structure first and then review legibility issues.

NOTE ▶ You will learn how to customize these titles later in this lesson.

14 Finally, before moving on, change the DVD title from its default Pop Art to something appropriate. The video will be shown in the studio, so its title should be something like the name of the business or perhaps something more specific like Spring 2004 Videos. Petroglyph is a simple title, so let's use that.

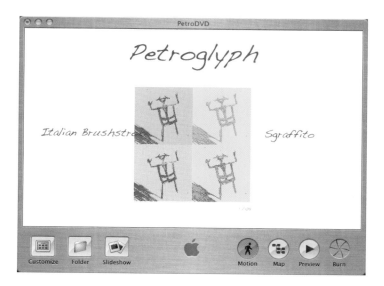

If the DVD were to contain only this pair of movies, you'd be done at this point. But Jennifer can do much more to make this disc useful and interesting.

Adding Photos and Slide Shows from iPhoto

While you're in iDVD, you can access your photos and entire albums in iPhoto. But before you go digging through them, you need to make a place in iDVD where your photos will go.

1 Click the Slideshow button at the bottom of the window.

This adds to your menu a link to a special type of slide show—which is different from what you'd get if you simply copied photos to the DVD like they were data files. (It's also different from using iPhoto to convert a slide show into a QuickTime movie of a slide show, something you didn't do in this book, but may have discovered at some point.) The slide show you place on this DVD will produce just as interactive an experience as you get with the Slideshow tool in iPhoto.

iDVD will add a link with the title My Slideshow (which, of course, you change when you're ready). Jennifer changes hers to Around Petroglyph.

2 Double-click the title of the new slide show.

This changes the main iDVD window into a slide show workspace. Displayed at the top is the title, along with how long (in minutes and seconds) the slide show will run, given the number of slides and each slide's duration. Time to add some slides.

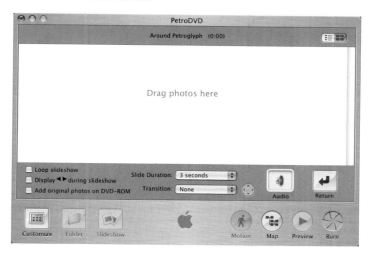

3   Click the Media button in the Customize pane, and choose Photos. From the menu of albums you've created while working on the projects in this book, select Company Press.

You may recall this album from Lesson 5, in which Jennifer created a linen-bound hardcover book. But because most customers won't see the book, a slide show of this material seems like suitable content for the DVD—she can show that in the studio.

You could drag one shot at a time to the large workspace on the right, but it's easier to grab an entire album and drag it there.

As soon as you drop the album, thumbnails begin to be created in the workspace.

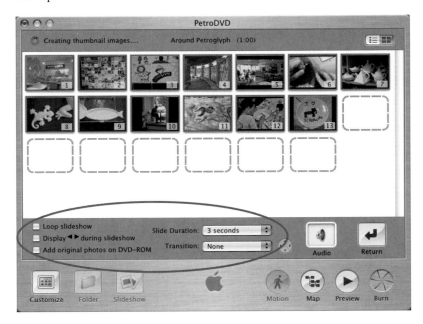

The controls at the bottom of the window let you specify whether you want this show to loop, how long each slide appears onscreen, and what kind of transition you want between slides.

 You'll also find an "Add original photos on DVD-ROM" check box. This option lets you include a folder of the slide show images at their best quality possible. Christopher chooses this option when he wants to distribute photos to the grandparents. They can watch the slide show first and, if they want, make prints from iPhoto, using the original files on the DVD. Jennifer has no need for this feature for her DVD, but it's a great option.

Because this slide show is running unassisted and in a public space, Jennifer decides to let the show loop indefinitely and to present each slide for five seconds, a little longer than she might ordinarily. She also likes to use dissolves as a transition between shots.

From this set of tools, you can also add audio to your slide show.

4   Access your iTunes Library from the Audio tab in the Media window.

5   Click and drag a song or playlist to the Audio button (also called the audio well) beneath the workspace.

When you drop the music, the audio well changes to reflect the file types it "holds" and to indicate that music will be played with this slide show.

If you decide you don't like the audio you've placed in the audio well, click and drag it from the well to the Desktop and watch it "vaporize."

Changing and Modifying Themes

You've now established some content for this disc (two movies and one slide show) and chosen a background image for the template. But before you leave this part of iDVD, it's a good idea to investigate the other themes and how to customize them. Because every theme manages its template components a little differently, sometimes it's interesting to see the benefits (or problems) of each.

You've been working in the Pop Art theme. Without changing any other features of your DVD, select some different themes.

1   Click the Return button at the bottom of the slide show workspace. This returns you to the previous workspace. It's not required, but it can help keep you oriented as you navigate iDVD.

2   Click the Customize button at the bottom of the screen. This should put you in familiar territory.

3   Change the theme to Drive In Two, and take a look at how the template changes, but how the menu items remain.

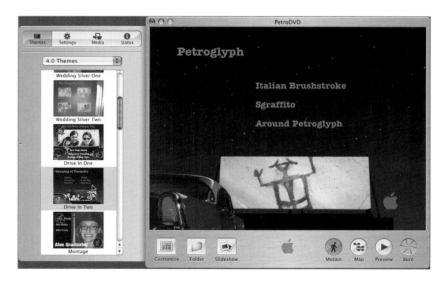

4   Change the theme to Blocks.

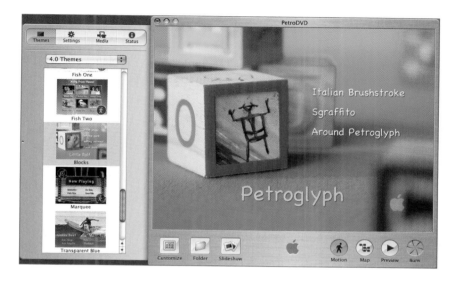

5   Change the theme to Montage.

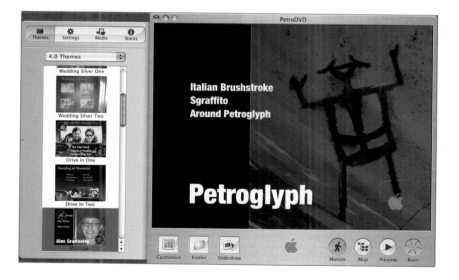

Notice that some themes have moving video in them already, some incorporate music, and others include ambient sounds. Templates that feature such built-in activity are designated by a Motion icon on the theme.

If the sound (or action or noise) bugs you, you can turn it off by clicking the Motion button at the bottom of the workspace.

Now the screen is probably calm enough to allow you to experiment.

Up until this point in iDVD, you've worked with the Customize tools, alternating between Themes and Media. Now let's work with a set of more specific tools.

6   Click Settings. This opens a set of tools for customizing the template you're looking at.

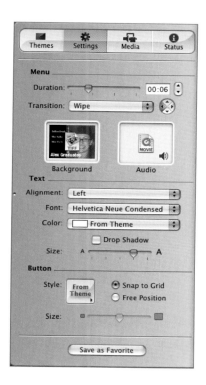

To customize the template, you can modify many of the preset attributes. When you're done, it will likely have little resemblance to the original Montage it began as. First of all, get rid of the music.

7   Click and drag the file in the audio well to your Desktop. It will disappear from its position in this template, and the well will be empty.

You could add your own tune here, but for now leave it blank.

8 Change the button style. Right now the style of button comes from the template: it's just the text with the title of the button. That's why the Style field says From Theme.

The disclosure triangle on the button indicates there's a pull-down menu of options for the button style. Click and hold it, and check out your options. Select the oblong square.

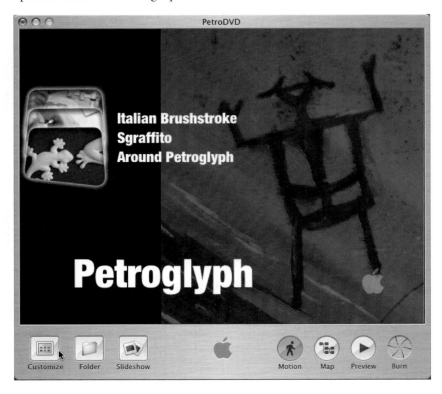

The buttons include windows with glimpses into each video or slide show. Unfortunately these buttons are stacked too closely to see fully. It's because they are locked to a grid in the template.

9   Click Free Position. This lets you drag the buttons around onscreen to the location you choose.

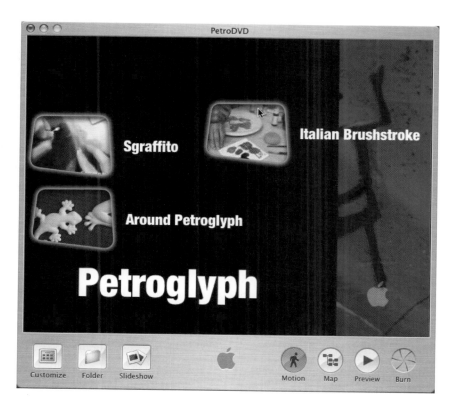

10 Reposition the buttons creatively.

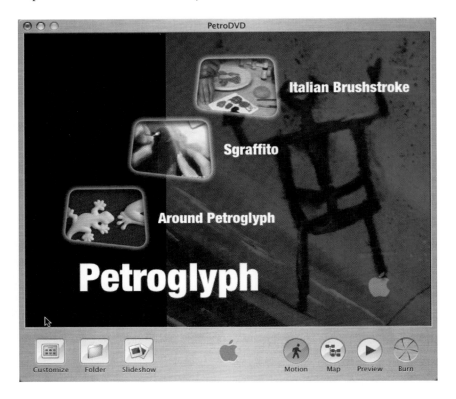

NOTE ▶ Other text attributes you can change include the size, the color, and, obviously, the font.

When you work with text onscreen, it becomes increasingly important to recognize the "safe" area of the screen. A computer monitor displays the entire frame of video from a videotape or DVD. But when you put that same material on a regular TV set, the edges are chopped off. Exactly how much depends on the set, but a video frame has a well-defined safe zone. Before you burn a DVD, you should always check to see that your most important material is within the safe area, particularly text.

11 Choose Advanced > Show TV Safe Area to turn on that option.

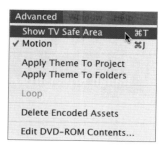

Some of the screen will be grayed out a bit; a red border separates the safe region from the risky.

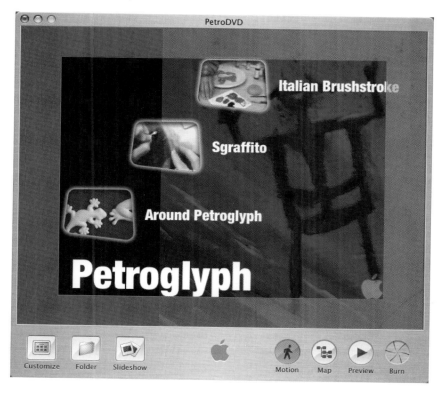

Adjust your DVD menu so that all the text is inside the safe area.

12 Click the Around Petroglyph button.

A slider appears over the clip allowing you to choose the image that is presented in the button. Slide it around and find a different image.

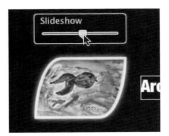

For buttons linked to video, you can choose whether you want the button to play the video or just show a single non-moving frame. To play the video, select the check box above the Movie slider.

TIP Moving the video is a pretty neat feature, but if you have lots of little movies going on at the same time on your menu, it's actually pretty distracting and somewhat irritating. An impressive demo, but consider using moving video in buttons sparingly.

These are some of the many ways you can customize menu templates. Any template can be saved (using the Save as Favorite button at the bottom of the column) or discarded at will.

13 Click Themes. Find the Pop Art template again and click it. The screen will return to its familiar facade.

What you've seen is that regardless of what theme you select, the button names and videos remain unaltered. The themes are just cosmetic overlays of the same content and structure. The structure of the DVD—that is, the way it is organized hierarchically and the way its audience navigates its menus to find the videos and slide shows—remains the same across all of these themes.

The DVD's structure, which you may want to see if you're confused about how the user access and experience are built, for instance, can always be viewed by clicking the Map button.

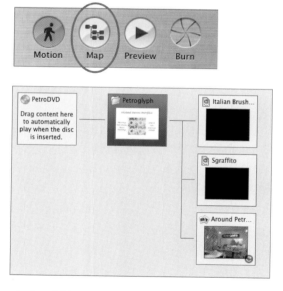

Now it should be clearer how your DVD is structured. The Map view is a good way to navigate your DVD while you're building it. It also gives you access to a unique option: You can set up an opening video (or slide show) that will play as soon as the DVD is inserted into a player—before the opening menu appears. The first square—called an autoplay well—is built into the structure of the disc, and is presented to the left and connected to the main menu—in this case, the Petroglyph Pop Art menu. The autoplay well is labeled PetroDVD. You can drag video or slide shows onto it to use as the opening sequence, which cycles endlessly until someone selects Play to see what's on the disc.

Jennifer will leave the autoplay feature alone for now, but it's an interesting option that she may use as she increases her library of videos from her studio.

Menus in Menus

While Jennifer's DVD is probably too simple to warrant complex organization, you have the option of adding more levels of menus to your DVD. For instance, if you have more videos or slide shows than will fit on the first menu page (for many themes, the limit is six items), you'll need to create another menu—a *submenu*. To create a submenu, you must first create a new page.

1   Create a new page by clicking the Folder button at the bottom of the screen. This adds a link to a submenu attached to your top menu.

The default name for the link is "My Folder"—but you can change this to whatever describes the new area.

TIP ▶ If you show the buttons as images, the folder button onscreen will show a folder icon. You won't see a video or slide images when you click the folder and slide the slider. Still, the button is a "well," and you can drag and drop an image from the photos in the Media Browser to this well to give it an image.

2   Double-click the folder and you reveal a new place (a new menu) to add your videos and slides. There will always be an arrow on this page, pointing left, which allows you to return to the previous menu. (On some templates it's harder to see than others.)

3   If you want to, experiment by adding videos and slides, following the same steps you did earlier in this lesson for customizing your first menu.

This submenu can have any theme, and doesn't need to match the theme of the top one. As you expand your DVD's structure, the Map view of the disc's contents becomes increasingly important. In the Map view, you can see which menus are submenus, what is linked to what, and any menu's theme.

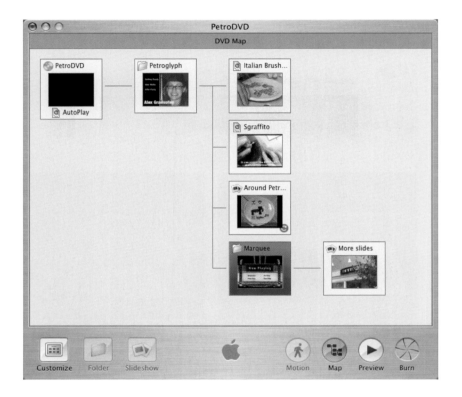

Previewing Your DVD

All this work preparing the DVD is pretty easy, but it's important to be able to test out the user's experience. Since the disc doesn't really exist yet (the work you've done to create menus for videos and slide shows are not yet burned to disc), you can't try it out in a DVD player. The alternative is to "preview" the disc's content.

The Preview button at the bottom of the screen lets you do exactly that.

1 Click the button, and the tools go away; now you can experience the disc exactly the way you will when it's burned.

An onscreen DVD remote control pops up, which you can use to play, stop, and test the chapters and other attributes of your disc's navigation. Of course, you can also just watch the disc's videos.

2 To end the preview, click the Preview button again and you'll return to the Customize pane. Continue this back-and-forth of building and previewing until the disc feels ready. Then it's time to burn your DVD.

Burning a DVD

Burning a DVD is easy for you to arrange, but it's a lot of work for a computer. The compression required and the encoding into the DVD format is what scientists call *computationally complex*, meaning it requires a lot of math. Your Mac's processor (G4 is good, G5 is better) and clock speed (the megahertz or gigahertz number that is bantered about) are the important elements. The faster the clock speed and larger the processor, the faster the burning of your DVD will go.

Just like burning a CD in iTunes, all you really need to do is click the Burn button. It will open up to reveal the "real" Burn button, with a warning symbol.

Click the Burn button, and iDVD will coach you through the rest of the process. Insert a blank DVD in your SuperDrive, and that's it.

How long iDVD takes to burn a disc is highly variable. A rule of thumb is twice the length of time required to play the disc—maybe an hour or two. Some advanced settings can augment the speed and quality of the disc you burn, but the defaults are generally appropriate.

When the recording is done, iDVD will eject the disc for you.

What You've Learned

- Keep all your media in the appropriate folders (Movies, Music, and Photos) in your Home folder. This makes accessing content from the Media Browser in iDVD easy.

- Use the Customize button to reveal a selection of menu templates.

- Drag and drop menu elements as each template indicates. Drag and drop content from the Media Browser onto the blank portions of the template; that prepares the content to be added to the disc.

- Personalize templates using the Settings button—in particular changing DVD button styles and position, background music, and fonts.

- Use the Show TV Safe Area feature to make sure the DVD will look good on a TV set, and to make sure you don't cut off words on menus.

- Use Map view to review the structure of your disc, and, if you want, to add an opening movie to the Autoplay well.

- Preview your DVD before burning to make sure the user's experience matches your expectations.

- Burn your DVD when you're ready; iDVD will coach you through recording the disc.

Index

Symbols

+ (plus) button, 69

A

adapters, 38

Add Chapter button, 324–325

AIFF audio files, 11

albums, 67–93

    bound books. *see* bound books

    building DVDs from, 337–341

    comments added to, 76–77

    cropping photos, 85–89

    defined, 54

    enhancing, 90–91

    keywords added to, 77–80

    ordering shots, 73–75

    organizing photos into, 69–73

    overview of, 67

    preparing, 68–69

    printing, 96–99

    ratings added to, 80–81

    red-eye correction, 91–93

    sharing, 96

    Smart Albums, 81–84

Apple, Freeplay music, 276

Apple iTunes Music Store, 8

archives, video, 267–270

arrow keys, 157, 260

aspect ratio, 87–89

audio

    editing dialogue scenes, 259–265

    file size, 29

    formats, 11, 280

    music. *see* iPod; iTunes

    narration. *see* narration

    slide show DVDs, 341

Audio button, 145, 341

audio well, 341

audio, iMovie, 202–219

    deleting audio clips, 208–209

    deleting picture clips, 207

    duration of shots, 215–218

    extracting from first clip, 205–206

    fade out transitions, 216

    gaps, 212–215

    labeling, 203

    narration tool, 219–224

    scrubbing, 210

    snap and sound effect cues, 209, 211

    synchronizing with video, 213–215

    Trim tool, 211

    unlocking clips, 207

waveforms, 209–210
workspace in Clip view, 204, 216
workspace in Timeline view, 204–205
autoplay feature, DVDs, 352
AUX input jacks, 37–38

B

background
    adding video titles, 134, 137–139
    shooting photos, 53
backwards compatibility, 323
bass, 283–285
batteries, digital cameras, 47
beats column, Loop Browser, 280
Blocks theme, 343
bound books, 99–110
    Book window, 101
    cover, 103–104
    layout, 105–108
    locks, 106–108
    order of photos, 100–101, 109–110
    overview of, 99–100
    page design, 103–104
    printing, 108–109
    resolution, 101
    text added to, 104–105
    themes, 102–103
    titles, 103
brightness, 90–91
Browse button, 278
Browser, iTunes, 19–22
Burn button, DVDs, 356–357
burning
    CDs, 28–30
    DVDs, 356–357
button style, DVD, 346–347, 350

C

camcorders
    capturing video into iMovie, 177–181
    close-up shots, 234
    good shots, creating, 181–183
    image quality, 46
    as microphone, 198–201
    motion guidelines for, 228–229
    overview of, 172–174
    saving cassettes, 267–270
    shooting basics, 175–177
    shots with relationships, 183–184
    sound quality, 197–198
    time-lapse videos, 150–153
    Web slide shows, 307–309
    zoom effects, 232–235
camera mode, 176
cameras
    camcorders. *see* camcorders
    digital. *see* digital cameras
captions, Web slide shows, 316
capturing video, 178, 181
CDDB (Compact Disc Database)
    adjusting information after
        importing, 14–19
    adjusting information before
        importing, 12–13
    obtaining disc data, 6–7
CDs
    backwards compatibility
        and, 323
    as source for iTunes, 7–8
CDs, custom
    after importing, 14–19
    browsing/viewing tunes, 19–22
    burning, 28–30

before importing, 12–13
launching iTunes, 2
making playlists, 23–26
playing, 3–5
selecting/importing songs, 9–11
song order, 26–28
as source for iTunes, 7–8
using automatic CD album
information, 5–7
chapters
adding to movies, 324–327
previewing DVD, 355
checkmarks, iTunes
defined, 5
importing songs and CDs, 9–10
chorus, 299
Classic Rock piano, 285–286
Clip pane, iMovie
cleaning up, 258
dragging clips to workspace
from, 189
editing time-lapse videos, 153–154
editing video, 191
first cuts, 251–252
importing videos, 180–181
labeling/deleting clips, 254
overview of, 121–122
reviewing coverage in, 249–250
using Command-T with, 188
Clip view
editing time-lapse videos, 154
editing video in, 190
overview of, 122
re-arranging workspace, 131

reordering shots, 142
separating picture from sound in
iMovie, 204, 208, 216
clock speed, 356
close-up shots
defined, 189
editing techniques, 254, 255–256,
262–264
function of, 237
shot/reverse combinations, 239–240
zoom effects, 234–235
columns, iTunes
alphabetically arranging, 19
changing width of, 19
narrowing search fields, 20
columns, Loop Browser, 280
ComboDrive, 322–323
Command-click
making playlists, 25
selecting multiple photos, 63
Command-T
editing time-lapse videos, 157–158
editing videos, 185, 188, 191–192
GarageBand editing, 288
making first cut, 252
Command-Z, 89, 91
comments, adding to albums, 76–77
Compact Disc Database (CDDB)
adjusting information after
importing, 14–19
adjusting information before
importing, 12–13
obtaining disc data, 6–7
compatibility, DVD players, 323

composition, photo, 49–53

compression

    DVDs, 323, 356

    QuickTime movies, 335

connectors

    getting video into iMovie, 177–178

    playing iPod through stereo, 36–38

Constrain pop-up menu, 88

contrast, 90–91

conversations. *see* narration

copying loops, 287

copying photos, 89

copyrights, music, 36, 276

counters, digital

    adding variation to songs, 296

    measuring time, 292

coverage, reviewing. *see* editing videos

coverage, shooting techniques, 236–243

    cutaway shots, 240–242

    establishing shots, 242–243

    multiple shots from each position, 237

    overview of, 236

    shot selection, 181–183

    shot/reverse combinations, 237–240

    story structure and, 244

covers, bound book, 103–104

Crop tool, 85–89

cross dissolves, 160

culling, 156

Customize button, 330, 342

cutaway shots

    editing techniques, 255–257, 264

    overview of, 240–242

    shooting techniques, 240–242

cuts, first, 156–161, 251–252

D

deletes

    Clip pane clean-up, 254, 258–259

    photos, 60–61

    playlists/Library, 26

    slide show narration, 208–209

    video, 159

desktop picture, 117

dialogue scenes, editing, 259–265

digital albums. *see* albums

digital cameras, 43–53

    composition, 49–53

    exposure, 48

    importing images into iPhoto. *see* iPhoto

    manual for, 47

    resolution, 44–46

    taking lots of shots, 47

digital counters

    adding variation to songs, 296

    measuring time, 292

direction setting, slide shows, 114

dock

    moving playlists to iPod, 34

    opening iDVD from, 328

    playing iPod through stereo, 38

Document folder, 328

documentaries, 202

dolly shot, 229

drag and drop, 353

Drive In Two theme, 342

drums, 279–281, 283

duration

    adjusting in movies, 142–144

    iMovie connecting to iPhoto, 127–128

labeling/deleting clips in Clip
     pane, 254
slowing down, 130
synchronizing audio with video,
     215–218, 222–223
wide shots, 189
DVD-ROMs
     building movie DVDs, 341
     compression and, 323
     defined, 322
DVDs
     players, 323
     slide shows. *see* slide shows, DVD
     videos. *see* videos, DVD
dynamic faders, 290
dynamic slide shows. *see* slide shows,
     dynamic

E
ECU (extreme close-up) shot, 234
Edit Volume check box, 303–304
editing photos
     cropping, 85–89
     enhancing, 90–91
     red-eye, 91–93
editing videos, 167–195, 247–273
     background music added, 266–267
     cutaway shots, 255–257
     dialogue scenes, 259–265
     first cuts, 251–252
     getting right shots, 181–183
     modifying shots in Timeline, 193–195,
          252–253
     moving video into iMovie, 177–181
     organizing, 169–172

overview of, 167–168
     playing sequence in Timeline, 254
     reviewing coverage in Clip pane,
          249–250
     saving, 267–270
     shooting videos vs., 168–169
     shots with relationships, 183–185
     time-lapse, 153–161
     trimming/arranging footage, 185–193
     uploading to Web, 270–272
     visual balance, 254
effects, transition. *see* transition effects
email, attaching photos to, 116
Enhance feature, 90–91
erasing photos, 56
establishing shots, 242–243
EWS (extreme wide shot), 233
exporting to iTunes, 300–301
exposure, photo, 48
Extract Audio function, 205–206
extreme close-up (ECU) shot, 234
extreme wide shot (EWS), 233

F
fade in transitions
     creating story structure, 244
     editing dialogue scenes, 265
     overview of, 139–142
fade out transitions
     adding to slide shows, 216
     creating story structure, 244
     editing dialogue scenes, 265
     exporting from GarageBand into
          iTunes, 303–304
     overview of, 139–142

Favs column, Loop Browser, 280
fields, search, 20
fill flash, 48
film rolls
    adjusting name on, 59–60
    viewing photos in Library, 58–59
Finish button, iMovie, 128–129
FireWire cables, 177–178, 268
fluid heads, tripods
    defined, 150
    panning and tilting with, 230
folders
    creating new, 309
    DVD submenus, 352–354
    keeping media files in Home, 326
foreground, 51, 52
formats
    audio, 11
    DVD, 323, 356
    still images from videos, 312
4-pin connector, 177–178
frames
    creating story structure, 244
    cropping to fit, 87–89
    defined, 127
    grabbing still images from
        videos, 310–311
    zooming to create, 231
Free Position setting, 347
Freeplay music, 276

G

GarageBand
    Classic Rock piano, 285–286
    copying loops, 287
    experimenting with, 285–287
    exporting music into iTunes, 300–304
    Loop button, 288–289
    measuring time, 292–293
    mixing music, 289–291
    overview of, 275–276
    Trim tool and, 288
    variation added to, 294–299
    video background music, 267
GarageBand, creating new music, 276–289
    bass, 283–285
    drums, 279–281, 283
    Grand Piano interface, 278
    Loop Browser, 278–282
    Loop tool, 282–283
    parameters, 277
Genre column, 22
Grand Piano interface, 278

H

hard disk, 176
Hollywood shooting techniques. *see*
    shooting techniques
Home folder, Mac, 326
HomePage, 315

I

i.Link, 177–178
iChat AV, 162
icons
    Burn Disc, 28, 30
    import, 10–11
    search, 20
    speaker, 5
    warning, 28

iDVD, 321–357
accessing photos/slide shows, 337–341
dropping movie onto template, 335–336
finding photos or movies, 332–335
getting iMovie ready to burn, 324–327
launching, 325–326
opening, 327–328
overview of, 322–323
previewing, 354–355
submenus, 352–354
themes, 342–352
IEEE 1394, 177–178
images. *see* photos
iMovie, 119–147
DVDs burned in, 324–327
editing videos. *see* video editing
fade in/fade out transitions, 139–142
iDVD opening in, 325–326, 328
interface, 120–123
iSight camera and, 161–165
iTunes music, 145–146, 302–304
loudness scale, 221–222, 267
moving video into, 177–181
overview of, 119
QuickTime quality vs., 335
slide duration and, 142–144
slide shows created with, 119–120
still photos for, 123–132, 309–312
titles, 133–139
trashcan, 254, 259

iMovie, audio, 202–219
deleting audio clips, 208–209
deleting picture clips, 207
duration of shots, 215–218
extracting from first clip, 205–206
fade out transitions, 216
gaps, 212–215
labeling, 203
narration tool, 219–224
scrubbing, 210
snap and sound effect cues, 209, 211
synchronizing audio with video, 213–215
Trim tool, 211
unlocking clips, 207
waveforms, 209–210
workspace in Clip view, 204, 216
workspace in Timeline view, 204–205
importing
background music to videos, 266–267
defined, 181
video into iMovie, 180–181
importing, iPhoto, 55–64
camera images, 55–59
changing roll information, 59–60
deleting photos, 60–61
launching, 56
overview of, 54–55
rotating photos, 62–64
importing, iTunes
adjusting information after, 14–19
adjusting information before, 12–13
songs and entire CDs, 9–11

Information button, 76–77
Internet
        low resolution of, 45
        uploading video to, 270–272
Internet slide shows, 306–319
        getting stills from video, 309–312
        overview of, 307–309
        putting digital files into iPhoto,
                313–318
interviews. *see* narration
iPhoto
        iDVD access to, 326
        iMovie connection to, 123–132
        JPEG format for, 312
        movie DVDs built from, 337–341
        Web slide shows, 308, 313–318
iPhoto, albums, 67–93
        bound books. *see* bound books
        comments added to, 76–77
        cropping photos, 85–89
        enhancing, 90–91
        keywords added to, 77–80
        ordering shots, 73–75
        organizing, 69–73
        overview of, 67
        preparing, 68–69
        printing, 96–99
        ratings added to, 80–81
        red-eye correction, 91–93
        sharing, 96
        Smart Albums, 81–84
iPhoto, importing, 55–64
        camera images, 55–59
        changing roll information, 59–60
        deleting photos, 60–61
        launching, 56

overview of, 54–55
        rotating photos, 62–64
iPhoto, sharing/printing
        bound books, 99–110
        other options, 116–117
        preparing for, 96
        printing paper images, 96–99
iPod, 32–41
        adding playlist without iTunes, 39–41
        customizing playlists, 35–36
        moving playlists to, 34–35
        overview of, 33
        playing music through stereo, 36–38
iSight camera
        getting video into iMovie, 178–179
        making videos with, 161–165
iTunes
        adjusting information after
                importing, 14–19
        adjusting information before
                importing, 12–13
        automatic CD album information, 5–7
        browsing/viewing tunes, 14–22
        burning custom CDs, 28–30
        burning DVDs, 326, 333–334
        iPhoto vs., 54
        making playlists, 23–26
        Music Store, 8
        playing playlists, 26–28
        playing songs and CDs, 3–5
        playlists added to iPod without, 39–41
        putting GarageBand music into,
                300–304
        selecting/importing songs/entire
                CDs, 9–11

slide show music, 114–115, 145–146
sources, 7–8
starting, 2
video music, 266–267

J
JPEGs, 312
jumps, 159

K
Ken Burns Effect
    defining, 124–126
    durations, 144
    synchronizing audio/video,
        215–216, 222–223
    working with, 128–132
key column, Loop Browser, 280
key, GarageBand, 285
keywords, 77–80

L
labels
    audio segments, 203
    CD, 30
    cleaning up Clip pane, 254
    video cassettes, 169–170, 267–270
layout, bound books, 105–108
LCD screen, camcorders
    overview of, 174
    playback mode, 176
    saving video cassettes, 269
legal issues, 36, 276
Library, iPhoto
    creating photo albums, 69–73
    deleting photos from, 60–61

iMovie connecting to, 123–132
overview of, 54
viewing photos in, 58–59
Library, iTunes
    adding music to slide shows
        from, 146
    adjusting information after
        importing, 14–19
    defined, 8
    deleting songs from, 26
    moving playlists to iPod, 34
    playlists vs., 23
lingo, motion, 229–230
The Little Digital Video Book (Peachpit
    Press), 172
locks
    audio clips, 207
    bound books, 106–108
log sheets
    overview of, 169–170
    with timecode, 171–172
Loop Browser, GarageBand
    adding bass, 283–285
    adding drums, 279–281, 283
    overview of, 294–299
    working with, 278–279
Loop button, 288–289, 294
loop columns, 280
Loop tool, 282–283
loops
    copying, 287
    defined, 278
    measuring time with, 292–293
    overview of, 280–282
    trimming, 288

loudness scale
mixing music, 267, 289–291
narration, 221–222

M

.Mac hosting accounts
making Web slide show, 315, 317
streamlining iLife with, 309
.Mac Slides option, 315
manuals, digital camera, 47
Map view
creating DVD submenus, 353–354
overview of, 351–352
markers, chapter, 324–325
measures
adding, 295–296
defined, 282
Electric Bass track, 285
time, 292–293
medium shots
editing techniques, 254, 262–263
shot/reverse combinations, 239–240
showing subject with, 237
zoom effects with, 233–235
megapixels
printing photos, 99–100
resolution, 44–46
menus, DVD
creating submenus, 352–354
customizing. *see* themes, DVD
microphones
camcorder, 196–201
iMovie narration tool, 219–224
MIDI loops, 280

mixdowns, 301
Mixer, GarageBand, 289–291
mixing
in GarageBand, 289–291
loudness scale, 267
mixdowns, 301
Montage theme, 343
motion
guidelines for camcorder, 228–229
lingo, 229–230
shooting repetitive, 235–236
Motion icon, DVD themes, 344
Movie slider, iDVD, 350
MP3 audio files, 11
MP4 audio files, 11
multiple shots, 237
music
with GarageBand. *see* GarageBand
with iPod. *see* iPod
with iTunes. *see* iTunes
Music Store, 8
Mute button, tracks, 291
My Rating, 80–81

N

naming conventions
editing dialogue, 263
film rolls, 59–60
iPod playlists, 36
movie DVDs, 328, 336–337
playlists, 23
shots in Timeline, 252–253
zoom shots, 235

narration
    with camcorder as microphone,
        198–201
    editing dialogue scenes, 259–265
    iMovie audio. *see* iMovie, audio
    iMovie narration tool, 219–224
    quality of, 197–198
navigation, DVD, 351–352
nondestructive editing, 195
numbering, video cassettes
    overview of, 169–170
    timecodes and, 171–172

O

omnidirectional microphones, 197
On-The-Go playlist, 39–41
Order Book feature, 109–110
Order Prints feature, 116
OS (over-the-shoulder) shot
    in dialogue scenes, 260
    overview of, 239–240
Over Black feature, 137–139

P

page design, bound books, 103–104
pans
    controlling with Mixer, 290
    defined, 229
    guidelines for, 230
Pause button, iTunes, 3
Pause slider, 136
PDF files, creating, 108–109
peak meters, 290

photo albums, 67–93
    bound books. *see* bound books
    comments added to, 76–77
    cropping photos, 85–89
    enhancing, 90–91
    keywords added to, 77–80
    ordering shots, 73–75
    organizing, 69–73
    overview of, 67
    preparing, 68–69
    printing, 96–99
    ratings added to, 80–81
    red-eye correction, 91–93
    sharing, 96
    Smart Albums, 81–84
photos
    cropping, 85–89
    enhancing, 90–91
    grabbing stills from videos, 309–312
    red-eye, 91–93
    shooting. *see* digital cameras;
        shooting techniques
Photos button, 215–218, 222–223
photos, importing to iPhoto, 55–64
    changing roll information, 59–60
    deleting photos, 60–61
    importing images from camera
        to, 55–59
    launching, 56
    overview of, 54–55
photos, sharing
    bound books, 99–110
    other options, 116–117

preparing for, 96
printing paper images, 96–99
Play button
iMovie videos, 131
iTunes, 3
slide shows, 115
playback
effect of rendering on, 132
getting video into iMovie, 178
saving video cassettes, 268
playhead
adding music to slide shows, 146
adding music to videos, 266–267
defined, 122–123
editing dialogue, 259–260
editing time-lapse videos, 155,
157–158
GarageBand, 281
playlists
adding music to slide shows,
114–115
adding to iPod without iTunes, 39–41
automatically generated, 8
burning CDs, 29
changing song order, 27–28
customizing iPod, 35–36
defined, 8
deleting songs from, 26
including songs in multiple, 26
making, 23–26
moving to iPod, 34–35
random play, 27
plus (+) button, 69
point-of-view, 50

preferences
iPod playlists, 35–36
photo rotation, 62
printing from photo album, 97–98
slide show, 112–113
Preview feature
bound books, 109
DVDs, 354–355
iMovie, 129
video titles, 135
Print button, 97
printing photos
for bound books, 99–110
options for, 116–117
Order Prints feature, 116
overview of, 95
from photo album, 96–99
processors, 356
production sound, 198
publishing
movies to Web, 267–270
slide show on Internet, 316

Q
QuickTime movies
building DVDs, 334–335
exporting movie to, 138
iDVD direct access to, 326–327

R
Radio, 8
random play
iTunes playlists, 27
slide shows, 113

ratings
  adding to photo albums, 80–81
  slide show, 111
  Smart Albums, 81–84
razor blade tool, 288
RCA plugs, 37
Record button, camcorders, 173, 174
Record with iSight feature, 163–164
recording
  audio while shooting video, 199–201
  saving video cassettes, 267–270
  using zoom, 231
Red-Eye feature, 91–93
relationships, between shots, 183–184
remote controls, time-lapse photography,
  150, 152–153
rendering, iMovies
  changing slide duration, 144
  overview of, 132
  video titles, 136–137
resolution
  bound books and, 101
  digital cameras and, 44–46
  printing photos and, 99–100
Reverse button, iMovie, 131
reverse shots
  overview of, 237–240
  shooting cutaway shots, 241
rewind, 180
ripping, 181. *see also* importing
roll information, 59–60
Rotate Photo button, iPhoto, 62–63
rotation, photo, 62–64
rule of thirds, 52

S

safe zone setting, 348–349
saving
  iMovie projects, 120
  movie DVDs, 328
  video archive quality and, 267–270
scenes
  cutaway shots, 241
  defined, 235
  determining video, 235–236
  editing dialogue, 259–265
scrubbing
  audio, 210
  time-lapse videos, 155
  video, 187
search, iTunes
  with Browser, 20–22
  search feature, 19–20
sequence, photo
  in Clip View, 142
  slide shows, 112–113
  videos, 185, 191–193
Settings button, DVDs, 344–348
Set-Up Assistant, iChat AV, 162
Setup Assistant, iTunes
  launching iTunes, 2
  obtaining disc data, 6
Shaker loop, 298–299
Share option, iMovie
  opening iDVD with, 328
  saving video cassettes, 268–269
  uploading video to Web, 267–270
sharing photos
  bound books, 99–110
  other options, 116–117

preparing for, 96
printing paper images, 96–99
Shift key, 63
shooting techniques, 227–245. *see also*
editing videos
approach to, 228
camcorder motion, 228–229
camcorders and, 172–174
determining scenes, 235–236
editing video vs., 168–169
getting right shots, 181–183
motion lingo, 229–230
overview of, 175–177
shots with relationships, 183–184
zoom effects, 231–235
shooting techniques, coverage, 236–243
cutaway shots, 240–242
establishing shots, 242–243
multiple shots from each position, 237
overview of, 236
shot/reverse combinations, 237–240
story structure, 244
shot/reverse combinations
cutaway shots and, 241
editing dialogue, 259–265
overview of, 237–240
shots
close-up, 234
cutaway, 240–242
from different positions, 237
establishing, 242–243
getting right, 181–183
medium, 233
over-the-shoulder, 240

relationships between, 183–184
story structure created with, 244
wide, 233
zoom effects with unmoving,
232–235
Show TV Safe Area feature, 349
Shuffle button, 27
shuttle controls, camcorder, 176
signage, 243
single shot, 260
6-pin connector, 177–178
size
audio files, 29
iPhoto, 60–61
titles, 135
sketches, 185
slice, 290
slide shows, DVD, 327–354
burning, 324–327, 356–357
dropping movie onto template,
335–336
from iPhoto, 337–341
opening iDVD, 327–328
overview of, 321–323
previewing, 354–355
submenus, 352–354
themes. *see* themes, DVD
slide shows, dynamic, 119–147
adding narration with camcorder,
198–201
adding narration with iMovie audio.
see iMovie, audio
adding narration with iMovie narration tool, 219–224

adjusting, 142–144
fade in/fade out transitions, 139–142
iMovie interface, 120–123
music from iTunes, 145–146
overview of, 119–120
photos from iPhoto, 123–132
titles, 133–139
slide shows, Internet, 306–319
getting stills from videos, 309–312
overview of, 307–309
putting digital files into iPhoto,
313–318
slide shows, quick, 111–116
Slideshow button, iDVD, 338
Smart Albums, 81–84
Solo button, tracks, 291
songs
with GarageBand. *see* GarageBand
with iPod. *see* iPod
with iTunes. *see* iTunes
ordering for custom CDs, 26–28
sound
editing dialogue scenes, 259–265
GarageBand. *see* GarageBand
iPod music. *see* iPod
iTunes music. *see* iTunes
narration. *see* narration
time-lapse videos, 156
Sources
iPhoto, 54, 313
iTunes, 7–8
Southern Rock Guitar, 295–297
spacebar, 157
speaker icon, iTunes, 5

speed
adding movie titles to black background, 138
adjusting video titles and effects, 136
editing time-lapse videos, 155
fade out transitions, 140
importing songs and CDs, 9–10
Split Video Clip at Playhead, 157–158
Start button, iMovie, 128
Start Slideshow button, 318
Steadicam, 229
stereo music, 36–38
still photography
dynamic slide shows. *see* slide shows,
dynamic
grabbing from videos, 309–312
tripod, 150
Stop button, 10
storage, DVD, 322–323
story structure, 244
style, video titles, 134–135
submenus, DVD, 352–354
SuperDrive
burning DVDs, 356–357
defined, 322
DVD formats, 323

T

television, resolution, 45
templates
dropping movie onto, 335–336
DVD theme, 330–332, 344–345
idiosyncrasies of, 336

tempo
    column, Loop Browser, 280
    synchronizing in GarageBand, 285
text
    bound books, 104–105
    safe zone setting for, 348–349
    videos, 133–137
    Web slide shows, 316
themes
    bound book, 102–103
    Web page, 271
    Web slide shows, 316
themes, DVD, 342–352
    Blocks theme, 342–352
    with built-in activity, 344
    button styles, 346–347, 350
    Drive In Two theme, 342
    dropping movies onto templates,
        335–336
    Map view, 351
    Montage theme, 342–352
    overview of, 329–332
    safe zone setting for, 348–349
    Settings tools, 344–345
    viewing DVD structure, 351
thumbnails, 340
tilts, 229, 230
timecodes
    getting video into iMovie, 180
    overview of, 171–172
    playback mode and, 176
    saving video cassettes, 269
time-lapse videos. see videos, time-lapse

Timeline view
    dialogue editing, 260–265
    duration adjustments, 143
    music added to videos in, 266–267
    overview of, 122–123
    picture separated from sound in
        iMovie, 204–208
    professionals using, 193
    sequence played in, 254
    shots modified in, 193–194
    shots rearranged in, 252–253
    time-lapse videos edited in, 155
    video edited in, 190
    workspace arrangements in, 131
titles
    adding transition effects to, 141
    bound books, 103
    movie DVDs, 331, 336–337, 338
    time-lapse videos, 160
    videos, 133–137
    Web slide shows, 316
tracking, 229, 230
tracks
    adding variation to, 294–299
    listening to chosen, 291–292
    measuring time, 292–293
    volume adjustment, 290–291
Tracks column
    creating workspace, 281
    mixing music, 289–291
    time scale adjustment, 292
training tapes, 151

transition effects
  cross dissolves, 160
  fade ins. *see* fade in transitions
  fade outs. *see* fade out transitions
  slide duration, 144
  slide show, 113–114, 216
  story structure and, 244
trashcan, iMovie
  emptying, 259
  restoring clips from, 254
Trim tool
  editing audio clips, 211
  editing cutaway shots, 257
  editing dialogue, 265
  modifying shots in Timeline, 194
tripods
  iSight camera vs., 161–165
  pans/tilts with, 230
  for time-lapse photography, 150,
    152–153

U
Undo command, photos, 89
Unlock Audio Clip function, 207
URLs, 317

V
video editing, 167–195, 247–273
  adding background music, 266–267
  cutaway shots, 255–257
  dialogue scenes, 259–265
  first cuts, 251–252
  getting right shots, 181–183

modifying shots in Timeline,
    193–195, 252–253
  moving video into iMovie, 177–181
  organizing, 169–172
  overview of, 167–168
  playing sequence in Timeline, 254
  reviewing coverage in Clip pane,
    249–250
  saving, 267–270
  shooting videos vs., 168–169
  shots with relationships, 183–185
  time-lapse, 153–161
  trimming/arranging footage,
    185–193
  uploading to Web, 270–272
  visual balance, 254
videos, 350
  dynamic slide shows. *see* slide shows,
    dynamic
  photo composition, 49–53
  recording audio when shooting,
    200–201
  synchronizing audio with, 213–215
videos, DVD, 327–354
  accessing photos/movies/music,
    332–335
  accessing photos/slide shows,
    337–341
  burning, 324–327, 356–357
  dropping movie onto template,
    335–336
  getting to know, 322–323
  opening iDVD, 327–328

overview of, 321–322
    previewing, 354–355
    submenus, 352–354
    themes. *see* themes, DVD
videos, shooting, 227–245
    approach to, 228
    camcorder and, 172–174
    camcorder motion, 228–229
    determining scenes, 235–236
    editing video vs., 168–169
    getting right shots, 181–183
    motion lingo, 229–230
    overview of, 175–177
    shots with relationships, 183–184
    zoom effects, 231–235
videos, shot coverage, 236–243
    cutaway shots, 240–242
    establishing shots, 242–243
    multiple shots from each
        position, 237
    overview of, 236
    shot/reverse combinations, 237–240
    story structure, 244
videos, time-lapse, 149–165
    finding project, 151
    integrating into still or moving
        videos, 151
    overview of, 149
    preparation, 150
    setting up camera, 152–153
    shaping raw materials, 153–161
    using iSight camera instead of tri-
        pod, 161–165
    Viewer, iMovie
    editing time-lapse videos, 154–155

    grabbing still images from video, 310
    overview of, 121
viewing
    enlarging photos in Library for,
        60–61
    keywords added to photos, 80
    photos in Library, 58–59
    tunes for custom CDs, 19–22
    video workspace, 122–123
volume
    exporting music into iTunes,
        303–304
    loudness scale. *see* loudness scale
Volume slider, 290
VU meter, 221

W
WAV audio files, 11
waveforms, 209–210
Web slide shows, 306–319
    getting stills from video, 309–312
    overview of, 307–309
    putting digital files into iPhoto,
        313–318
Web, uploading video to, 270–272
wide shots
    duration for, 189
    editing dialogue, 264–265
    editing techniques, 187–190, 254
    as establishing shot, 242–243
    shot/reverse combinations
        with, 239–240
    showing "where" with, 237
    zoom effects with, 233–235